The Afterlife *of* Sympathy

The Afterlife of Sympathy

Reading
American
Literary Realism
in the Wake of
Uncle Tom's Cabin

FAYE HALPERN

University of Massachusetts Press
AMHERST AND BOSTON

Copyright © 2024 by University of Massachusetts Press
All rights reserved
Printed in the United States of America

ISBN 978-1-62534-785-5 (paper); 786-2 (hardcover)

Designed by Sally Nichols
Set in Minion Pro
Printed and bound by Books International, Inc.
Cover design by adam b. bohannon

Library of Congress Cataloging-in-Publication Data

Names: Halpern, Faye, author.
Title: The afterlife of sympathy : reading American literary realism in the wake of "Uncle Tom's Cabin" / Faye Halpern.
Description: Amherst : University of Massachusetts Press, 2024. | Includes bibliographical references and index. |
Identifiers: LCCN 2023046466 (print) | LCCN 2023046467 (ebook) | ISBN 9781625347855 (paperback) | ISBN 9781625347862 (hardcover) | ISBN 9781685750558 (ebook)
Subjects: LCSH: American fiction—19th century—History and criticism. | Realism in literature. | Sentimentalism in literature. | LCGFT: Literary criticism.
Classification: LCC PS374.R37 H35 2024 (print) | LCC PS374.R37 (ebook) | DDC 813.40912—dc23/eng/20231206
LC record available at https://lccn.loc.gov/2023046466
LC ebook record available at https://lccn.loc.gov/2023046467

British Library Cataloguing-in-Publication Data
A catalog record for this book is available from the British Library.

Chapter 1 was previously published as "Word Become Flesh: Literacy, Anti-Literacy, and Illiteracy in *Uncle Tom's Cabin*," in *Legacy* 34, no. 2 (2017): 253–77, published by the University of Nebraska Press. Chapter 3 was previously published as "Searching for Sentimentality in Henry James's *The Bostonians*," in the *Henry James Review* 39, no. 1 (2018): 62-80, published by Johns Hopkins University Press. Used by permission.

This book is dedicated to my father,

Michael Halpern.

I miss you.

Contents

INTRODUCTION
1

CHAPTER 1
Word Become Flesh
Literacy, Anti-Literacy, and Illiteracy in *Uncle Tom's Cabin*
29

CHAPTER 2
William Dean Howells, Mark Twain, and the Sentimental Red Herring
51

CHAPTER 3
The Unmastering of Henry James, or, Searching for Sentimentality in *The Bostonians*
92

CHAPTER 4
Constance Fenimore Woolson's Rhetorical Passing
115

CHAPTER 5
Weaponizing Sympathy
Charles Chesnutt's Narrative Experiments
139

AFTERWORD
A Case against the (Solely) Discerning Reader
186

Notes 197
Works Cited 219
Index 237

The Afterlife *of* Sympathy

Introduction

WHEN I WAS a grad student writing about popular antebellum sentimental women writers, I gave a friend in the program part of my dissertation to read. Having done so, she asked me why I felt so much contempt for the authors I was writing about. I had not been aware of my contemptuous tone, but when my friend pointed it out, I felt a flash of pride that my distance from these authors was registering in my prose. It has taken me many years to understand that my reaction was less odd than oddly representative—and more years than that to feel dismayed by my earlier reaction.

I eventually came to understand that my contempt for sentimental writing came from my having internalized an important protocol of the discipline I was trying to join. I had become a critical reader, and critical reading acts like kryptonite on sentimental novels. Yet when I remember the time that I spent writing my dissertation, another detail comes to mind: the tissues that I used to mark my place in these novels. So it wasn't just contempt I felt; there were also the tears these novels elicited from me despite my contempt. But the tears remained a secret, even from myself. I forgot about the tissues for a long time. Instead, it was my evolving skills as a critical reader that shaped my dissertation and my first book on these antebellum sentimental writers, *Sentimental Readers*. The book you are now holding in your hand or reading on your screen reflects my continued interest in critical reading and sentimental writing. This book moves the time frame forward into the postbellum period, but it continues my investigation into the question of why sentimentality evokes such resistance on the part of contemporary literary critics by focusing on the role of sentimentality and sympathy in American literary realism.

For most of the nineteenth and twentieth centuries, accounts of literary realism granted sentimentality a minimal role.[1] Sentimental writing, so the story went, was done in—and good riddance!—by a chastened postbellum nation's newfound commitments to objectivity and mimetic accuracy and superseded by the rise of literary realism, which shared these commitments.[2] Unlike the antebellum sentimental tradition, the realist tradition was constructed as much by the movement's authors as it was by twentieth-century American literary historians, who largely took the realists at their word. The ninth edition of *The Norton Anthology of American Literature* includes not only realist fiction but also realist manifestos by the authors of this fiction ("Realism and Naturalism"). These manifestos contend that sentimentality had exceeded its expiration date. "Without taking them too seriously," intones William Dean Howells in the April 1887 "Editor's Study" column reprinted in the *Norton*, "it still must be owned that the 'gaudy hero and heroine' are to blame for a great deal of harm in the world" (957).

This story began to change toward the end of the twentieth century.[3] Literary critics started to document how much realist authors grappled with sympathy and sentimentality.[4] In *Sentimental Twain*, Gregg Camfield meticulously documents Samuel L. Clemens's lifelong engagement with sentimental moral philosophy, his early rejection of moral idealism mellowing into a belief that "good literature is a manifestation of the heart" (236). Furthermore, Camfield demonstrates how, even during periods when Clemens's commitment to scientific materialism was at its strongest, he still included sentimental scenes in his novels. For example, Camfield identifies as sentimental a scene from *Huck Finn* I will also consider: Jim's revelation, to Huck, of his regret at his cruel treatment of his deaf daughter. Like Camfield, Hildegard Hoeller looks at how Edith Wharton toggles between realism and sentimentality throughout her career. Kristin Boudreau's *Sympathy in American Literature* offers a nuanced account of changing ideas about sympathy as these ideas manifested in fictional works from the early republic through the early twentieth century, including a close look at how Howells critiques philanthropy. In *Questionable Charity*, William Morgan argues that the literary realists modernized sentimentality, rejecting an ideal of virile manliness in favor of sentimental manhood and embracing sentimentality's "ideology of humanitarian concern" (19) while critiquing its tendency toward complicity. More recently, Marianne Noble has returned to Camfield's project of documenting nineteenth-century authors' philosophical inquiries into sentimentality and sympathy. In her thoughtful and humane *Rethinking Sympathy and Human Connection in Nineteenth-Century Literature*, Noble uncovers how a range of authors revised their earlier ideas about sentimental sympathy to develop a conception of sympathy that honors people's essential differences.[5]

I want to discuss some of the characteristics of these illuminating works to clarify how my own builds on them. These scholars have explored sympathy as an intellectual and political resource, a means by which authors could answer questions about epistemology, social cohesion, masculinity, and intersubjectivity. Another way to put it is that they almost all offer thematic understandings of sentimentality and sympathy,[6] to use a concept from James Phelan. Phelan uses "thematic" to categorize literary criticism that responds to the ideas a text offers as well as "the cultural, ideological, philosophical, or ethical issues being addressed by the narrative" (*Living* 20). Many of these works also evince a skepticism about sentimental sympathy. For example, Boudreau worries that sentimental sympathy can result in self-negation by "transfusing [the self] with an alien identity" (10), which can happen when a sympathizer completely identifies with a person in pain.[7] Finally, these authors, though focused on texts and ideas from the past, hope their insights about them also bear on the present. For example, Noble expresses the wish that the strain of nineteenth-century thinking about sympathy that she uncovers will afford "the inspiring understanding that our own era so desperately needs" (*Rethinking* 37).

My book builds on these scholars' insights about the role of sympathy and sentimentality in American literary realism in three ways. First, I view sympathy as not just an intellectual resource for the authors I consider but a narrative one. That is, instead of mainly focusing on how authors have thought about sentimental sympathy as a concept—as a tangle, a solution, a problem, a conduit, a trick, a siren song, and so on—I focus on how they mobilize it in their writings and use it to evoke sympathy from their readers. What narrative techniques do they use? What does the successful evocation of sympathy accomplish for different realist authors? Differentiating sympathy as an idea from sympathy as a narrative resource (without insisting on clean margins) allows one to recognize that authors can oppose sentimental sympathy on intellectual or aesthetic grounds or even on the grounds of self-interest but still come to rely on it (see chapter 2) or, conversely, be fascinated by it but avoid using it themselves (see chapter 3). Seeing it as a narrative resource for realist authors also gives me license to use narrative theory to analyze realist writing; narratological concepts and models bring into prominence features of literary realism that haven't received much attention.

Second, my focus on sentimental sympathy as a narrative resource has led me to see it as more ethically flexible than other literary critics have found it to be. Although I agree that sentimental sympathy can have negative ethical consequences, I don't believe it to be inevitably harmful; in some contexts, it can even have positive ethical effects. Because the view of sentimental sympathy by literary critics has been so uniformly negative, my claim about its ethical flexibility might well register as a defense. This defense rests on how sentimentality works on readers. I mean that in a few senses: that sentimental writing can create an intimate relationship between texts and readers, that this relationship is powerful, and that it can be ethically valuable. For example, sentimental sympathy keeps us turning pages to find out what happens to characters we have come to care about. It can further the aims of not just white authors but minoritized ones. The relationship between text and readers that sentimental sympathy engenders is an intimate, uncritical one. It behooves literary critics to separate our justified ethical worries about sentimental sympathy from our understandable but less ethically defensible reaction to sentimental sympathy as something that threatens the sense we have of ourselves as superior readers, whose superiority derives in no small part from our ability to read with critical distance.

Third, like other books that have focused on sympathy in the nineteenth century, this study is presentist but in a particular way: I use my search for sentimentality in literary realism as an occasion to meditate on how contemporary literary critics read. I'll now flesh out these three points as well as demonstrate how they result in a new way to think about realist versus sentimental characters before offering a summary of the book's content.

SENTIMENTAL SYMPATHY

As this book's title suggests, *Uncle Tom's Cabin* (1852) plays an important role in what follows. In fact, it plays multiple ones. It figures both as a work that influenced the realist authors who wrote in its wake and as a handbook of sentimental narrative techniques. As a particular work, it threads its way through my book as I contribute to this new story of American literary realism. My fullest explication of Harriet Beecher Stowe's novel and the reading practices it teaches appears in the first chapter, but it also appears in the second chapter, in Howells's retrospective account of Stowe, whom Howells transforms from a wildly popular and effective purveyor of abolitionist outrage into a local color miniaturist. It appears again in the final chapter, as I explore the ramifications of acknowledging Charles Chesnutt's understanding of himself as writing in the tradition of *Uncle Tom's Cabin* even as twentieth- and twenty-first-century literary critics have placed him in an African American literary tradition.

But as a handbook of sentimental techniques, *Uncle Tom's Cabin* plays an even larger role because it enables me to demonstrate the affordances of sentimental writing, ones that appealed to realist writers even though some of them claimed the opposite. *Uncle Tom's Cabin* is a natural centerpiece for this inquiry since it is as concerned with teaching readers how to read fiction as it is about teaching them how to fight against slavery. In fact, Stowe sees these two projects as inextricable. The fight against slavery proceeds via her plan to train readers to read sympathetically. When one of Stowe's characters, the fugitive Eliza, forges an interracial bond of sympathy with Mrs. Bird, the wife of a senator, over their anguish at losing a child, Stowe is modeling in the world of the novel what she wants to happen in the real world. Stowe knows that this text-to-world transfer is much more likely to occur if readers stop seeing Eliza and Mrs. Bird as fictional characters and instead see them as people, as vivid as the people they encounter in their real lives. This invitation makes for both immersed readers and alienated contemporary literary critics.

The sympathy that Stowe invites her readers to experience guides my analysis of realist works. Sympathy is a complex and much-debated concept. One source of its complexity derives from the development in the early twentieth century of the closely related concept of empathy. The cognitive narratologist Suzanne Keen defines sympathy as feeling for and empathy as "feeling with" (xxi), but in the nineteenth century, such a distinction didn't exist, which is why I use the more historically accurate term "sympathy" in this book (and I've suggested elsewhere that even now it's difficult to retain such conceptual distinctions).[8] Empathy clawed back some of what earlier theorists had put in sympathy's domain. Another aspect of sympathy's conceptual complexity derives from the different conceptions of sympathy/empathy that have circulated in the last two centuries. The social psychologist C. Daniel Batson identifies eight different contemporary conceptions of empathy, from "Knowing Another Person's Internal State" (4) to "Feeling Distress at Witnessing Another Person's Suffering" (7). In what follows, I do not explore, as does Noble in *Rethinking Sympathy*, a form of sympathy that acknowledges the essential mystery of another person, a type of sympathy that Noble describes as depending on "a benevolent non-knowing" (10). Instead, I attend to how (and why) a range of realist narratives rely on a more familiar but currently much more maligned model of sympathy: the kind found in *Uncle Tom's Cabin*, what I call "sentimental sympathy."

How might we understand this more familiar type of sympathy? It matches the type of sympathy that Batson calls "Intuiting or Projecting Oneself into Another Situation" (6) and that the philosopher Amy Coplan calls "self-oriented perspective taking" (although they would both call it "empathy"). It occurs when a person (the sympathizer) imagines what they would feel if they were to be transported into another person's set of circumstances, with the result that the sympathizer concludes how much they have in common with the object of their sympathy. Thus, we might also call this "sameness-asserting sympathy." Coplan opposes this type of sympathy to "other-oriented perspective taking" or what we could also call "difference-insisting sympathy," which results when a person imagines what another person with their own distinctive set of beliefs and experiences likely feels in their particular set of circumstances rather than what the sympathizer would feel if they were in their shoes. Coplan prefers this second type of sympathy. As Coplan puts it, "One individual's response to a set of circumstances is rarely a reliable indicator of what another's will be" (9). In this preference for difference-insisting sympathy, Coplan aligns herself with contemporary literary critics, who agree with her about sameness-insisting sympathy's capacity to produce error. But that's just the beginning of what contemporary literary critics object to when it comes to sentimental sympathy.

THE ETHICS OF SYMPATHY

For the literary layperson, empathy has become a common justification for reading fiction. For example, almost every author talk I've attended in recent years has ended with some form of the claim that fiction is valuable because it allows readers to form empathetic bonds with marginalized others. Such talks also assume that empathy will inspire readers to help the real-world counterparts of their literary objects of sympathy. But literary critics resist what they see as these simplistic, too-hasty conclusions about literary empathy. In *Empathy and the Novel*, Keen describes how people might avoid situations that they know will evoke an empathetic reaction because they find it too distressing or exhausting, and even when people do put themselves in the way of feeling empathy, there is no empirical evidence that such a reaction leads to benevolent acts in the real world, or what Keen calls "pro-social action." Continuing the critique of empathy as an unalloyed good regardless of context, Erin McGlothlin discusses the ethical complexities of Holocaust novels that invite an empathetic response to their first-person Nazi narrators. Keen and McGlothlin are narratologists, but other kinds of literary critics also evince critical resistance to empathy. Instead of seeing literary empathy as a tool to end social injustice, literary critics see it as a path to cultural appropriation or political apathy or even what Noble calls "autoerasure" (8), meaning what happens when a person so strongly identifies with someone else that their own identity is erased.[9]

Yet while I agree that sympathy can have negative effects, I suggest that it can also have positive ones. In an interview with Rebecca Lane and Jeffrey Zamostny, Noble tells a story about being teased as a child and how that experience does not give her license to presume she understands people who are experiencing mockery on sexual or racial grounds: "Suppose I were to say 'You can get over it, buck up. I know exactly what you're going through.' In fact, I don't know what they're going through. Their situation is different from mine . . . I might just say, 'Come on, toughen up. All children go through that'" ("The Limits of Empathy" 162). But it is just as likely that someone who'd been teased for something small would stand up for those being attacked for their gender or race. That is, the effects of sympathy are not always quietist, and the power of such a sympathetic reaction is a force that can be channeled toward good actions as well as bad ones. I use "force" to highlight one of sentimental sympathy's most important features: the strength of the reaction it can produce in readers. However much difference-recognizing sympathy forestalls the ethical problems that sentimental sympathy raises in certain contexts, I do not believe it inspires a very powerful emotional reaction.[10] Sentimental sympathy's power to affect so many readers so deeply is one reason it becomes compelling for the American literary realists, who otherwise take great pains to teach readers to recognize and assess the distinctive perspectives and life circumstances of their characters rather than identify with them.

SYMPATHY AS NARRATIVE RESOURCE AND SUPPLEMENT

In this book I contend that sentimental sympathy functions as a narrative resource for the realist authors who follow the antebellum sentimentalists, even those realists like William Dean Howells and Mark Twain who publicly disavowed it. Framing it as a narrative resource challenges two traditions in literary studies: the literary critical tradition of disparaging sentimentality and the pedagogical tradition of teaching students to be critical readers.[11] Lauren Berlant's influential assessment of sentimentality suggests how these two traditions often converge. Berlant is well known for their skepticism about the possibility that sentimental texts can induce people to agitate for political change, but their work might be even more motivated by the urge to identify how sentimental texts make their consumers into unobservant readers: Berlant highlights "the forces of distortion in the world of feeling politics" (*Female Complaint* 40–41). According to Berlant, sentimentality exhibits the "will to appropriate and inhabit difference... [which] necessarily involves distortion, mistranslation, and misrecognition" (40). The acuity of the consumer of sentimental texts is blurred by her tears. Although Berlant does not discuss literary pedagogy per se, one can infer Berlant's strong preference for critical reading, which presumably enables readers to resist the faulty conflations encouraged by sentimental texts.

As my discussions of Berlant suggests, and as we've seen in the previous section, sentimental sympathy is as much a cause for concern today as it was in the nineteenth century, even as the reasons differ. Susan Ryan discusses how nineteenth-century reformers worried that "a too-thorough identification between helper and helped risked a degree of social leveling that most donors would have resisted" (19).[12] Contemporary literary critics fear the same thing, minus the elitism: sympathy risks "leveling" the experiences of the marginalized so that they seem to match the experiences of the white and/or middle-class reader—and, as Xine Yao points out in *Disaffected*, if a marginalized person refuses to sympathize or accept sympathy, white people use it as a reason to deny their humanity.

Literary critics' aversion to sentimental sympathy derives from ethical concern, but it may not solely do so. I wonder if there might be another reason driving the discipline's recoil. Batson observes that "to feel for another, one must think one knows the other's internal state... [b]ecause feeling *for* is based on a perception of the other's welfare.... To feel for someone does not, however, require that perception be accurate" (10). Batson allows us to see potential inaccuracy as simply the price of admission to a feeling of care. Why is this potential inaccuracy so troubling to literary critics? I suspect there is another kind of aversion propelling that inability to countenance sentimental sympathy's ethical complexity when otherwise the discipline is one that loves complexity: an aversion to being swept up and immersed in a character's fate.

Sentimental sympathy threatens the reading practices that set English professors or "professional readers," to use John Guillory's term, apart from lay readers. Professional readers have a vested interest in disparaging sentimentality. Recognizing this ulterior motive has inspired me to use my analysis of sentimentality as a tool to pry apart some of my discipline's assumptions about how we ought to train our students to read and how we should read ourselves. It's my hope that a richer portrait of American literary realism gives us, ironically, some critical distance on critical distance so that we can see the affordances of sympathetic reading. Critical reading is indeed antithetical to sympathetic reading, so much so that both literary realists and contemporary professional readers, their legatees,[13] require sympathetic reading to supplement it. I want to emphasize this point about supplementarity because it lies at the heart of my qualified defense of sentimental sympathy. Just as I am not arguing that the realists always write sentimentally (a rather absurd proposition), I am not advocating that sympathetic reading is more valuable than critical reading. I am arguing instead that sentimental sympathy has ethical and narrative value and that this value is different from—and called into service by—critical reading's ethical and narrative value.

There are signs that professional readers might be open to giving sentimental sympathy another hearing. I join Eve Sedgwick and Rita Felski in trying to make visible the limits of the discipline's critical stance toward its objects of analysis and also their efforts to supplement it. The way I've chosen to do that is by illuminating the affordances of sentimental sympathy and the kind of sympathetic reading practice it fosters, a species of reading practice that falls into the category of what Michael Warner has called "uncritical reading" and John Guillory has called "lay reading." Chapter 1 looks closely at how critique limits our understanding of a sentimental work like *Uncle Tom's Cabin* by disabling the critic from understanding its power, so that the critic's own deficiency gets projected back onto the novel. In subsequent chapters I look at how various realist authors invite their readers to lay aside critical distance at least briefly, or to consider what is lost when one doesn't. The marginalized realist authors Constance Fenimore Woolson and Charles Chesnutt, whom I consider in the final two chapters and the afterword, meditate on the costs of critically discerning reading practices and engage in ingenious acts of rhetorical passing that enable them to demonstrate how discerning readers can be in fact the most gullible readers of all. Yet despite my efforts to push against the limits of critique, I also recognize the irony of this commitment:

in your hands is a book that critiques critiquers (most obviously in my paranoid reading of Howells and Twain) and tries to get some critical distance on critical distance. But perhaps Felski herself would forgive me for my methodological impurity since a rigid insistence on methodological purity seems a salient feature of critique itself.

This project tries to redress what Michael Millner has called "our [discipline's] limited understanding of the emotions of reading" (xvii) and, I'd add, the limited value we attach to the emotional reactions that fiction inspires in readers. A familiar account of this rejection would begin with W. K. Wimsatt and Monroe C. Beardsley's foundational essay "The Affective Fallacy," first published in 1949, which famously separated "what [a poem] *is* and what it *does*" (1246), warning that attending to a poem's emotional effects on the reader results "in impressionism and relativism" (1246). In *Affecting Fictions*, Jane Thrailkill takes on the work of overcoming the affective fallacy with regard to the literary realists. Her illustration of how realist fiction demonstrates the value of emotion has been particularly inspiring to me in writing this book.[14] But whereas Thrailkill focuses on a variety of emotions, I focus on sympathy. I add to Thrailkill's account by looking at how realist authors made it easy for critics intent on ignoring the emotional aspects of what they read. They value sympathy but try to hide it. For example, as Hoeller shows Wharton to be doing, Twain and Howells say one thing in their manifestos and treatises on fiction but do another in their fictional works. Thanks in part to such public claims, realism came to be associated with objectivity and disinterestedness and sentimentality with the opposite.[15] As Daniel H. Borus writes, "Although literary realism did not fashion the claims to scientific precision that sociology did, it was an essential component of the intellectual movement of the late nineteenth century" (14). Borus echoes William Roscoe Thayer's contemporaneous account of realism, which also suggested its objectivity even as it sought to disparage it for this quality. Thayer calls the realists "Epidermists" (470), who write as if they were cameras "see[ing] only the outside[,] ... [t]he surface, the cuticle of life" (477).[16]

The difference between what realist authors and tastemakers espouse and what Wimsatt and Beardsley contend can seem significant: realist tastemakers were defining what constitutes good literature, while Wimsatt and Beardsley were defining how critics ought to read it. This book, however, suggests a link between the two by demonstrating that many nineteenth-century fictional works, most especially *Uncle Tom's Cabin*, are also reading primers, with the caveat that they are teaching not basic literacy but more advanced interpretive skills. Realist novels are no exception. Twain's depiction of Emmeline in *Adventures of Huckleberry Finn* mocks not just sentimental poetesses but readers like Huck, who are moved by sentimental poetry like hers. Huck has no taste because he has no critical distance. But Twain's readers, if they're reading Twain's novel properly, will not make the same mistake. In the "Explanatory" that precedes the novel, Twain directs his readers to attend to the differences in the dialects his characters speak, but he'll also teach readers, implicitly, to attend to a different set of differences: differences between Huck's worldview and that of the implied author. Though the novel asks readers to feel affection for Huck, the novel also trains readers to recognize that Huck is a (mostly) bad if amusing reader not just of the world but of sentimental writing. Twain gives his readers the tools to do better.

Bad reading is something that pains literary critics not just because they believe their own good reading practices are what distinguish them from lay readers[17] but because most academic literary critics don't simply write about literature but teach students how to read it. Protocols against reading emotionally have cast a long shadow on not only our criticism but our teaching as well. For example, in an article on teaching close reading in a large lecture class, Teresa Tinkle and her colleagues deem students who "respond[ed] emotionally" to literary texts (512) as producing shallow, "impressionistic" (513) interpretations. We teach our students to resist becoming flooded with emotion by what they read but, if it does happen, to avoid writing about it in their academic essays: "And then the scene with Little Eva giving away her hair made me cry"—how does one grade *that*?

Sentimental sympathy brings professional critics back to their forgotten roots as immersed and susceptible readers, failing to register what was going on around them because they were so lost in a book. Perhaps because sentimentality, from the perspective of literary critics, is an abject and threatening form, its presence has been both overstated and understated. In regard to the former, it has been easy for critics to overlook how, in *Uncle Tom's Cabin*, sentimental passages coexist with satirical and analytical ones; the novel frequently invites readers to experience feelings other than sympathy. In regard to the latter, as I noted earlier, for most of the twentieth century, critics saw American literary realism as having no truck with sentimentality.

Sentimentality need not be something whose mere presence so overwhelms a novel that it becomes a sentimental one. In the introduction to *The Female Complaint*, Berlant notes in passing that interest groups who do not otherwise participate in what they call "feeling politics" can deploy sentimental rhetoric "tactically" (22).[18] Fredric Jameson also opens up a way of seeing sentimentality as a potential ingredient in something that is not otherwise sentimental: he sees realism as made up of "heterogenous materials" (7). While he does not name "sentimentality" as one of these materials, he does view realism as made up of a mixture of older and newer narrative forms, poised as it were between the older *récit*, with its story of an exemplary life that evokes conventional emotions from a reader, and the modernist scene, with its evocation of affects that escape socially prescribed meanings. Jameson considers these two narrative forms as producing an irresolvable tension in realist works. In the case of American literary realism, however, it might make more sense to see sentimentality as something that enables the realist project rather than threatens to dissolve it precisely because sentimentality produces effects on readers that the American literary realists required and couldn't produce via realist narrative methods.

Up until now, my discussion of sentimentality as a narrative resource has emphasized the "resource" part of that formulation by suggesting how valuable the realists found sentimental sympathy to be and the different uses they put it to. Let me now turn to the "narrative" part of this formulation. This book analyzes the narrative techniques that realist authors use, and it draws heavily on narrative theory to do so. A narratological approach to realism is rare but not without precedent. Jameson himself, while insatiably curious about the political effects of realist works, also analyzes how they function narratively. I myself could not have embarked on this project without the particular lens on literary texts afforded by a subset of narrative theory known as rhetorical narrative theory, which, among other things, equips literary critics to analyze how different authors construct their narratives to invite different emotional reactions.

Rhetorical narrative theory was pioneered by Wayne Booth, who did not believe in the "affective fallacy." It has been carried forward by, among others, Peter Rabinowitz and James Phelan, who have developed conceptual models that illuminate the relationships between narrators, readers, and authors. I could not have developed the idea of sentimentality as a narrative resource without Phelan's "ARA" (author-resources-audience) model of narrative communication.[19] Literary critics are used to exercising their intellects when they engage with texts as well as, though usually less explicitly, their values; analyzing how a text triggers sentimental sympathy has not been nearly as explored because of the reasons I have listed. It's a story that a rhetorical narrative approach allows the literary critic to tell.

FROM THEME TO RHETORIC

In my previous book *Sentimental Readers*, I discussed the benefits of identifying sentimentality as involving more than seeing if a text contains a certain kind of plot (e.g., orphan-learns-to-be-true-woman plot),[20] character type (e.g., clear-cut heroines and villains), or theme (such as domesticity or interpersonal relationships). In identifying sentimental works simply in terms of whether or not they contain these elements rather than what kind of relationship the text invites the reader to form with it, we hamper our ability to distinguish sentimental works from works that exhibit these elements but aren't in fact sentimental. Stephen Crane's *Maggie*, with its tragic, rejected heroine, would fall into this category of false positives (a work that can initially seem sentimental but is not), as would *The Bostonians*, with its prominent marriage plot. That critics do not call these works sentimental shows that there's an intuitive rejection of such a static definition even as it continues to guide much criticism. Crane wants us to scorn sentimentality; James wants us to ponder it. Neither author wants us to experience the sympathetic, intimate, uncritical relationship with the text that sentimental writing invites.

Phelan invites us to see that a narrative "is ultimately not a structure but an action, a teller using resources of narrative to achieve a purpose in relation to an audience" (*Somebody Telling* x). That orientation is particularly useful when it comes to identifying sentimentality. Sentimentality is not static but active; it's not hermetic but relational. Sentimental authors want their fictional works to be experienced as real, not just in the sense that they want readers to ignore their works' status as fiction but in that they want their readers to see their characters as existing (and yearn to meet them) and to experience the scenes within them as extremely vivid. For its intended readers, the sentimental novel ceases to seem like a text at all, becoming instead a living reality.[21] The sentimental novel wants to make the text–real world interface as permeable as possible in another way. Sentimental novels don't just feature characters feeling certain strong emotions like sympathy; they strive to transfer the strong emotions the characters are experiencing to their readers. *Adventures of Huckleberry Finn*, with the exception of its crucial sentimental scenes, does not work this way. As I described earlier, Huck ardently admires Emmeline's poetry while the novel's intended readers feel an amused contempt.

If I'm right that sentimental writing can be identified best through the relationship it strives to create between itself and its readers, it will serve us well to break that relationship down further in order to discuss it more precisely. Sentimental literature develops certain kinds of relationships between what Phelan calls "tellers" (implied authors and narrators), characters, and readers.[22] My discussion of sentimental rhetoric and realist writing will often draw on these and other concepts from rhetorical narrative theory.

A rhetorical narrative approach allows me to attend to what I see as a crucial aspect of *realist* fiction as well: realist narrators and realist narration. What I find in this regard will likely come as a surprise. Critics have credited modernist authors with creating the kinds of narrators and narration that enable them to explore subjectivity and the subjective nature of knowledge, for example, Mrs. Dalloway and her famous streams of consciousness or the unreliable narration of J. Alfred Prufrock. Realist narration, as I mentioned earlier, has been seen as objective. Ryan Simmons discusses the "objectivity of narration" in Chesnutt's novel *The Marrow of Tradition* (102), and Nancy Glazener calls attention to "the omnisciently narrated [realist] novel that was to become the main tradition of nineteenth-century fiction" (104).[23]

But this book demonstrates that realist novels do not often rely on omniscience or produce objective knowledge about the storyworld; to the contrary, realist narration burrows deep into particular characters' consciousnesses. Even when it does not feature subjective first-person narration, it almost always relies on focalized narration (narration filtered through the perception of a particular character). Realist authors favor this kind of narration to demonstrate how their characters often get things wrong. Furthermore, when we look at realist narration more closely (and with the precision tools of narrative theory), it becomes clear that realist narration proceeds almost always through either *unreliable* narration or *unreliable* focalization. The first-person narrators that I consider in this book, including Huck, Hank Morgan (the narrator of *A Connecticut Yankee in King Arthur's Court*), John (the frame narrator of Chesnutt's conjure tales), and the narrators of Woolson's short stories "Solomon" and "'Miss Grief,'" are all unreliable even if the unreliability of some of them is a complex affair. As for the works I consider that do not feature first-person narrators and hence the possibility of unreliable narrators,[24] they proceed via unreliable *focalization*, from *The Bostonians* through *A Hazard of New Fortunes* to *The Marrow of Tradition*. *Uncle Tom's Cabin* is the only book—and not a realist one!—featured here that is not shot through with unreliability. Yet I did not cherry-pick only realist works that unfold via the perspective of unreliable narrators and unreliable characters; instead, it's a defining feature of postbellum realist works.

What accounts for previous critics' overlooking or at least de-emphasizing this feature of realist narration? Phelan has shown narrative unreliability to be much more supple and subtle than originally theorized. It can be easily missed by literary critics who believe unreliable narration to be more binaristic or sensational than it often is. Unreliable narration does not act like a light switch whereby a narrator is either completely unreliable or completely reliable. Instead, as Phelan has demonstrated, unreliable narrators are usually unreliable only along some axes and perfectly reliable along others; for example, they misinterpret the motives of another character but accurately report what the character looks like. Further, they can become less unreliable along particular axes as the fictional work progresses (*Living*, ch. 1). I would add to Phelan's observations that unreliable narrators are often unreliable in unremarkable ways. For example, Howells's Basil March does not try to justify pedophilia (like Humbert Humbert) or ask us to overlook any murders he happens to have committed (like many of Poe's narrators). What Basil March gets wrong is much less spectacular: he tends to aestheticize suffering in a way the reader is meant to reject. Paradoxically, the effect of realist unreliability might account for the sense of its objectivity. As Simmons has noted, the realists believed that the knowledge any individual can achieve is partial (4), and, I'd add, they believed that one can achieve a more accurate picture of the world by putting these partial perspectives together (and here is where the realists part ways with the modernists). Hence, the common realist technique of focalizing the narration through a series of (unevenly) unreliable characters.

What is the effect of all this unreliability in realist novels? Works featuring unreliable characters and narrators by definition insist that readers take a stance of critical distance toward the unreliable character or narrator. Booth, the coiner of the term "unreliable narrator," defines unreliable narration in terms of distance: "Probably the most important of these kinds of distance is that between the fallible or unreliable narrator and the implied author who carries the reader with him in judging the narrator" (*Rhetoric of Fiction* 158). Most realist works therefore require the reader to carefully evaluate first-person characters and third-person focalizers (a phenomenon I discuss at length in chapter 3). The reader needs to decide when and to what degree they are unreliable, an evolving determination that often depends on assessing the character's own assessments of the reliability of other characters, in an endless web of discernment. It's hard work. Signs of unreliability can easily be missed or misread by actual readers, whose own values and beliefs can make it difficult to recognize instances of unreliability that conflict with them, for example, if the implied author asks them to recognize a perspective as unreliable that they themselves share. This difficulty trains readers to read critically, yet it also provides the means for two realist writers whom I look at, Chesnutt and Woolson, to make a sly case that distanced, discerning readers might be in pressing need of self-reform. But critical distance doesn't foment a reader's immersion in a storyworld or attachment to a character. Sentimental sympathy does.

Just as realist works use sentimental sympathy to supplement the critical distance they cultivate in readers, I understand my rhetorical narratological approach to *supplement* a thematic approach, allowing me to illuminate different aspects of realist and sentimental texts and ask different questions of them. Yet I do not want to suggest that thematic and rhetorical approaches operate distinctly. For example, an analysis of the nature of *Uncle Tom's Cabin*'s racial politics can be enriched by understanding the sentimental sympathy Stowe establishes between her characters and tries to catalyze between her characters and readers. There's only one way I think a rhetorical approach does better than a thematic one: in identifying sentimentality. Otherwise these two approaches focus on complementary aspects of a particular narrative.

Given the fresh insights a rhetorical approach can generate, what might account for the general avoidance of it? To focus on the rhetorical aspects of a narrative requires the literary scholar to grapple with different kinds of readers. For example, the critic needs to consider who the author imagined they were writing to, an intended reader whose reading practices might be very different from the critic's own. Instead, most pieces of literary criticism set up the critic as a representative reader. This practice results in a strange contradiction: On the one hand, the piece of criticism suggests that the critic's interpretation is readily available to everyone who has ever read that work. On the other hand, because the discipline values intricate, original literary interpretations, literary criticism inevitably highlights the ingenuity of the critic's own interpretation, suggesting that only this particular critic, with their mad skills, was able to generate it. To avoid this contradiction, the critic would need to acknowledge in their criticism that different readers interpret texts differently. Of course, reader-response criticism has primed us to accept just this situation even as the discipline has tempered the impact of reader-response criticism by insisting, partially through essays like "The Affective Fallacy," that only interpretations from critics who adhere to the discipline's own reading protocols are interesting.

Attention to how realist authors use the resources available to them to achieve their particular purposes presents another problem for contemporary literary scholars: realist novels invite us to employ critical reading practices that we find congenial, ones in fact that our professional identity is staked on. This consonance makes it difficult to see that these reading practices are historically contingent, one choice among many. Ironically, it's difficult to get critical distance on critical distance, to see it as a particular reading strategy rather than the *only* reading strategy. That realist reading practices are also poisoned arrows directed at the heart of sentimentality becomes, on this view, a trivial observation. Sentimental novels deserve to be trivialized, literary critics think, because of their arrant artifice and manipulativeness. Sentimental novels ask the literary critic to become at times a kind of reader that literary critics resist being: an uncritical one. Because books issue invitations rather than death threats, readers can choose not to become members of the intended audience. But we ignore the distinction between the actual and intended audience (one emphasized by rhetorical narratologists) at peril to our literary analyses. If we ignore it with a sentimental novel, we will fail to understand its emotional impact; we will also tend to consider past readers dupes, so that the history of reading starts to resemble those old charts that illustrated the steps of the evolution of man from apes, but instead of man being at the pinnacle, we have the contemporary literary critic. But our literary analyses can run into problems in the inverse situation: with realist novels, we slip into the intended audience with so little resistance we don't even hear the gears clicking into place.

In other words, attending to the rhetorical aspects of narratives presents what can seem like existential problems for literary scholars. It means confronting an implicit assumption that guides most contemporary literary critics: that the discerning interpretations they offer are central to understanding the text they are analyzing. Surely this is a blameless sentiment. But in what follows, I explore the limitations of focusing on our own discerning interpretations to the exclusion of other, uncritical ones. There are benefits to pursuing a rhetorical reading of realist narratives: it allows us to focus on how realist authors encourage the members of their intended audience to read. Such an approach allows us to see that realist authors were not just making a case for *what* authors ought to focus on—for example, strata of people who had not received much literary attention in the past (what gives rise to the characterization of realist writing as democratic).[25] A rhetorical narratological approach allows us to set into relief the *reading practices* that realists like Howells and Twain encourage readers to embrace as well as the ones they proscribe but nonetheless rely on.

It will come as a shock to very few that recognizing our own investment in realist reading protocols does not actually threaten the existence of literary criticism. Yet it still might help us push back against its limits. The limits this book tries to push beyond are what Felski calls "the limits of critique" (*Limits*). Felski compares critique to "slic[ing] into a literary work to expose its omissions and occlusions, its denials and disavowals" (16). She invites literary critics to imagine roles for themselves beyond that of coroner,[26] to think about how discernment, distance, and the refusal to get caught up in the emotional power of a text might deaden the practice of literary criticism and, I'd add, literary pedagogy. This book extends Felski's project by looking at a chapter in American literary history that set the discipline on the path of critique but which itself contains possibilities for bushwhacking new ones. One of those new paths begins with reevaluating what we think we know about characters and characterization. This reevaluation is made possible by seeing sentimental sympathy as a narrative resource. I offer the next section as both a foretaste and a cornerstone of what's to come.

WHAT MAKES A CHARACTER VIVID?

"Is it true—true to the motives, the impulses, the principles that shape the life of actual men and women?" Howells asks in a well-known formulation of realism's aspirations (*Literature and Life*). Of course, this question is also a statement about the superiority of realist literature and an implicit rebuke to what Howells calls "romanticistic" works by authors like Sir Walter Scott and Nathaniel Hawthorne and to sentimental ones as well, which his question not only dismisses but also retroactively characterizes as false to reality.[27] Twain augments this characterization with his well-known skewering of sentimental poetry via the figure of Emmeline, the prolific poetess we met earlier, always on the scene to write a tribute to the newly deceased. It turns out Emmeline is also a painter, one of whose paintings Twain describes in detail: it features "a woman in a slim black dress, belted small under the arm-pits, with bulges like a cabbage in the middle of the sleeves ... and white slim ankles crossed about with black tape, and very wee black slippers, like a chisel" (111–12). Twain suggests the cause of sentimental authors' distortions: they don't take the time to observe how things really are, a fault he does not share, as he makes clear in his famous, amusing takedown of James Fenimore Cooper.

I cannot make a case for the narrative affordances of sentimental sympathy without acknowledging what seems like its most fundamental failing: its refusal to represent how people really are. Despite Thayer's accusation of the realists' fixation on surfaces, most readers find realist characters to be three-dimensional, in contrast to the flat and improbable characters we find in sentimental writing. Camfield suggests how this failing came about: according to him, sentimental writers need their characters to be both real and ideal; they are caught "between describing reality [and] an idealized preconception of reality" (12). In other words, sentimental authors simplify their characters instead of depicting the complexity of real people. Even Jane Tompkins, the great modern defender of *Uncle Tom's Cabin*, concedes its impoverished characterization when she asks her scholarly readers to set aside "some familiar categories for evaluating fiction," including "psychological subtlety" (126). Although Tompkins will offer many other reasons to value Stowe's novel, she too accepts the judgment that Stowe's characters are cardboard cutouts.

Yet I'd suggest Stowe's characters were at least as believable—and in fact more vivid—to her contemporaneous readers, and a not inconsiderable portion of readers since then, in comparison to a character like Margaret Vance in Howells's novel *A Hazard of New Fortunes*, whom I'll return to shortly. I want to consider the question of what makes a character seem real in order to understand how sentimental characters can seem so vivid to many readers. Camfield might attribute this to the extent to which sentimental authors did value realistic depiction, but I'd suggest it has just as much to do with the extent to which they valued the typical.

Critics often turn to E. M. Forster to understand how authors create lifelike, or as he puts it "round," characters. He famously argues that round characters are ones that evince a number of different characteristics: they are not just good or evil; they cannot be summed up in a single phrase. It is even better when these characteristics do not easily fit together: "The test of a round character is whether it is capable of surprising in a convincing way" (118), for example, someone is loyal, generous, and a blowhard. For Wimsatt, it is not so much a capacity to surprise as the possession of self-consciousness that creates a lifelike character: "A kind of awareness of self (a high and human characteristic), with a pleasure in the fact, is perhaps the central principle which instead of simplifying the attributes [of a character] gives each one a special function in the whole" (qtd. in Knapp 63).

These theories seem to exhibit the modernist bias that Tompkins refers to in linking believability to psychological subtlety. But is it a modernist bias? I'd say instead that it's a realist one. The narrator of *A Hazard of New Fortunes* appears to echo (or, better, foreshadow) Forster's and Wimsatt's ideas when, in discussing a character in the storyworld to which he's the guide, he notes that "she [Margaret Vance] was like every one else, a congeries of contradictions and inconsistencies, but obedient to the general expectation of what a girl of her position must and must not finally be" (254). We have here not just a large number of qualities but a set of qualities that can't easily coexist with one another (filled with "contradictions and inconsistencies"). In other words, she's a character, not a character type, and all the more vivid because of it. Melanie Dawson detects this same rejection of the typical in illuminating how Howells and other realist authors depict emotions. Realist authors resolved they would do better than sentimental writers by tempering what they saw as overblown descriptions of emotion with an attention to how emotions arise out of local contexts and out of the distinctive histories and preferences of individual characters, what Dawson calls "the value of local and limited, or small-scaled enactments of emotion" (56).

Realists had a vested interest in proclaiming that realist characters were more lifelike than previous ones, so if we want to be impartial, we should not automatically discount the possibility that earlier readers might have found sentimental characters lifelike, no matter how one-note, unsurprising, or lacking in self-consciousness. And in fact, they did find them so. How else can we account for the dramatic reactions of readers to sentimental characters whose fates we would expect readers to be indifferent to?[28] Although he doesn't analyze sentimental characters specifically, Herbert Grabes provides a possible answer. Taking a cognitive approach, he focuses on the mental processes readers undergo in "figuring-forth" (222) characters who come to take on an independent life in their readers' minds. Curious about how readers take the scanty, piecemeal information about a character that narratives offer and make the character into a whole, he postulates the important role of "social schemata, prototypes, and stereotypes" (226). According to Grabes, "such 'mental models' . . . consist of combinations of certain characteristics whose unity is guaranteed by communal experience and convention" (226). That is, readers piece together scattered bits of information into a whole character by supplementing them with extratextual information that has been supplied by the social schemata their culture has bequeathed them.

It's quite possible that readers find characters particularly vivid who fit neatly into such schemata, as sentimental characters do. This possibility is given weight if we connect Grabes's idea to an observation that Robyn Warhol makes about sentimental novels in the course of listing what makes them so effective at evoking their readers' tears. Warhol notes that "the plots of sentimental novels rely upon repeated moments . . . which serve to 'mythologize' experience in that they draw upon the culture's store of cherished beliefs" ("As You Stand" 119). She offers examples of these cherished beliefs: "Family *will* prevail; sisters *are* friends forever; true love *will* prevail; courage *will* be rewarded; Christian forbearance *will* put an end to slavery—oh, it *is* a wonderful life!" ("As You Stand" 120). What Warhol is likening to myths, I would liken to the schemata and prototypes that Grabes identifies. I'd like to call them instead "cherished cultural narratives" to make clear that they're also templates for how to shape a story. A large subset of them involve a certain type of character embarking on a life-changing trajectory or changing the people around them in life-altering ways. In the antebellum era, we have the angelic small child who teaches the adults truths they cannot see for themselves; in our own era, we have the decadent bachelor who is humanized by having to care for a small child.[29]

These cherished cultural narratives allow members of that culture to piece together the narrative and characters involved in it from only a few clues, for instance, a shot of the bachelor waking up hungover next to a woman whose name he cannot remember.[30] They also transfer to these characters the strong emotions that the narratives in which they appear evoke in their readers or viewers. (Hollywood movies are, we know, expert in drawing on these cherished cultural narratives.) To put this in cognitive terms, two reasons why the "flat" characters in sentimental novels register as vivid to many readers is that they both reduce cognitive load and evoke strong emotion. As George Sand wrote in her review of *Uncle Tom's Cabin*, "Where do we find creations more complete, types more living, situations more touching and more original, than in Uncle Tom?" "Types more living"—Sand recognizes that characters who present as types do not forestall identification but often hasten it.

We can see why contemporary literary critics who think highly of their own cognitive-load-bearing capacities might not like the connection between typicality and vividness. Nor did the realists. Dawson describes how typicality registered with Howells in the context of *Annie Kilburn*: "As with Basil March and his wife, [Annie's] substitution of the 'typical' for the specific allows her to circumvent the possibility of emotional connection with the poor" (60). According to Dawson, Howells believes that typicality prevents someone from feeling a strong emotional attachment, including a reaction of sympathy, because without specific knowledge of the individual *qua* individual, fellow-feeling cannot develop.

Yet Dawson's analysis, which seems accurate as far as Howells's view goes, does not evaluate if this view is true. According to Howells, we need information about the individual character, his particular circumstances, his history, in order to experience fellow-feeling. Yet there's reason to think this view is false. For Stowe at least, the reader needs simply to know that this fugitive enslaved woman standing in front of her is also a suffering mother. From that sketchy information, the reader's brain and heart rapidly fill in the rest of the picture via recourse to the cherished cultural narrative of maternal sacrifice. More information—Where is this fugitive from, coastal North Carolina or one of the urban mansions of New Orleans? Is that homespun or coarse linen her dress is made from? Is she fleeing from an impecunious owner or a jealous slave mistress? Is she feeling fear and sadness, or could this combination also be mixed with glee at the reaction she hypothesizes her owner will have to the news that she is missing?—is unnecessary because she already feels deep sympathy for her. And as much as Stowe's reader feels for this fugitive, she believes the same amount *in* her, in her existence as more than a character on the page. Her status as a character is obliterated in the moment of sentimental sympathy. She becomes a person. Eliza's vividness cannot be disarticulated from her typicality. In fact, typicality, especially when combined with a cherished cultural narrative, foments sentimental sympathy, and sentimental sympathy foments vividness.

Because sentimentality has normally been analyzed thematically rather than rhetorically, we have come to associate it with the cherished antebellum cultural stories that were circulating when sentimental novels were in the ascendant, for example, "children too good for this earth" or "Black people helping white people let God into their hearts." But these stories no longer resonate with (and some are even offensive to) contemporary literary critics. Winfried Flück argues along these lines when he proposes that *Uncle*

Tom's Cabin lands with many modern readers to the extent it represents the crime of slavery through the discourse of families being sundered but loses them when it relies on biblically typological thinking to represent slavery's breach of the moral order.[31] I propose that we see sentimentality defined not by *particular* cherished cultural stories. Instead, sentimental writing features the cherished cultural stories of their intended readers, not readers past or future. Just because a novel doesn't feature, say, "a dear old-fashioned hero and heroine . . . who keep dying for each other all the way through" (Howells, *The Rise of Silas Lapham* 174) doesn't mean it's not sentimental.

Sentimental authors write to specific groups of readers, and different readers are affected more or less strongly by different cherished cultural narratives—and this functions both diachronically (antebellum cherished cultural narratives are not the same as ones today) and synchronically (within the same time period, different readers will respond to some cultural narratives and not others). As a teen, I read serious literature compared to my friends: not the Sweet Valley High books, but *I, Claudius*. But I probably cried over that novel more than they did over theirs (*I, Claudius*'s cherished cultural story: "person with disability is underestimated and goes on to triumph"). This anecdote also illuminates another principle: we are primed to identify cherished cultural narratives in novels deemed sentimental, but they exist in many other literary traditions, including in realist literature in the nineteenth century and literary fiction in ours. Jim's revelation of his ill-treatment of his deaf daughter in *Huck Finn* makes him vivid not just because Jim suddenly has many more and conflicting characteristics, including self-consciousness, but because what he says fits neatly into a cherished cultural story: "parent who realizes and tries to atone for how they wronged their children." Thinking about Yao's *Disaffected*, I wonder whether stories about minoritized characters remaining immune to calls on their sympathy are deeply moving for many contemporary readers.[32]

If the existence of cherished cultural narratives can affect vividness, so too can different reading practices. Literary scholars interested in the question of how literary characters come to feel real to their readers tend to discuss characters without looking at how different reading habits encourage or close off this connection. Grabes is not an exception to this rule, but he does hint at how one could begin such an analysis. He writes that the experience of registering literary characters as vivid—that is, as figures that seem "as much alive as those we meet in everyday life"—"will be felt most strongly by the literary scholar who still has the ability to read or to watch a film or theater performance without immediately analyzing it" (222). He does not pursue this idea; instead, it's a path he leaves open. What if analysis isn't just a technique that a reader brings along with her as she opens up a novel's pages but a requirement (if one wants to be a member of the intended audience) that some authors build into their novels via the rhetorical choices they have made? Realist novels compel analysis, whereas sentimental novels discourage it. Of course, a reader can still engage in analysis regardless of the type of novel it is, as literary critics inevitably do. But the act of analysis will have different effects on a given novel: in some cases, it will allow the novel's characters to bloom, and in some, it will cause them to wilt.

One form of uncritical reading that English professors commonly encounter in the classroom has its roots in sympathetic identification: a student identifies with a character so much as to prevent them from seeing that character as a textual construction. Instead, the character seems to the student to be a real person. This tendency often results in papers where the student simply records their connection to that character or considers whether that character should have acted the way they did. The English professor version of the Hippocratic oath might go, "First, do not write about characters as if they're real people."

Yet it is an impoverished model of reading to suppose that readers must never imagine characters to be real people. Rabinowitz corrects such an arid notion by recognizing that the richest kind of reading requires a person both to accept the premise of many authors that they are offering a true account and also acknowledge that the characters they encounter are textual constructs: "A viewer is hardly responding appropriately to *Othello* if he rushes on the stage to protect Desdemona from the Moor's wrath. . . . Neither, however, is it proper to refuse to mourn Desdemona simply because we know that she will soon rise, return to her dressing room, remove her makeup, and go out for a beer with Roderigo" ("Truth" 125). I'd add to Rabinowitz's point by suggesting that fictional works vary in how much they ask readers to see characters as real people. A student's impulse to see a character as a real person in a sentimental novel or sentimental passage might reflect their sensitivity to a particular book's own reading lessons rather than being a symptom of a bad way of reading. Particular fictional works encourage particular relationships to characters, and sentimental works encourage a particularly intimate, credulous relationship between readers and characters.

Certainly, any particular reader can refuse a text's invitations, and no one is better at refusing such a sympathetic, uncritical relationship between reader and character than the contemporary literary critic. But if students often try, problematically, to identify with a character even when a book wants them to have a different kind of relationship, literary critics suffer the converse problem in feeling distanced from a given character even when a book encourages intimacy. I will return to this idea of the vividness of sentimental characters throughout the book.

OVERVIEW OF THE BOOK

This book explores the different relationships a range of postbellum realist authors had with sentimentality. It does so in order to clarify what sentimental sympathy allowed them to accomplish and also, in the process, suggest some new possibilities for how literary critics read and teach. Chapter 1 sets the stage for the rest of the book by describing how Harriet Beecher Stowe's *Uncle Tom's Cabin* trained its readers to read. *Uncle Tom's Cabin* has been interpreted in many ways, but in this chapter I view the novel as a reading primer that teaches its readers to adopt an "intensive" practice of reading instead of accepting the "extensive" reading practices that were developing among secular readers in the antebellum period. Even then, the novel's sense of what true literacy entails went against the times. Today, its understanding of literacy seems even more objectionable: the novel's notion of a literacy grounded in communal orality—in groups of people reading aloud to one another—upends a notion of literacy grounded in the silent, isolated activity of decoding words on a page, an act construed today to be at the center of adult literacy. According to contemporary protocols of reading, the novel is teaching a kind of illiteracy. Analyzing *Uncle Tom's Cabin* in terms of a history of reading can explain the novel's tremendous but uneven power across time and with different readers. We know a lot about the resistance that contemporaneous southern white readers exhibited toward the novel, but another group of organized resistance, we will see, comprised realists like Twain and Howells. This opposition continues with contemporary professors of literature, whose very identity as a particular kind of reader becomes threatened by the reading practice advocated by Stowe.

Chapter 2 contextualizes the current moment in literary criticism by returning to an earlier point in the evolution of critical distance, when Twain and Howells publicly championed realist works of fiction over and against sentimental ones and enabled subsequent literary critics to see the sentimental appeal as what James Baldwin calls "the mark of dishonesty" (496). Howells and Twain have a contradictory relationship to sentimentality. In a rare novel like *Annie Kilburn*, which mocks sentimental reform, Howells manages to align his anti-sentimental pronouncements with a refusal to engage in sentimental writing. By contrast, in *The Rise of Silas Lapham* and Twain's *Adventures of Huckleberry Finn* and *A Connecticut Yankee in King Arthur's Court*, anti-sentimental pronouncements and parodies are offset by sentimental scenes and characters. Reading Twain and Howells against the grain of their anti-sentimental pronouncements and parodies allows us to see what they would have lost if they had actually given up sentimentality—and why it's no coincidence that their most famous, most resonant works incorporate it.

Henry James forms a less contradictory but more poignant relationship to sentimentality. Chapter 3 views *The Bostonians* not as an expression of James's mastery over sentimentality but as a meditation on its power. James is fascinated by sentimentality but unable or unwilling to engage in it himself. His narrative technique of shifting unreliable focalization fails to provide the incontrovertible assessment of Verena Tarrant, the sentimental orator at the novel's center, that the reader desires. James's refusal of mastery over this sentimental character opens up a new way to position him in relation to sentimentality and provides us with an alternative to prevailing critical methods of reading sentimental fiction.

The last two chapters focus on Constance Fenimore Woolson and Charles Chesnutt, who employ sentimentality strategically and ingeniously. Both authors use the strategy of what Rabinowitz calls "rhetorical passing." Woolson and Chesnutt "passed," for a long time, as local colorists whose descriptions of bark removed any possibility of a bite. Against this view, I uncover their incisive, clever critiques of realist discernment in Woolson's case and white supremacist thinking in Chesnutt's, and how sentimental sympathy enables them both to mount them.

Chapter 4 turns to Constance Fenimore Woolson. Though she has long been seen as a "[Henry] James-obsessed spinster" ("Introduction" 7), as Victoria Brehm puts it, and a minor regionalist writer, I show that Woolson is in fact a keen critic of the protocols of reading realist literature. Woolson sets realist reading protocols against sympathetic reading in her tour de force short story "'Miss Grief'" and in another short story, "Solomon." Both feature narrators whose unreliability has often gone unnoticed by both critics and readers, whose fancied discernment renders them unable to appreciate sentimental writing. Woolson tallies the costs exacted by the discriminating reading touted by the white male realists, costs that accrue particularly painfully to women writers and other marginalized artists. This chapter illuminates how one woman writer managed both to capitalize on realism's fancied sophistication and to critique that sophistication and the normative force it exerted. She was not alone in her skepticism.

The final chapter turns to Charles Chesnutt, another ingenious, marginalized realist author who in the nineteenth century was seen by many readers as simply entertaining. In his conjure stories, Chesnutt also creates an equivocally unreliable narrator. Contemporaneous white readers identified with this white frame narrator against the Black tale teller, Uncle Julius, whom they dismissed as merely charming. Chesnutt has become central to the African American literary tradition, but he himself saw his second published novel, *The Marrow of Tradition* (1901), as belonging to the tradition of *Uncle Tom's Cabin*. My reading of this novel explores what happens when we place him in this tradition. Chesnutt not only uses but weaponizes sympathy in the fight against racial injustice. In *The Marrow of Tradition*, he entices his white readers to sympathetically identify with his white characters in order to induce these readers to recognize their own complicity in white supremacist thinking. Sympathy, as wielded by Chesnutt, tries to force readers to engage in self-critique, with mixed results.

The book closes with an afterword that reflects on the impossible situation in which Chesnutt found himself—how to induce readers of his fiction to use sentimental sympathy as a means of recognizing not just the pain of others but failures in themselves—and what that can teach us about contemporary academic reading practices. In reflecting on my own experience reading *Marrow*, I acknowledge that I never read it the way Chesnutt intended but argue that that should not make me (and others who read as I do) feel excepted from Chesnutt's attempts to make his readers look at themselves critically and overcome the limits of their self-regard.

The discipline of literary criticism has excelled in demonstrating how certain practices and beliefs that have been seen as always already to have existed have arisen at particular times and for the particular benefit of some and not others. This kind of paranoid literary criticism aims to limit the power of those practices and beliefs. In locating an overlooked origin point of my discipline's commitment to critical reading, I am not, however, attempting such an unmasking or calling for a renunciation of this extremely useful way to read fictional texts, as if that were even possible. Instead, I want to suggest that, just as the realists supplemented their realism with sentimentality, so contemporary literary critics can supplement their current skill set by recognizing the power of sympathetic reading and appreciating it in themselves and their students. No book teaches sympathetic reading the way *Uncle Tom's Cabin* does even as that reading practice was going out of style.

This book would not have been possible without the insightful feedback and support of many of my colleagues, starting with the members of my writing group, Gillian Silverman and Claudia Stokes. I also want to thank James Phelan for turning me on to narrative theory so many years ago, and his unflagging generosity in reading my work and discussing narrative theory with me since then. Thanks as well to the two anonymous readers who provided extensive and immensely helpful feedback on my book; to my editor at the University of Massachusetts Press, Brian Halley; and to my copyeditor, Amanda Heller. Thank you as well to the other colleagues who have helped me explore nineteenth-century American literature and narrative theory over the years, including Debby Rosenthal, Michael Tavel Clarke, Peter Rabinowitz, Brian McHale, and Amy Shuman. I also thank the participants in the Society for the Study of American Women Writers regional reading groups and Project Narrative Summer Institute seminars that I've attended. Last but not least, I want to thank Jeremy, Toby, and Norah for their love and support.

Much of the work of this project was funded by a grant from the Government of Canada's Social Sciences and Humanities Research Council (SSHRC).

CHAPTER 1

Word Become Flesh

Literacy, Anti-Literacy, and Illiteracy
in Uncle Tom's Cabin

THIS CHAPTER IS about how *Uncle Tom's Cabin* teaches us to read.[1] It opens the novel to new avenues of inquiry by situating it within the history of reading in the United States. This chapter also provides the foundation for the analyses of the postbellum realist works that follow. To demonstrate how a range of realist writers continue to rely on the sympathetic reading that Stowe's novel teaches, I first establish what this reading practice entails and the sentimental techniques it relies on.

For Stowe, the abolition of slavery is intimately tied not just to *"feel[ing] right"* (404), as she says at the end of *Uncle Tom's Cabin*, but to reading right. Seeing the novel in this way clarifies the reading practices of both secular and religious antebellum readers. It also illuminates the reading practices of contemporary literary critics. Modern critics, even feminist ones, are often bewildered about how *Uncle Tom's Cabin* so deeply engaged such a wide audience in the antebellum United States. In answering that question, we can gain insight into why it leaves so many contemporary readers, especially literary critics, unaffected. Although the novel is directed at certain people (everyone, really, who was living in the United States in 1851) and uses a particular strategy (sentimental sympathy) to persuade them of its antislavery message, it also assumes that many readers taking up the book do not know how to read it. It is the novel's job to teach them.[2]

Uncle Tom's Cabin is deeply concerned with literacy. While Sarah Robbins reads the novel within the tradition of nineteenth-century domestic literacy narratives, my argument attends to the novel's iconoclasm: how the reading practices it teaches its readers are an attack on antebellum notions of literacy. Rather than inculcating among its readers the secular reading practices that were becoming ascendant in the antebellum period, *Uncle Tom's Cabin* teaches what I call "anti-literacy." Conventional reading practices lead to moral illiteracy as far as Stowe is concerned. Yet for modern literary critics, it is Stowe's recommended reading practices that compromise literacy. The realists had much to do with this contemporary assessment, as subsequent chapters will detail, but for now it's enough to say that the shift from Stowe's very successful moral literacy project to present-day analyses of how her most famous novel degrades literacy attests to the immense but uneven power of *Uncle Tom's Cabin*, both across time and for different readers. The novel's presupposition that its potential readers will not know how to read it (and that the novel itself will teach them) levels and potentially enlarges its intended audience to encompass everyone. Not all its readers, however, begin as equally eager pupils.

READING IN *UNCLE TOM'S CABIN*

There are endless scenes of reading in *Uncle Tom's Cabin*, occurring in many locales, featuring diverse people, and involving different kinds of media. Genteel white men spend time in their parlors reading the newspaper; the slave catcher Marks reads a list in a tavern; the son of Tom's enslaver teaches Tom how to read; and many, many characters read the Bible. Despite its seeming variety, reading in the novel can be grouped into two categories: good ways of reading and bad ones. Yet the practices associated with these categories are not what we might expect. Just as Jane Tompkins has identified the revolutionary way that *Uncle Tom's Cabin* reverses the political values of its time, so the novel reverses the practices that most of Stowe's contemporaries (and almost all modern readers) associate with each of these categories.

The novel effects this reversal gradually. It begins by meeting its white readers where they are.[3] Thus in an early chapter, the narrator invites "us" (18), her white readers, to spend "An Evening in Uncle Tom's Cabin" (17). But if Stowe lures "us" in with a frisson of the taboo, she also assuages her jumpy white readers by keeping them apart from and above such a locale and its inhabitants. The domestic appointments of the cabin inhabited by Tom and his wife reveal at the same time their aspirations and their ignorance of just how things are done. For example, the narrator points out the portrait of George Washington hanging over the fireplace, "drawn and colored in a manner which would certainly have astonished that hero" (19), thus allowing her readers a chuckle that acknowledges their own sophistication.

In the midst of this tour, we come upon a scene of reading instruction. George, the son of Tom's enslaver, is philanthropically teaching Tom to write his letters, which Tom, like many novice reader-writers, is reversing: "'Not that way, Uncle Tom,—not that way,' said [George], briskly, as Uncle Tom laboriously brought up the tail of his *g* the wrong side out; 'that makes a *q*, you see'" (19).[4] Chloe is thrilled to entertain "Mas'r George" that night, feeding him before she feeds her own children. What secures George so exalted a place in Chloe's social hierarchy is not just his father but his literacy: "'How easy white folks al'us does things!' said Aunt Chloe ... regarding young Master George with pride. 'The way he can write, now! and read, too! and then to come out here evenings and read his lessons to us,—it's mighty interestin'!'" (19). George's literacy is also remarked upon by the enslaved men and women who join Chloe and Tom for a religious meeting, which George leads. After George supplements his reading of some verses from the Bible with "expositions of his own" (27), Chloe and Tom's friends tell him that "a minister couldn't lay it off better than he did"; that "'twas reely 'mazin'!" (27). In George we find a model of conventional literacy, the performance of which garners him effusive praise from the group of enslaved men and women who have attended the meeting and presumably from Stowe's white readers.

Yet even in this primal scene of literacy we can see how Stowe introduces an alternative to the conventional understanding of it. Christopher Castiglia has argued that such antebellum scenes of instruction between Blacks and whites "establish hierarchical relations of power" (210), but this grim depiction of power relations may be less totalizing than his Foucauldian analysis suggests. Depicted as struggling with conventional literacy at the beginning of the scene, Tom, by the end of it, is shown leading his unofficial congregation in prayer in a way that puts George's meager efforts to shame: "Nothing could exceed the touching simplicity, the child-like earnestness, of [Tom's] prayer, enriched with the language of Scripture, which seemed so entirely to have wrought itself into his being, as to have become a part of himself" (27). This description of Tom's ministerial abilities follows the paragraph in which George's efforts in religious instruction are recorded. It now appears that George's are derivative (he was "well trained in religious things by his mother" [27]); Tom's prayers well up from his very being, not effortful at all, and result from his lack of conventional literacy.

Stowe's invocation of Tom's "child-like earnestness" is not simply evidence of Stowe's romantic racialism (although it is also that).[5] Because she believes children to be eloquent in a way that no trained rhetorician can be, it is also part of an ethically defensible effort to make her white readers skeptical about George's rhetorical superiority. The description of Tom's abilities as a speaker invites the reader to reread the description of George's efforts with a more critical eye. We might detect something excessive in the attendees' lavish praise of George ("a minister couldn't lay it off better than he did") as opposed to the "abundance of the responses which broke out everywhere around [Tom]" (27) after Tom's prayers. That a minister couldn't "lay it off" better than George suggests that the enslaved men and women attending this meeting might be laying it on. Stowe shows us elsewhere in the novel that she was well aware of the ability of the enslaved to tell white people just what they wanted to hear.[6]

Stowe juxtaposes George's conventional literacy to Tom's, and her conclusions about their relative merits are, even at the beginning of this novel, unconventional. Yet they are—I think intentionally—easy to overlook. What might linger as much as Tom's power as an unofficial preacher are the images of what Hortense Spillers has called Tom's dyslexia (193) and George's accomplishments. So sensitive to readers' discomfort at what Stowe would call the "rude dwelling" that the narrator has invited them to enter, Stowe has the narrator make every effort to put them at ease. The narrator's description of Tom's effectiveness as a minister is sprinkled with distancing quotation marks: "In the language of a pious old negro, he 'prayed right up'" (27). But reading retroactively, we can limn the contours of a different valuation of literacy from the one we might first have discerned: George's as learned but unpersuasive, leading to social stratification; Tom's as natural and thus powerful, leading to community. But to be able to read this realignment into this early scene and to understand it more fully, we must trace other scenes of reading that follow it.

The literacy of slave catchers presents a useful problem for Stowe's reading instruction:

> Marks had got from his pocket a greasy pocket-book, and taking a long paper from thence, he sat down, and fixing his keen black eyes on it, began mumbling over its contents: "Barnes—Shelby County—boy Jim, three hundred dollars for him, dead or alive.
> "Edwards—Dick and Lucy—man and wife, six hundred dollars; wench Polly and two children—six hundred for her or her head." (63)

Marks reads in a dehumanizing way. Real people turn into abstractions, enslaved men and women into dollar amounts. Thus Stowe introduces her readers to the logic of equivalence that undergirds the slave system, and, as a sentimental novelist, she focuses on how this logic breaks up families. These are not just any enslaved men and women Marks is turning into dollars, but husbands and wives, mothers and children. The logic of equivalence deracinates Dick, Lucy, and Polly. This transubstantiation takes place because of a particular kind of document, the slave advertisement, and the reading practices it has engendered.

The function of Marks's list is literalized in an uncanny way a few chapters later. Whether or not Stowe intended this parallel, it is as if the Lucy of Marks's "Dick and Lucy" has come alive. We meet Lucy on a boat that is taking Tom farther south. When we first meet her, she does not believe that her enslaver has sold her and her child to a slave trader. To prove it to her, the slave trader, Haley, has a man passing by read the bill of sale aloud: "'Why, it's a bill of sale, signed by John Fosdick,' said the man, 'making over to you the girl Lucy and her child. It's all straight enough, for aught I see'" (115). Transformed into a dollar amount, her son subsequently sold away, Lucy throws herself off the side of the boat. Marks's document evacuates the enslaved of personhood; the Lucy scene allows the reader to *picture* that personhood. We have moved from reader to witness: these are not just words on a page but bereft mothers and open water.

Even when they do not involve perusing slave advertisements, acts of reading often distract men from what goes on around them, even when that reading material purports to convey exactly that. Miss Ophelia, keen for her cousin St. Clare to free the girl Topsy, begs him to write up the papers. The aristocratic, languorous St. Clare resists. Stowe figures his languor as inextricably tied to his reading habits: "'Well, well,' said St. Clare, 'I will;' and he sat down, and unfolded a newspaper to read" (282). For Stowe, advertisements for freedom seekers stand synecdochically for newspapers, and newspapers stand synecdochically for conventional literacy. St. Clare's reading does not just provide a pretext for his congenital and stereotypical southern ennui; it distracts him from the immediacy of the slavery problem. His face covered by sheets of paper, he literally cannot see what is right in front of him. Despite what Benedict Anderson would argue 130 years later, Stowe figures the newspaper here as atomizing readers, rendering them unable to act for the greater good. In fact, newspaper reading is what kills St. Clare: he dies while intervening in a fight in a café; he had gone there to read the papers. As the novel progresses, conventional literacy picks up more insidious associations: from social privilege and a source of benevolence to class bounding and the power to dehumanize.

HOW TO READ *UNCLE TOM'S CABIN*

Susan Suleiman suggests that one of the generic characteristics of the didactic novel, or as she terms it the *roman à thèse*, is a high degree of redundancy (149). Characters reappear in different guises; plots repeat. Stowe often deploys a form of redundancy we might term "inversion." For example, the enslaved Eliza travels north on a path to freedom, while Tom travels south on a path to martyrdom. Why does Stowe favor this form of redundancy? Stowe's eschatology might predispose her toward the lesson of Matthew 20:16: "So the last will be first." But it is also a feature of oratorical eloquence in this period. Recall Frederick Douglass's famous chiasmus in his *Narrative*: "You have seen how a man was made a slave; you shall see how a slave was made a man" (47). The daughter, sister, and wife of ministers, Stowe knew the discipline of rhetoric and oratory intimately. Although she spurned the eloquence of senators, as we will shortly see, Stowe nevertheless embeds oratorical figures in her novel—just not on the level of her sentences. Inversion, or chiasmus, plays out on the level of the plot.

Just as Douglass's famous chiasmus represents a turning point in his narrative, so the scene of Marks's dehumanizing reading finds its chiasmatic inversion in another scene of reading, one featuring a character named Senator Bird, who voted for the Fugitive Slave Bill. We meet the senator and his wife as we follow Eliza north. Just as the Birds are arguing about whether to help fugitives, Eliza appears at their door, "a young and slender woman, with garments torn and frozen, with one shoe gone, and the stocking torn away from the cut and bleeding foot, . . . laid back in a deadly swoon upon two chairs" (74). The senator promptly encourages his wife to do all she can to help Eliza. The narrator accounts for this remarkable turnabout thus:

> He was as bold as a lion about it [the Fugitive Slave Bill], and "mightily convinced" not only himself, but everybody that heard him;—but then his idea of a fugitive was only an idea of the letters that spell the word,—or, at the most, the image of a little newspaper picture of a man with a stick and bundle, with "Ran away from the subscriber" under it. The magic of the real presence of distress,—the imploring human

eye, the frail, trembling human hand, the despairing appeal of helpless agony,—these he had never tried. (80–81)

Bird reads just like Marks: people turn into "letters that spell the word," nowhere more so than in newspapers. But the presence of an actual suffering fugitive makes that method of reading untenable. Bird will atone for his sinful way of reading.

So here is the chiasmatic inversion that has taken place at the level of plot: "You have seen how a man dehumanizes the enslaved; you shall see how the enslaved humanizes a man." Until the senator's encounter with this "real presence of distress," reading was an abstract mental process: words comprised letters, which the senator could decode. The senator must learn a new way to read—adopt what I'm calling a sympathetic reading practice—so that the word becomes flesh. He realizes that words should conjure pictures of people—and sometimes they will uncannily conjure real people themselves, as happens repeatedly in this novel. But not just any kind of people: the iconic image of "a newspaper picture of a man with a stick and bundle" features an enslaved man whose only ties, presumably, are the ones securing his bundle. In *Uncle Tom's Cabin*, this iconic image turns into an actual crying woman whose bundle is her child.

If conventional literacy turns enslaved people into words, sentimental literacy turns words into enslaved people. We see this with Senator Bird, whose perusal of an ad about an enslaved freedom seeker conjures "the real presence of distress." But we can see this process even more clearly in Tom's practice of reading. For Tom, reading his Bible on the ship conveying him south, "every passage breathing of some old home scene, and recalling some past enjoyment, his Bible seemed to him all of this life that remained, as well as the promise of a future one" (132). Again, we have the living—and this time, breathing—Word.

But the way Tom reads the Bible has not just the power to conjure scenes from memory; it has the power to make one's mental images present in the external world. Nowhere might we see this more than in a scene that describes how Tom and his new enslaver's daughter read together: "Tom and Eva were seated on a little mossy seat, in an arbor, at the foot of the garden. It was Sunday evening, and Eva's Bible lay open on her knee. She read,—'And I saw a sea of glass, mingled with fire.' 'Tom,' said Eva, suddenly stopping, and pointing to the lake, 'there 'tis'" (238). The scene goes on to ring variations on Tom and Eva's matching what they are reading to the topography around them, culminating with the sickly Eva's pointing to the sky, which Tom has just referred to in a hymn that speaks of "spirits bright." Eva notes, "'I'm going *there*,' she said, 'to the spirits bright, Tom; *I'm going, before long*'" (239). What Tom and Eva read allows them to see their surroundings and invest them with spiritual significance, a process that Candy Gunther Brown ascribes to evangelical literature generally.[7] Before Bird's conversion, even if he had seen a freedom seeker, he would not have recognized her as a distraught mother. Conventional, secular literacy, Stowe teaches us, produces a kind of perceptual disability: it robs words of their power to induce readers to see the world around them in its spiritual fullness, as we can register when St. Clare elsewhere comments on Tom's reaction to a biblical passage. "'Tom,' said his Master, 'this is all *real* to you!' 'I can jest fairly *see* it Mas'r,' said Tom. 'I wish I had your eyes, Tom'" (277), St. Clare responds.

Reading, for Stowe, is an intensely visual experience. Marianne Noble, building on work by Jeannine DeLombard, describes how sentimental authors evoke sympathy via depicting an eyewitness to suffering ("Sympathetic Listening"). Before Stowe wrote *Uncle Tom's Cabin*, she informed the editor of *The National Era*, the abolitionist paper where her novel would be serialized, of her plans: "My vocation is simply that of a *painter*, and my object will be to hold up in the most lifelike and graphic manner possible slavery.... There is no arguing with *pictures*, and everybody is impressed by them, whether they mean to be or not" ("Letter to Gamaliel Bailey"). This conception of reading is literalized in a comic moment in the novel where words literally become a picture. Tom has received a letter from his old reading instructor, George, which Tom never "tired of looking at . . . and even held a council with Eva on the expediency of getting it framed, to hang up in his room. Nothing but the difficulty of arranging it so that both sides of the page would show at once stood in the way of this undertaking" (236). Hanging the letter is equivalent to hanging a portrait of those whom Tom left behind. Stowe knows that her audience envisions itself more sophisticated than Tom and Eva; they need this very serious lesson about the fungibility of words to be coated in humor to ingest it. Why is viewing pictures a compelling metaphor for reading? For Stowe, good reading—sympathetic reading—is equivalent to seeing the people that the words on the page represent as if they are real.

Stowe suggests that the act of reading should be pictorial, but she also wants it to be oral and communal. The scene of Tom and Eva reading together that I related earlier slides, in a barely perceptible way, from Bible verses to hymns, from passages that one reads to oneself, as Tom does on the ship to New Orleans, to stanzas meant to be sung in a group. Reading frequently turns into singing in *Uncle Tom's Cabin*. It's what happens in that primal scene of literacy, which we begin to see serves as a template for the rest of the novel: the self-important intoning of the Bible by "Mas'r George" turns into group singing by the enslaved men and women he's addressing. Once they are together, Eva and Tom never read silently or alone.[8] In fact, once we become aware of it, we can register how Stowe believes silent, isolated reading to be a force that pulls against the family, whether it is a distraction from the important work of freeing an enslaved girl or an instrument for breaking up enslaved families. In contrast, reading aloud to others strengthens social bonds.[9]

Until now, I have been talking about literacy on the diegetic level: How do different characters read, and how do they influence other characters to read well or badly? But as her "Concluding Remarks" suggest, Stowe wanted, as do all authors of didactic works, for the storyworld of her novel to have real-world effects.[10] These effects would be produced by her actual readers adopting the reading practices of the intradiegetic ones, the ones in the novel.[11] How do actual readers take on the habits of fictional characters? Sentimental novels encourage sympathetic identification, which, according to Glenn Hendler, "works through a logic of equivalence based on affect; any being capable of suffering, regardless of race, age, or any other personal characteristic, can evoke sympathy, especially from a female character (or reader) who has suffered herself" (688). Mrs. Bird, whose young son has recently died, identifies with Eliza, whose son is in danger of being sold away from her. Sentimental sympathy erases class and racial difference, which many contemporary literary critics, as I discussed in the introduction, find to be a cause of grave ethical concern.

I want to note a different aspect of sentimental sympathy, one that becomes apparent if we linger for a moment on the relationship between the intra- and extradiegetic realms, those within and outside the world of the novel, in the *roman à thèse*. For sentimental sympathy to affect an actual reader, she must imagine a given character is a person, just like her. Critics have focused on the racial and gender politics of such an equation,[12] but let me focus for a moment on the textual ones. The actual reader must imagine that the character is not a fictional creation but a person. In other words, critics have emphasized that sentimental sympathy allows the reader to think (or deceives the reader into thinking, as most critics tend to believe) that someone, marked by racial or class difference, is a person *just like her*. But it also requires that the reader think she is a *person* just like her.[13]

If sentimental sympathy invites extradiegetic readers to ignore the fictionality of a novel's characters, so too does the novel's disparagement of conventional literacy. I described before how Stowe locates the ground zero of enslavement in the habit of turning people into words. The solution, as Senator Bird learns, is to turn words back into people. If we consider how *Uncle Tom's Cabin* wants its internal dynamics to become real-world lessons, we can acknowledge how much this text discourages the reader from seeing it, ultimately, as a written screed. Instead, it teaches readers to see it as a series of pictures come to life.

There are many strategies Stowe uses to do this. I discussed one, revealed by Robyn Warhol, in the introduction: the mobilization of cherished cultural narratives. Warhol has discussed others. For example, Stowe's many apostrophes ask the reader to contribute to the "living dramatic reality" of the novel, "to convince the reader that the redundant message is not only true, but of personal importance" ("Poetics" 290). They invite the reader to visualize a scene as if they could enter into it. Here is a representative apostrophe: "While this scene was going on in the men's sleeping-room, the reader may be curious to take a peep at the corresponding apartment allotted to the women" (299). Not all of Stowe's interventions are titillating like these "peeps" into the women's sleeping quarters, but they all prime readers to accept the idea that this novel is not distracting readers from reality, as newspaper reading does, but bringing them close enough to see it for themselves. There's a third strategy Stowe uses to make her novel seem less like a representation of the world and more like a doorway into it. Stowe has the habit, detailed earlier, of turning what someone is reading about into scenes that take place in the storyworld of the novel. Senator Bird reads about a freedom seeker and lo, a freedom seeker *actually appears*. Such a technique makes the storyworld of the novel seem real by process of elimination, as when one dreams about waking up from a dream. What's left must be reality.

Contemporaneous readers did register the novel's "living dramatic reality." In 1852 the abolitionist William Lloyd Garrison wrote of reading *Uncle Tom's Cabin*, "We confess to the frequent moistening of our eyes, and the making of our heart grow liquid as water, and the trembling of every nerve within us, in the perusal of the incidents and scenes so vividly depicted in [its] pages"

(50). He articulates the emotional impact of this novel through recourse to the vividness of the scenes Stowe created. We might have expected Garrison to respond thus to a novel whose antislavery thesis so closely echoed his own. But even those most opposed to the antislavery message of the novel noted its vividness. "A Carolinian," author of "Slavery in the Southern States," wrote: "We have a variety of vivid scenes to illustrate the power of the master in separating the families of slaves, in destroying their moral character, and in scourging them even to death. In these sketches her zeal has got the better of the authoress, and she has drawn a most wild and unreal picture of slavery" (433–34). The vividness, the pictorial quality of the novel—the Carolinian's descriptions closely echo Stowe's own letter to the editor of *The National Era*, although, of course, this proslavery author laments these characteristics. Negative reviewers found *Uncle Tom's Cabin* false, but false in a particular way: they did not dispute how lifelike it seemed. In fact, its vividness—what we could call its "reality effect"—is exactly the problem because, according to these critics, it gave a real-seeming but false picture of slavery that ignorant northern readers would take to be true.[14]

These comments suggest how Stowe created an alternative reality for the reader. As Barbara Hochman has written about at length, many readers became so immersed in this novel that their extratextual lives halted for the time it took them to read it.[15] As Eunice Beecher, the wife of Stowe's brother Henry Ward Beecher, reported: "The clock struck twelve, one, two, three, and then, to my great relief I heard Mr. Beecher coming upstairs. As he entered he threw 'Uncle Tom's Cabin' on the table, exclaiming: 'There, I've done it! But if Hattie Stowe ever writes anything more like that! I'll—well, she has nearly killed me anyhow!'" (qtd. in Hochman, *Reading Revolution* 83). A lifelong friend of Stowe's, Georgiana May, reacted similarly: "I sat up late last night long after one o'clock, reading and finishing 'Uncle Tom's Cabin.' I *could not* leave it any more than I could have left a dying child" (qtd. in Noble, *Masochistic* 141). Stowe's sentimental strategies found purchase with many readers, those sympathetic to Stowe's message and those not.

STOWE'S ANTI-LITERACY

What I have been calling the "conventional literacy" that Stowe opposed was both historically specific and ideologically charged. If we look at how literacy was being construed in the mid-nineteenth century, we can understand why I want to call the kind of literacy Stowe was teaching "anti-literacy," as opposed to framing it simply as an alternative practice. Stowe was advocating a set of reading practices that had lost significant ground among secular readers in the antebellum period. She was asking them to reject the reading practice that was increasingly registering as constituting adult literacy: reading quickly and reading alone. She was calling for the return of reading practices that had been common in the early republic and in Europe for many centuries, and that persisted among evangelical American readers.[16] Although the oral nature of reading had by no means disappeared (nor would it disappear even in the postbellum period),[17] it was becoming, to use Raymond Williams's term, residual (6).

In "The Uses of Literacy in New England," David D. Hall marks the mid-nineteenth century as a time of radical transition in terms of what he calls "reading style" (54) and what I have been calling "reading practice." A culture of "intensive" reading was being superseded, if not wholly replaced, by one of "extensive" reading, to use an influential heuristic developed by Rolf Engelsing. Instead of reading a handful of mainly religious books over and over with an attitude of reverence (Hall, "Uses" 54), people were reading more and varied books more casually and secularly. The publisher and author Samuel Goodrich describes this older reading style in his reminiscences, published in 1856: "Books and newspapers—which are now diffused even among the country towns, so as to be in the hands of all, young and old—were then [in the early nineteenth century] scarce, and were read respectfully, as if they were grave matters, demanding thought and attention. They were not toys and pastimes, taken up every day, and by everybody, in the short intervals of labor, and then hastily dismissed, like waste paper" (86).

Thomas White evokes the experience of this older form of literacy in his *Little Book for Little Children*: he advises his young readers to underline parts of the book or make marks in the margin to ease the task of finding places they want to return to, "places you find most relish in, and take most special notice of, that that doth most concern thee" (qtd. in Hall, "Uses" 64). White evokes Tom's own habit of making marks next to passages in his Bible to spur the recollection of home scenes, to facilitate the Book's bodying forth the most cherished parts of his identity. Hall, writing not about passages in sentimental novels but about passages in eighteenth- and early nineteenth-century books more generally, notes that they "became embodied in their [reader's] memories" ("Uses" 65). He concludes that "the distance between books and life was very short, if any real distance existed in the first place" ("Uses" 67). Reading as intensive, as oral, as immediate—we might say with some confidence that Stowe was mounting, in the pages of *Uncle Tom's Cabin*, a strong defense of and primer in an earlier form of literacy, one that was being superseded by other reading practices.

Yet we must complicate this historical shift further in the antebellum context. These practices were less residual among certain communities of readers, including Stowe's own evangelical reading community. Evangelical readers kept alive the practices of intensive reading—thinking of books as personal companions, reading orally—at the same time that they took advantage of a burgeoning print culture, as Brown describes in *The Word in the World*. Stowe faced the same problem they did: to balance what Brown describes as "purity and presence," the desire to remain true to the Word while also achieving a presence in the larger culture.

With her Christianity-infused best-selling novel, Stowe achieved this balance by disarticulating two things that usually go together in the history of reading: the number and kinds of books available and the ways their readers read them. In the traditional account, intensive reading practices develop alongside a culture of print scarcity, extensive reading practices alongside an increase in number and kinds of reading material, for example, newspapers, magazines, and novels, rather than just the Bible and John Bunyan's *Pilgrim's Progress*. On this view, it can seem that Haley's bad reading habits come from his reading newspapers rather than the Bible; the genre he is reading determines how he reads it. Yet for Stowe, whose early published work appeared in evangelical newspapers,[18] what you read is not nearly as important as how you read it. Genre and medium only loosely determine reading practice, as other evangelicals in this period demonstrated, concerned with spreading the Word by making sure that those in the evangelical community possessed a large number of evangelical texts in all sorts of genres.[19] Stowe sketches out a possible way to counteract the welter of secular reading material that people in this period were being confronted with: read it by all means, but read it in the right (intensive and sympathetic) way.

How well did contemporaneous readers learn her lessons about the right way to read? What is remarkable about Stowe's lessons in literacy is how effective they were. Let us return to one of Stowe's contemporaneous readers mentioned earlier, Georgiana May. According to Hochman, "May reproduces Stowe's words, not as explicit citation, but as a kind of deep recycling which assimilates the reader herself into the action of the book" ("Devouring" 90). Should we conclude from reactions like this one that Stowe was endorsing a set of reading practices that her antebellum readers could easily slip on again or that they had never abandoned? It would be tempting to say yes, but the abundance of Stowe's literacy lessons in *Uncle Tom's Cabin*, and their carefully calibrated increases in difficulty, lead me to suspect it was not that easy for them to slip on this set of reading practices. Beecher and May were, after all, trained in the same evangelical, intensive reading practices that Stowe was. It's more plausible that Stowe imagined a large part of her audience as having moved away from them.

We know that different readers read for different things in different ways. Not every contemporaneous reader would receive Stowe's literacy lessons in the same way. Some would find in them confirmation; others would find in them new possibilities. But the tremendous impact her novel had—its ability to appear as brilliantly vivid to supporters and detractors of abolition alike—attests to the effectiveness of Stowe's pedagogy, its ability to train a wide swath of contemporaneous readers in what was, for many of them, only a vaguely familiar or newly unfamiliar set of reading practices.

ANTI-LITERACY AS ILLITERACY

How much should we value Stowe's form of anti-literacy, what I am calling "sympathetic reading," today? My students are quick to defend Tom's way of reading against Haley's and the senator's. Yet we also need to tally its cost. It is a convenient feature of Stowe's novel that she allows us to do so without poking our head above her pages. Suleiman notes the "overflow effect" of many *romans à thèse*: how they contain within their pages material that "subverts" their theses (206). St. Clare is just the sort of reader that Stowe wants to retrain. He specifically challenges the reading practice that Stowe champions. More objectionable even than the choice of his reading material is St. Clare's habit of denying the reality of the Bible via his skills as a critical reader, as we witness when he hypothesizes to Miss Ophelia about what would happen to biblical interpretation if slavery suddenly ceased to be profitable: "What a flood of light would pour into the church, all at once, and how immediately it would be discovered that everything in the Bible and reason went the other way [from condoning slavery]!" (168). St. Clare suggests that even the Bible can be interpreted polysemously and self-interestedly. This is a hermeneutical position Stowe finds very dangerous, not just because it's heterodox but because it suggests a way of reading that replaces immersion with proto-Marxist literary analysis.[20] Readers like St. Clare cannot feel the living dramatic reality of what they read because they are engaged in the intellectual exercise of generating different interpretive possibilities. He is the only character whom Tom, Eva, and Miss Ophelia all proselytize, but he cannot be converted. I suggest, only half-jokingly, that we can register Stowe's acknowledgment of the powerful draw of this way of reading by noting that Stowe has to kill him off.

Communal, oral, immediate—these traits characterize intensive reading, but they also characterize, in later eras, the reading practices we associate with children. Stowe's humorous passage about Tom and Eva's attempt at framing George's letter shows that she makes the same association. I can see, with some effort, that Stowe uses this scene to show what she believes adults lose by approaching texts with less reverence than this enslaved man and this child, but later generations are hard-pressed to see the scene as anything but amusing. Stowe thinks that children reveal best practices when it comes to speaking and reading, but contemporary Americans have come to see the literacy of children as a necessary but rudimentary stage in the more complex literacy they need to develop.

It is precisely those actions that Stowe associates with Eva and Tom which she wants all her readers to adopt—reading aloud and in groups, hearing the same text read to them repeatedly—that we most associate with the rudiments of literacy. It is how young children learn to read and *not* how adults should read.[21] Until the early twentieth century, teachers in primary schools had beginning readers read aloud and in turn to test their reading proficiency. It was seen as an educational advance, part of the movement of "reading for meaning," when schools began to emphasize silent reading practices for their students (Pearson and Goodin). A contemporary report from the International Reading Association describes "the principal way in which most accomplished adolescent and adult readers read—independently and silently" (Hiebert and Reutzel xi). In a renegade article, "The Case for Slow Reading," Thomas Newkirk laments the premium our schools place on fast, silent reading. He describes how schools see the "slow reading" practices that he's extolling, which are remarkably similar to the ones that Stowe is teaching us, as "antiquated, inefficient, and mismatched to the ways people read outside school" (8).[22]

Up to this point in the chapter I have stressed how reading practices change across time, which can lead some people, like Newkirk, to become nostalgic. Yet reading practices vary synchronically, too. Groups of people or members of different "interpretive communities," to use Stanley Fish's phrase, read differently from one another. This rather commonsensical observation can be nuanced if we use a model of audience developed by Peter Rabinowitz to precisely isolate the difference between the kind of reader Stowe is trying to create (a kind of reader who resembles the "lay reader" of today) and a professional reader.[23]

The concept of the reader is simplified in most thematic criticism. The literary critic takes herself to be a stand-in for all readers, her reading practice assumed to match those of all other readers. We can gain a lot of interpretive traction if we dispense with that substitution and replace it with Rabinowitz's more complex model of audience, developed in his article "Truth in Fiction." His model illuminates the different audiences "implied in" (125) any fictional narrative—the different kinds of readers a fictional text invites us to be: "actual" reader, "intended" reader, and "narrative" reader.

The first kind of reader doesn't, in fact, require an invitation. No matter who you are (assuming you are not a chatbot), you are an *actual reader*; you bring to your fiction reading certain areas of knowledge and ignorance, certain values and predilections. You might or might not be close to the author's *intended audience*,[24] the audience that the author imagines will be reading their narrative, the audience to whom the author imputes certain "beliefs, knowledge, and familiarity with conventions" ("Truth" 126), including the knowledge that what they're reading is fiction. If a work is from the distant past, you might have drifted far from an author's intended audience. Do not despair. If you do not know a certain fact or have a particular set of values an author assumes you do, you can do research or pretend to have the values the author assumes readers to have and join the intended audience.[25] The third kind of audience a reader can choose to become is one that is probably not as familiar to many of my readers: the *narrative audience*. As a member of the narrative audience, you become the reader for whom the narrator (not the author) is writing, the one who thinks the storyworld of the novel is the real world. For example, if you're a narrative reader of *War and Peace*, you think that "Natasha and Pierre, and Andrei 'really' existed and that the events in their lives 'really' took place" ("Truth" 126).[26]

All these readerly positions exist at the same time, and Rabinowitz and James Phelan would argue (and I would agree) that the most fulfilling reading experience arises when you become part of both the intended and the narrative audience. If you refuse to become a member of one or the other, problems arise. If you resist making yourself into a member of the intended audience (by refusing, say, to fill in facts about the Spanish Civil War that Hemingway assumes you know), you might not be able to follow the plot of *For Whom the Bell Tolls* (this is an example Rabinowitz uses himself). If you refuse to become part of the narrative audience by saying something to yourself like "that would never happen!" or "that character is completely improbable!"[27] then you will find finishing that novel becomes a chore. Alternatively, if you find yourself searching for the grave of Charlotte Temple, you have joined the narrative audience but not the intended one, who know Susanna Rowson's novel is fiction. Rabinowitz's model allows one to understand why different readers respond differently to different narratives. For example, I am allergic to Westerns, so I am inevitably bored and/or outraged by them (a refusal to become part of the narrative audience). My undergraduate students, before I fill them in on Puritan pronoun conventions, are convinced that Mary Rowlandson does not love her infant daughter because she refers to her baby as "it" (they have not made themselves part of her intended audience).

Rabinowitz's model of audience allows us to understand, first, that actual readers might have particular reading practices that dispose them to join or refuse to join the other kinds of audiences implied by a fictional text. He also allows us to understand how certain texts can interact well or badly with such predilections. I want to focus now on professional readers. Janice Radway remarks that "professional, academic reading is only one kind of reading and a relatively specialized one at that, and as such, it cannot be used simply and in unqualified fashion as a model for all other forms of reading or as a stand-in for the acts of reading it wishes to reconstruct" (291). For English professors, used to conference presentations and collaboratively written articles, the oral and communal nature of intensive reading might not present much of a problem, assured as we are that we still do most of our reading silently and independently. I would wager that it is the immediacy and immersiveness of the reading experience Stowe endorses that most sticks in our craw, the lack of distance she insists on between her book and her intended reader's life. She invites us to be robust narrative readers, the kind who find themselves immersed and uncritical. This is a real barrier for many literary critics. For one thing, it erases our hard-won distance from novice students and their ease with narrative reading, which leads these students to identify with characters or imagine what they would do if they were transported to the world of the novel. These are our forms of collegiate pre-literacy, with our efforts going to instill critical distance.[28] My fondness for St. Clare, polysemic interpreter and wielder of irony, is no surprise; for me, he is the kind of reader I fancy myself, and have tried to teach my students, to be. For another thing, Stowe's invitation to be a narrative reader requires that literary critics allow themselves to be immersed in her novel's particular storyworld, one whose sentimental "excess" is an aesthetic hard sell for many literary critics and whose racial essentialism is, justifiably, an ethical one.[29]

I do not want to romanticize how easy it would be for literary critics to adopt the reading lessons Stowe teaches us. Rather, I would argue that residual forms of adult reading practice can become in later eras signs of pre-literacy or even illiteracy. Of course for Stowe, what she is teaching is not at all anti-literacy. But for literary critics, it is. My own reading practices, I suspect, were developed in specific reaction to the kind of immersive, uncritical reading that Stowe advocates. Yet I would suggest that many literary critics have not simply abandoned these practices. For example, Radway opens her wonderful article "Beyond Mary Bailey and Old Maid Librarians" by calling attention to the way that she views *It's a Wonderful Life* one way when watching it with her family at Christmas and another way when she writes about it in her scholarly essays. As I mentioned in the introduction, even when, as a grad student, I was most concerned with appearing as if I fit into the discipline, I experienced bouts of sympathetic reading, although I conveniently forgot about them for a long time.

CREATING AN AUDIENCE FOR *UNCLE TOM'S CABIN*

Stowe links the end of slavery to better ways of reading, and we can understand the effects of this linkage by again consulting the powerful model of audience I introduced earlier. As I mentioned in the course of laying out that model, even when authors create a highly mimetic world, they do not believe that their intended reader believes the fictional characters and events contained in the novel are real. I want to suggest that Stowe troubles this distinction through the particular way that her novel seeks to change her actual readers. Howells does not expect his contemporaneous readers to finish *The Rise of Silas Lapham* and then seek out the paint that Silas produces, no matter how much the novel proclaims its high quality, but Stowe does expect her readers to close *Uncle Tom's Cabin* and picture an actual enslaved mother the next time they read an advertisement for an enslaved woman who has endeavored to escape. But did she want her readers to believe that Eliza really exists? In some sense, yes: her "Concluding Remarks" begin by asserting that "the personal appearance of Eliza, the character ascribed to her, are sketches drawn from life" (400).[30]

Stowe followed *Uncle Tom's Cabin* with *A Key to Uncle Tom's Cabin* (1853). The second sentence of its first chapter begins with her claim that *Uncle Tom's Cabin* "has been a collection and arrangement of real incidents,—of actions really performed" (5). This claim reinforces the understanding that Stowe wrote her *Key* to counter proslavery critics like the author of "Slavery in the Southern States," who claimed Stowe had drawn a "most wild and unreal picture of slavery" (A Carolinian 434). As Stowe notes in the opening chapter of *A Key*, *Uncle Tom's Cabin* "is *treated* as a reality—sifted, tried, and tested, as a reality; and therefore as a reality it may be proper that it should be defended" (5). Cindy Weinstein has argued that *A Key* not only reveals what really goes on under slavery; it also teaches us a method to distinguish the "reality" of Stowe's depiction of slavery from the false facts provided by those southerners who defended it.[31] Weinstein calls *A Key* a "hermeneutic *tour de force*" (91), which suggests that the text may be thought of as the teacher's guide to the literacy manual that is *Uncle Tom's Cabin*.

That many readers treated *Uncle Tom's Cabin* as depicting reality rather than presenting a fictive universe invites us to think further about the distinction between intended and narrative audience. We might conceive of the distinction as a switch: turn off the distinction and we have nonfiction; turn it on and we have fiction. I acknowledge that even its most sympathetic readers did not read *Uncle Tom's Cabin* as nonfiction in an obvious way. While readers did not believe Eliza to be a real person, the novel invited them to think that a person just like Eliza did exist, not only because Stowe told her readers so but because she trained her readers to turn words about an enslaved person into a living picture of one. We do know that many readers believed that Tom did in fact have a real-life correlative, Josiah Henson, a belief that both Henson and Stowe encouraged.[32] Thus it seems equally false to suggest that antebellum readers retained a certainty that the people and events in *Uncle Tom's Cabin* were unreal or made up or existed only in the imagination of its author. The Black activist and physician James McCune Smith resolved at an 1852 meeting of the American and Foreign Anti-Slavery Society that "the warm thanks of this meeting be presented to Mrs. Harriet Beecher Stowe, for writing the inimitably beautiful and *truthful* story called *Uncle Tom's Cabin*" (qtd. in Banks 213; emphasis added). Here the aesthetic qualities of *Uncle Tom's Cabin* (it is "beautiful") are nestled right up against its nonfictional ones (it is "truthful").

I suggest that in the case of *Uncle Tom's Cabin*, the distinction between intended and narrative audiences operates less like a switch than a dimmer.[33] This suggestion does not derive from the fact that Stowe changed many of her readers' beliefs about slavery. She did more than that. She taught them a way to read that turned words into people, a way to read that turned her novel into a "living dramatic reality." For these readers, *Uncle Tom's Cabin* is closer to a historical account than to how we normally understand fiction to function.

But the dimmer switch analogy also, I hope, captures the temporal dimension of Stowe's lessons in what we would now classify as anti-literacy. The novel works on the reader gradually. *Uncle Tom's Cabin* has as its intended audience both no one before they have read the novel and everyone after they have. Or one could say that its intended audience is everyone even before they have read the novel precisely because Stowe knows that the novel itself will teach them how to read it. Regardless, the distinction between intended and narrative audiences narrows as readers progress through the novel.

We know that Stowe envisioned a huge audience for this novel, and it is telling that she reveals this to us at the end of her novel, not at the beginning. In her "Concluding Remarks," she invokes "men and women of America" and names them regionally and by occupation, for example, "generous, noble-minded men and women, of the South. . . . Farmers of Massachusetts, of New Hampshire" (403–4). These apostrophes, a characteristic feature of antebellum sentimental writing, are one of the formal manifestations of her lessons in the anti-literacy of intensive, sympathetic reading. Apostrophes in which authors address their readers suggest immediacy—the author is right there!—and invite readers to share the author's urgent emotions. Jonathan Culler's account of apostrophe suggests that they might do even more than that: the act of apostrophe seeks to bring both the poet and the object of the apostrophe to life in a mutual act of co-creation. Culler is discussing the subset of apostrophes addressed to inanimate objects; Stowe's apostrophes address readers. But there's a way that the reader is an inanimate object as well. The reader whom the author addresses in writing is inevitably an abstraction, separated from the author in space and possibly in time. Stowe's apostrophes function like all apostrophes: they emphasize voice and deny their own identity as something written. As Culler observes, "The vocative of apostrophe is a device which poetic voice uses to establish with an object a relationship that helps to constitute him" ("Apostrophe" 157). Stowe addresses an object, the reader, and in the process makes both the reader and the author come alive. In other words, Stowe's apostrophes, through their vocative force, put author and reader in the same room and make them intimates. Stowe's lessons in anti-literacy ensure (she hopes) that by the end of the novel, she can use her sentimental techniques to bring to life an audience comprising every single person in the nation.

If only. That traditionally canonical authors like Nathaniel Hawthorne mocked works like *Uncle Tom's Cabin* might very well have proceeded from their awareness that these popular women novelists' apostrophes challenged emergent models of literacy that their own works depended on.[34] For modern critics, apostrophe, as Culler shows, is nothing but embarrassing: "It represents that which critical discourse cannot comfortably assimilate" (151). The unprecedented popularity of *Uncle Tom's Cabin* attests to its success in transforming its actual readers into both its intended and narrative audience and then narrowing the distinction—readers who would, by necessity, feel the power of this novel because they would come to see the novel and characters as real, a kind of literacy that is hard for the English professor not to see as naïve, as, in fact, a marker of only basic literacy. Those students who find themselves weeping at *Uncle Tom's Cabin*, they have so much to learn! Certainly students need to learn about the problem of romantic racialism, but we are on less firm ground if we object just as much to Stowe's methods to invite immersion.

Let me end by introducing a narrative that literary critics have long associated with literacy. I would claim that *Uncle Tom's Cabin* is as concerned with literacy as Douglass's *Narrative*, both linking it to the achievement of freedom. The kind of literacy that Douglass endorses, however, is very different from the kind that Stowe does. Douglass prizes eloquence, with its oratorical connotations, and his imagined reader is not a witness but an overhearer.[35] As Noble argues, "In his writings, Douglass indicates that sympathy gained through listening and speaking is superior to sympathy grounded in visual signs of physical suffering" ("Sympathetic Listening" 54). Douglass asks his readers to fictionalize themselves into the sort of people who subscribe to the eloquence and ideals that nineteenth-century America, in its best version of itself, had to offer.[36] Stowe offers something a lot less appetizing: the chance to become an unfashionable—a too immersed, too credulous—reader. If Stowe had left this fictionalizing for readers to perform on themselves, she would not have met with much success. Instead, Stowe goes to work on their defenses, teaching them gradually but inexorably to be the kind of sympathetic reader she needs them to be. This is not a foolproof lesson plan, and her most difficult group of pupils comprises, I would wager, contemporary literary critics, whose identity as critical readers becomes threatened.

Stowe believed she was making intimates of her readers; today we see her as making them credulous. Professional readers replace credulity with critical distance. How does one learn to be a critically distanced reader and fancy they value it to the exclusion of other ways of reading? Howells and Twain will teach us.

CHAPTER 2

William Dean Howells, Mark Twain, and the Sentimental Red Herring

IN *Maggie: A Girl of the Streets*, Stephen Crane's narrator describes the audience of a vaudeville show that Maggie, his main character, is attending: "Many heads were bent forward with eagerness and sympathy. As the last distressing sentiment of the piece was brought forth, it was greeted by that kind of applause which rings as sincere" (27). He leaves little doubt as to how his intended readers are meant to view this audience: contemptuously. This is a contempt so powerful that Crane violates the consistency of his focalization, that is, the perspective through which the scene is rendered. The first sentence focuses on the bent-forward heads of the vaudeville audience to signal where the narrative point of view will issue from next. And so it does: it's the vaudeville audience and not the narrator who finds the sentiments conveyed in the song "distressing." To keep the lines consistent, the second sentence should end something like "greeted by sincere applause" rather than "greeted by that kind of applause which rings as sincere," which is not how the audience members themselves would think about their own clapping. We can conclude that the narrator (who reflects Crane's own views) finds himself as distressed as the vaudeville audience. His distress, however, comes from imagining that his readers might think the narrator, whose judgments are meant to be shared by *Maggie*'s readers, would react similarly to the sentimental dreck that is so captivating to the vaudeville audience. In this and other instances, Crane teaches his readers that no praise of sentimentality can be sincere even if the consumers of the sentimental performance intend it to be. The "rings as" is both a distancing technique and a safeguard against readers overlooking Crane's exposure of the vaudeville audience's incapacity to recognize worthwhile art. His readers must try to do better. Conveniently, the text in their hand will teach them to do that very thing.

As I wrote in the introduction, sentimentality depends on the circulation of sympathy. In the paradigmatic sentimental scene, the reader sympathetically identifies with a character who, in turn, spends a great deal of time sympathizing with others. Today, sympathy is associated with one person looking down upon another, feeling sorry for that person; recall Suzanne Keen's description of it as a "feeling for" (4) rather than empathy's "feeling with" (viii). *Maggie* excels in placing its intended readers above its characters, yet in most cases this height differential does not lead to sympathy. For example, we have nothing but contempt for Maggie's mother, Mary, as when Mary, having thrown Maggie out of the house after discovering her unmarried daughter's sexual relationship, declares her resolution never to let Maggie return: "She kin cry 'er two eyes out on deh stones of deh street before I'll dirty deh place wid her. She abused an' ill-treated her own mudder—her own mudder what loved her an' she'll never git anodder chance dis side of hell" (48). The novella prepares the way for the intended reader's contemptuous reaction to Mary by having shown Mary to be a gluttonous, abusive drunk, but this reaction clicks firmly into place in this passage with our detection of Mary's hypocrisy: Mary is much more guilty of mistreating her children than Maggie is of mistreating her mother. But perhaps "hypocrisy" is the wrong word for it if we see hypocrisy as requiring self-awareness. It seems doubtful that Mary knows herself well enough to realize she's not a loving mother. Rather, our contemptuous reaction to her is caused in large part by her incapacity to feel sympathy herself. For what is the mother doing in this passage but remaining aloof from Maggie's tears of pain? Maggie, by contrast, is highly sympathetic in both senses: prone to experiencing sympathy for others and thus able to evoke it.

We might think that Maggie's problems would be solved if the people around her could feel sympathy themselves. Yet the novella shows readers that this is no solution. Maggie's highly developed ability to sympathize with others dooms her. It fosters a dangerous naïveté that unfits her for survival in her naturalist milieu. *Maggie* uncannily evokes antebellum sentimental novels in the way it places a figure who cries out for sympathy before the reader, yet the novella also demonstrates that Maggie got what she deserved by failing to read the people around her in even a minimally discerning way.[1]

For Crane, the tragedy of the Bowery can be revealed only by creating a character worthy of the reader's sympathy because of the character's own capacities in this area. Crane invites us to have a relationship to Maggie unlike the relationships we are invited to have with other characters in the novel. The sympathy we are asked to feel for her places the reader at her level, not above or below her, and puts us into intimate relation with her; we care about her fate, and that makes the ending tragic rather than satisfying (as we might feel if it were Mary who dies). Yet Crane asks us to overlook his own reliance on sympathy because of *Maggie*'s larger pedagogical project, one he seems to share with William Dean Howells and Mark Twain:[2] to train the reader out of their own practice of sympathetic reading. Sympathy is central to Maggie's and *Maggie*'s functioning at the same time that it is repudiated by Crane through the majority of the relationships that he sets up between his tellers (implied author and narrator), characters, and readers. These relationships depend on the reader's discernment and critical distance. Crane both judges sympathetic reading practices to be worthless, if not fatal, and invites us to sympathize with Maggie in order to get caught up in the novella and feel the tragic heft of Maggie's mortal trajectory. Yet the novel resists acknowledging this necessity and structural contradiction by explicitly casting aspersions on sympathetic reading practices, both Maggie's and the reader's.

This analysis sets out in miniature the story I tell in this chapter of Twain and Howells and their similarly contradictory relationship to sentimentality. Twain and Howells have been central to the construction of a realist tradition. Within the "Editor's Study" columns that the ninth edition of the *Norton Anthology of American Literature* reprints, we find Howells suggesting that this new realist literature offers a *"true* picture of life" (958). In another "Editor's Study," from 1890, Howells laments the reader "who must be spoon-victualled with a moral minced small and then thinned with milk and water, and familiarly flavored with sentimentality or religiosity" (qtd. in Abeln 31). Yet might not these mini–realist manifestos, which implicitly proclaim realism's rejection of sentimentality, be taken as realist fiction as well? I join with other recent scholars in casting doubt on the story about realism's antithetical relationship to sentimentality that is being spun here and that was taken up by many critics in the twentieth century.

In this chapter I demonstrate some of the affordances of sentimentality to explain why Howells and Twain found it impossible to give it up and to describe how they hid their dependence. It is no coincidence that Howells's and Twain's best-known and most beloved novels are ones that explicitly attack or make fun of sentimentality while at the same time they rely on it. To sow the ground for that claim, I consider the skeptical descriptions of sentimentality offered by Twain and Howells and other realists before turning to an analysis of Howells's relatively unknown novel *Annie Kilburn*, the rare realist work that attacks sentimental sympathy *and* avoids sentimental writing. I then consider more well-known novels by Howells and Twain, novels that cannot maintain *Annie Kilburn*'s consistency—to their great advantage. This chapter shows what happens when we acknowledge the affordances of sentimental writing explicitly rather than just enjoy it unknowingly or surreptitiously.

REALIST CHARACTERIZATIONS OF SENTIMENTALITY

As Gregg Camfield has demonstrated, Twain had a habit of mocking the sentimental idealism he would eventually endorse, and Kristin Boudreau has similarly shown Howells to be someone whose thinking about benevolence, a concept related to sentimental sympathy, changed over time. In offering this account of Howells's and Twain's disparagement of sentimental writing, I run the risk of seeming to suggest that these are the only ideas about it they ever had. But to take the opposite approach, to emphasize how varied and evolving their assessments of sentimentality and sentimental writers were, also runs a risk: it makes it hard to register how influential their disparagement of sentimental writing (regardless of other ways they felt about it) has proven to be. At certain points, Howells and Twain thought, influentially, that its badness could be registered in both the aesthetic and ethical realms, and the charges they laid against it have continued to resonate into the present day, especially among literary critics. These characterizations have also shaped the way that American literary realism is taught: as a break with antebellum sentimentality.

With that qualification in mind, I now turn to their charges. Twain lays them out via the exquisitely tin-eared verse penned by *Huck Finn*'s Emmeline Grangerford, who has already gone to her reward by the time Huck encounters her family. Here is the final stanza of her "Ode to Stephen Dowling Bots, Dec'd.":

> They got him out and emptied him;
>   Alas it was too late;
> His spirit was gone for to sport aloft
>   In the realms of the good and great. (113)[3]

Emmeline is said to be modeled on the real-life author Julia A. Moore, who produced a best-selling, much-mocked volume of poetry, *The Sentimental*

Songbook (1876).⁴ Huck goes on to describe Emmeline's working methods: "She could rattle off poetry like nothing" (*Adventures* 113). He also describes her avidity in eulogizing the dead: "The neighbors said it was the doctor first, then Emmeline, then the undertaker" (113). Twain is satirizing not just popular elegiac poetry (which he himself wrote while a journeyman printer)⁵ but sentimental writers more generally. Twain's accusation that they're carelessly prolific echoes Nathaniel Hawthorne's oft-quoted characterization of "the damn'd mob of *scribbling* women."⁶

But there are more implicit accusations against sentimental writing in this parody, also having to do with its aesthetic qualities. The poem bears witness to the sentimentalists' bad ear (and Twain's sensitive one), although Huck, that ingenuous lover of all things tacky, is unable to register this. Nonetheless, the intended reader is not meant to read like Huck; we accept the accuracy of Huck's transcription but disagree with his evaluation. Because Emmeline's poetry is presented through the eyes of this endearing (at least until the end of the novel) but unreliable narrator, another implicit slur against sentimental fiction arises: good fiction, the kind that Twain is writing, works on multiple levels and requires cleverness to appreciate. The pleasure in reading "Ode to Stephen Dowling Bots, Dec'd." derives not just from our laughter at the poem but from its affirmation of our own literary taste. By implication, Emmeline's intended readers, sentimental readers who would read this ode as if it were moving and well wrought, have terrible taste.⁷

Howells augments Twain's skeptical portrait of the aesthetic failings of sentimental writing in *The Rise of Silas Lapham* (1885) by pointing out ethical ones. Within this novel lies a fictitious novel called *Tears, Idle Tears*, which becomes a topic of dinner table conversation among the characters and serves as an occasion for Howells both to deepen their characterization through their reactions to this fictitious novel and to present his own opinion of sentimental literature.⁸ Like Twain, Howells puts praise for it in the mouth of a character whose judgments the reader is meant to reject, the spinsterish Miss Kingsbury. She has this to say about *Tears, Idle Tears*: "It's perfectly heart-breaking, as you'll imagine from the name; but there's such a dear old-fashioned hero and heroine in it, who keep dying for each other all the way through and making the most wildly satisfactory and unnecessary sacrifices for each other. You feel as if you'd done them yourself" (174). Another young woman at the table disagrees and comments that the novel "ought to have been called 'Slop, Silly Slop'" (174). But it's the Reverend Sewell, whom other critics[9] and I read as a stand-in for Howells himself (Sewell's opinions on sentimentality are remarkably similar to ones Howells puts forth in his manifestos), who really puts his finger on the problem with such sentimental novels, calling them "ruinous" (175). He expatiates further: "The novelists might be the greatest possible help to us if they painted life as it is, and human feelings in their true proportion and relation, but for the most part they have been and are altogether noxious" (175). Howells reinforces Twain's association of sentimentality with bad art and naïve reading practices, but Howells sees this bad artistry as having an ethical dimension: sentimental novels lead readers to act in self-destructive ways, just as Lapham's otherwise intelligent daughter Penelope is poised to do, as if infected by the characters of *Tears, Idle Tears*. (In her case, she is poised to forsake the man she loves and who loves her to spare her sister's feelings.) Howells also brings out a dimension of sentimentality that Twain only hinted at. Miss Kingsbury, as I described, makes the comment that *Tears, Idle Tears* makes "you feel as if you'd done [those self-sacrifices] yourself." Howells thus suggests that sentimental fiction drains one's will to act on behalf of others because one feels one has already acted simply by feeling sympathy; tears are "idle" after all.

Twain lays out similar ethical charges. He offers a more pointed attack on the connection between sentimental persuasion and real-world action by lampooning the sentimental conversion scene. For Stowe and other sentimental authors, these conversions drive social revolution and provide evidence of the power of sympathetic identification. In Twain, such conversion scenes are played for laughs—and also to mount a serious critique. Early on in *Adventures of Huckleberry Finn*, Pap swears to Judge Watson and his wife that he will give up drinking.

> So they shook [Pap's hand], one after the other, all around, and cried. The judge's wife she kissed it. . . . The judge said it was the holiest time on record, or something like that. Then they tucked the old man into a beautiful room, which was the spare room, and in the night sometime he got powerful thirsty and clumb out on to the porch-roof and slid down a stanchion and traded his new coat for a jug of forty-rod. (49)

In Twain, tears are the mark of a scoundrel.[10] Twain lays the foundation for the skepticism of modern literary critics that you can ever really know what someone else is feeling. The judge doesn't understand Pap in the slightest even though he thinks he does. Twain does not go so far as to put forth the idea that sentimental sympathy can lead to cultural appropriation, but you can see how the judge's mistake points in that direction. The judge imagines he feels what a person from a different economic class feels; it's not a large leap to imagine a white person claiming they can feel, understand, and take on for themselves other kinds of difference.

In representing sentimental fiction as aesthetically challenged and ethically self-indulgent, Howells and Twain are formulating reactions and concerns that continue to resonate with contemporary critics. At the same time, they are also making a case for realist fiction as its opposite and superior. In "Novel-Writing and Novel-Reading," Howells calls the writing that came before the realists "painted and perfumed meretriciousness" (8). One problem with what he calls "romanticistic" writing is its deployment of types and paragons rather than rounded characters, a topic I discussed in the introduction.[11] Howells writes disapprovingly of Balzac's tendency to mark some characters out for his readers' sympathy and others for their abhorrence. Realist writing, by contrast, is distinguished, in Howells's words, by its "truth to human experience" (9). For Howells, what is true can be judged by the reader's "own knowledge of life. Is it like what he has seen or felt?" (9). Yet novelists have a role not just in presenting what will resonate with readers' "knowledge of life"; they can also sharpen readers' perception and help them see that the characters they read about in sentimental novels lack that admixture of good and bad qualities that characterizes real people. Twain's famous attack on "romanticistic" writing, directed at Cooper but applicable to the Emmeline Grangerfords of the world, extends Howells's critique of sentimental characterization to sentimental depictions of objects and events in the real world. Twain notes that the events depicted in the Deerslayer series could never happen in real life. For example, after observing how in the storyworlds that Cooper creates streams do not wash away footprints, Twain comments, "No, even the eternal laws of Nature have to vacate when Cooper wants to put a delicate job of woodcraft on the reader" ("Fenimore" 183). Thus, Twain and Howells make the case in both their fiction and their manifestos that sentimental characters and events are, in a word, unrealistic.

Yet if we look at the reception history of the most famous sentimental novel of the nineteenth century, we realize that Twain and Howells are offering an idiosyncratic, retrospective account of sentimental writing that has come to seem like a timeless consensus view. As I discuss in the first chapter, one of the curious things we find when we turn to contemporaneous reviews of

Uncle Tom's Cabin is that not only Stowe's supporters but also her detractors remarked on the verisimilitude of the novel. For example, in his 1853 "Review of Uncle Tom's Cabin," A. Woodward writes, "If Stowe's 'vile aspersions of southern character, and her loose, reckless and wicked misrepresentations of the institution of slavery' continued to be spread, America would soon tumble into 'revolutions, butcheries, and blood'" (qtd. in Reynolds 152). Like those who praised Stowe, the ones who damned her emphasize the novel's political efficacy, which proslavery reviewers link to its ability to present a false picture of slavery that yet seems true. And none of these damning reviewers attacks the novel's literary quality: they do not call it bad literature in an aesthetic sense, just in a political one. Furthermore, its problem is its political efficacy, not its political impotence.

If we turn to critical assessments of *Uncle Tom's Cabin* written in the 1880s and 1890s, the view of it has changed so significantly as to make *Uncle Tom's Cabin* seem like a different novel. It is no longer politically provocative. No doubt this stems partly from the fact that slavery is more generally acknowledged to have been an evil institution. Yet the novel has also been defanged by its association with regional fiction and personal testimony. An 1888 *New York Times* article, "Some Reminiscences of an Old Friend of Mrs. Stowe," begins with a line similar to the ones that would have launched a typical proslavery reader's attack on the novel in the 1850s: "Miss Cushing told me that one of the most remarkable facts connected with 'Uncle Tom's Cabin' was that its author, previous to writing it, had never lived in a slave State" (2). The article diverges from this path, however, by making Stowe into a charming local colorist: the "casual observations" of the South that Stowe made,

> together with what she had picked up from some of her relatives and others who had sojourned in the South, united with wonderful imaginative powers, a certain sort of intuition, and a nature rich in sympathies, embracing the widest range of human sufferings, enabled her to create and marshal a procession of realistic characters that, with the description of natural scenes, produced a diorama no less marvelous in coloring than true to the life in graphic portraiture. (2)

Still a vivid writer, Stowe has nonetheless become a charming fabricator of landscapes and the folk who inhabit them—a local color writer—rather than a political writer who helped cause a rift in the national polity.[12]

In an unsigned review of a new edition of *Uncle Tom's Cabin* that appeared in the *Atlantic Monthly* in 1879, which has been attributed to Howells himself, the novel becomes a function of Stowe's moral character:

> As one reads the wonderful book [*Uncle Tom's Cabin*] now, it seems less a work of art than of spirit. The art is most admirable: it is very true and very high,—the highest that can be known to fiction; but it has fearful lapses, in which the jarring and grating of the bare facts set the teeth on edge: there are false colors in character; there are errors of taste; but there is never any lapse of its wise humanity, never any flickering of its clear light, never any error of heart or of purpose. ("Recent Literature" [1879] 407)

The novel becomes an extension of the artist, as if it were less crafted than emanated. Although the review goes on to associate *Uncle Tom's Cabin* with the end of slavery, in these lines of praise, it's as if the novel's moralizing owes less to its anti-slavery politics than to the fact that Stowe was a large-hearted woman.

Another aspect of Twain's and Howells's characterization of sentimentality—more powerful for not being quite as overt—is its association with women. It was Emmeline who wrote about Stephen D. Bots, not her brother Buck;[13] it is Stowe's characteristics as a woman that allowed her to write *Uncle Tom's Cabin*. Claire Parfait notes how in the 1850s, critics thought the novel had unsexed Stowe, but by the 1880s and 1890s, the novel is understood as growing out of her womanliness. That Stowe has gone from wrenching to charming, from a political giant to a local color miniaturist, from a great artist to a great woman—this transformation results from Twain's and Howells's larger attack on sentimental fiction. What is notable about this portrait of sentimentality has been its durability. We see it reflected in Herbert Ross Brown's claim that the sentimentalists were "escapists, artfully evading the experiences of their own day from which letters derive much of their strength" (360). We see it reflected in Ann Douglas's reading of the poetry of Lydia Sigourney (another possible model for Emmeline Grangerford) as "rancid." What's more, it's not just the haters of sentimental fiction who were influenced by realist aspersions but the lovers of it. The feminist celebrators of sentimental fiction who rescued it in the 1970s and 1980s did so on the basis of its being a woman's genre. Today's scholars of sympathy share many of the same ethical worries brought forth by Twain and Howells.

Yet however merited, Twain's and Howells's concerns contradict the fact that they inserted sentimental scenes and characters into their own novels.

Their charges are not simply justifiable concerns about sentimental writing but red herrings. Their association of sentimentality with women, bad art, and bad faith, made both within their fiction and outside of it, naturally leads readers to believe that they eschewed it. Yet Twain's and Howells's most canonical, most resonant writings feature sentimental scenes and characters. This contradiction should encourage us to revisit their charges against sentimental writing and sentimental sympathy.

Howells *was* able to sustain his unsentimental commitments in one of his lesser-known novels, *Annie Kilburn*, which I turn to in the next section. *Annie Kilburn* demonstrates why the very feature that would seem to make it a perfect realist work by Howells's and Twain's standards, namely, its lack of sentimentality, leads Howells to renounce his renunciation of sentimentality in later novels. Howells's and Twain's decision to write sentimentally in many of their realist novels invites us to think beyond the potential problems associated with sentimental writing and sentimental sympathy and consider their narrative affordances. As I show in what follows, Twain's and Howells's need for these affordances is exacerbated by the realist celebration—and cultivation—of readers' critical distance.

ANNIE KILBURN'S UNSENTIMENTAL EDUCATION

Annie Kilburn (1888) embodies an important aim that Howells had regarding realism: to distinguish realist novels from sentimental ones, and specifically the sympathetic, uncritical relationship that sentimental novels establish between their characters and readers. *Annie Kilburn* functions as a counter-example to both Howells's novel *The Rise of Silas Lapham* (1885), which precedes it, and *A Hazard of New Fortunes* (1889), which follows it. I suggest we see *Annie Kilburn* as Howells's corrective to *Silas Lapham* and a standard that *A Hazard of New Fortunes* will not be able to sustain, much to its advantage. *Annie Kilburn* is Howells's anomalously consistent fictional response to the antebellum sentimental writing that he and Twain, as well as Henry James and Edith Wharton,[14] characterized in such a way to distinguish their own writings. By analyzing *Annie Kilburn*'s lack of sentimentality, I hope to clarify how sentimental writing involves not just a set of themes but a set of techniques that affect the intended reader in specific ways. These techniques lead in turn to certain narrative affordances and explain why Howells couldn't sustain the effort to write without sentimentality.

Annie Kilburn tells the story of its titular character's return to her birthplace after living abroad and caring for her father, who has died just before the novel begins. The novel opens with Annie's return to Hatboro', Massachusetts, to "try to do some good" (645). Her efforts coalesce around an attempt to forge sympathetic ties between the upper and lower classes in the town. The novel is an explicit meditation on interclass sympathy, but in the process, it becomes a meditation on sympathetic reading practices: how readers, including Annie herself, must abandon their uncritical ways of seeing the world and feeling for the less fortunate, including, primarily, her practice of "reading sympathetically" the people around her. Howells uses her problems in this area to indict another sense of "reading sympathetically": the sympathetic reading practice taught by Stowe, which I discussed in the previous chapter and which Howells does not want his own readers to persist in employing.[15]

Annie Kilburn allows us to make a distinction between how Howells thought of sympathy thematically and how he handles it rhetorically, even though in this novel they align. Sympathy in *Annie Kilburn* is a problem to be worked out not just at the level of the plot but at the level of the relationships it sets up between its characters and readers. As I suggested earlier, critics of the novel have generally offered thematic analyses, in many instances uncovering and debating the intricacies of Howells's views of charity as manifested in the novel. But in *Annie Kilburn* the arguments against sympathy are realized—and reinforced—in the rhetorical relationships it establishes. And perhaps because Howells knew that the novel's thematic critique of sympathy would prime readers to be on the lookout for whether the novel relied, in a performative contradiction, on forging sympathetic bonds between its characters and readers, he achieves a remarkable and anomalous self-consistency.

But why see the novel as a meditation on antebellum sentimentality and its use of sympathy at all? Instead, critics have made the case for a more international theme, the influence of Tolstoy on Howells. For example, Arthur Schlesinger Jr.'s introduction to *A Hazard of New Fortunes* suggests Tolstoy changed the course of Howells's oeuvre: "[Howells's] early novels were amusing, urbane, freshly observed domestic comedies. Then in 1885 he began reading Tolstoy" (xii). In an article-length elaboration of this line of inquiry, Sarah B. Daugherty sees *Annie Kilburn* as Howells's meditation on Tolstoy's ideas about community and the unity of man—and also a rejection of Tolstoy's simplifications.[16] Despite Howells's ambivalence toward Tolstoy,

Daugherty claims that "Howells was surely a brave fighter in the realism war, defending serious artists such as Tolstoy against the onslaught of entertainers and sentimentalists" ("Howells, Tolstoy" 38). One can see why Daugherty stresses Howells's ties to a serious writer like Tolstoy, and I subscribe to her understanding of American literary realism as part of an international phenomenon. But Daugherty has an implicit counterargument that shapes her account: she wants to dispute Howells's close ties to American popular writers, and it's this element of her argument that I suggest we resist.

What if we see the novel as Howells's chance to work out his relationship not just to Tolstoy's views of charity but to more homegrown ideas as well? One reason to argue for a more pluralist interpretation of the novel lies in a characteristic of realist authors in general: just like the journalists they read and often began as, realist novelists gravitated toward writing about national hot-button issues of the day. Even Henry James, that most serious and international of artists, was, as we will see in the next chapter, drawn to write about the American woman question. *Annie Kilburn* allows Howells to scrutinize not just Tolstoyan ideas about the universal brotherhood of man but also the American culture of benevolence.[17]

His scrutiny is not especially kind. If we consider the novel at the level of theme, we discover that Howells mounts, via his consideration of the culture of benevolence, different attacks on sentimentality and its central mechanism, sentimental sympathy.[18] As Daugherty does, Howells defines realism in both *Annie Kilburn* and *Criticism and Fiction* (1891) through the opposition he sets up between it and sentimentality: realism's naturalness becomes legible against sentimentality's artifice; realism's rigor against sentimentality's fuzzy thinking; realism's timeliness against sentimentality's obsolescence. In *Criticism and Fiction*, Howells takes up the poet and literary critic John Addington Symonds's assertion that great art is "simple, natural, and honest" (2).

Turning to *Annie Kilburn*, we find Symonds's dictum put into action from the start. Early in the novel we learn of a statue that the villagers had asked Annie, while she was still living in Rome, to commission in honor of the fallen soldiers of the Civil War. Upon her return, Annie wincingly confronts it. The statue has been placed on the village green, where it looms over both the town and Howells's readers. The novel recounts in detail how the abomination came about. Annie found the committee's recommendation for a "simple notion of an American volunteer at rest, with his hands folded on the muzzle of his gun, as intolerably hackneyed and commonplace" (651). Instead of trusting the simple honesty of the committee's plan, Annie lamentably decided to go down what Howells wants us to see as a sentimental path:

> Instead of going to an Italian statuary with her fellow-townsmen's letter, and getting him to make the figure they wanted, she doubled the money and gave the commission to a young girl from Kansas, who had come out to develop at Rome the genius recognised at Topeka. They decided together that it would be best to have something ideal, and the sculptor promptly imagined and rapidly executed a design for a winged Victory, poising on the summit of a white marble shaft, and clasping its hands under its chin, in expression of the grief that mingled with the popular exultation. (651)

Emmeline Grangerford was apparently too busy writing her odes to take the commission, so Annie had to find someone similarly gifted. What results is a statue that expresses the ideal rather than the real: the white marble shaft denying the existence of the blood and mire of Civil War battles, carnage that the villagers would have known about from the many newspaper accounts of the war; the grief and exultation of the figure's expression confirming the sickly sentiments and belief in a "good death" that, as Ellen Gruber Garvey has shown, manifested in popular Civil War poetry like "Mortally Wounded" (166).[19] What results is also an artwork sloppily put together ("the sculptor promptly imagined and rapidly executed" the statue) rather than a carefully crafted artwork. On the one hand, as Daniel Borus reminds us, careful craft was a characteristic of realist writing proclaimed by the realists: "The 'simple, natural, honest' account [what they considered their accounts to be] was art that appeared artless" (78). On the other hand, what results from the home-grown sentimental artist is not art at all. We have in this description of the unfortunate statue the fictional application of Howells's charges against sentimental writing. These negative associations apply to both this sculptor and her creations: conventional, timid, provincial, naïve. Of course the sculptor is a "young girl from Kansas."

Other attacks are forthcoming. Annie begins the novel with a rather formless idea of doing good: "But I have a longing; I feel that I must try to be of some use in the world—try to do some good—and in Hatboro' I think I shall know how" (645). Howells attacks the antebellum sentimental reformers by depicting them as philanthropic dilettantes, as if Stowe, once she put her mind to doing some good, picked the cause of slavery out of a hat. Annie's inchoate longing gains form in her support of an ill-considered scheme by some other rich villagers to hold a theatrical entertainment where the different classes might mingle. Planned solely by members of the local upper crust, who determine that the different parts in the play will be performed only by their associates and that the entertainment will be held on the grounds of one of the grand houses in the village, the evening does not, unsurprisingly, end with class harmony and a confirmation of the unity of man. Instead, it ends with "the straggling workpeople, who represented the harmonisation of classes, keeping to themselves as if they had been there alone" (771).

Just as sentimental art and reform efforts come under attack, so too does sentimental sympathy, its central mechanism. Annie had dreamt of fostering interclass community in a manner reminiscent of the way *Uncle Tom's Cabin* imagines sympathy fostering community between the enslaved and the white people within whose power it is to end slavery. "God tells us all to love one another" (684), Annie believes, a sentiment that Stowe would have heartily endorsed. Annie, however, also recognizes the failure of this attempt at interclass sympathy and turns to the novel's Tolstoy figure, the minister Mr. Peck, lamenting her inability to use her wealth to do good. The minister sensibly remarks to her:

> "Money is a palliative, but it can't cure. It can sometimes create a bond of gratitude perhaps, but it can't create sympathy between rich and poor."
> "But *why* can't it?"
> "Because sympathy—common feeling—the sense of fraternity—can spring only from like experiences, like hopes, like fears. And money cannot buy these." (684)

Here it seems that Howells might share a premise with the sentimentalists: that sympathy arises out of shared experiences (although the antebellum sentimentalists favor shared experiences of suffering). In *Uncle Tom's Cabin*, scenes of sympathetic reading follow a formula: a well-off white observer witnesses the acute suffering of someone who is enslaved, often an enslaved mother; this observer recognizes qualities that he or she shares with the enslaved, for example, she loves her children just like the enslaved mother does; the observer acknowledges their shared humanity and the injustice of the enslaved person's situation; the witness devotes herself or himself to rectifying the injustice within the storyworld of the novel. At the same time, the reader-witness to this intradiegetic interaction is inspired to take up the mantle of reform in the extratextual world. The problem in Hatboro' seems to be that the working-class inhabitants just aren't that badly off—there's no real suffering to witness—a fact the novel alludes to more than once.

Yet it's not just a lack of suffering that thwarts the sentimental reformers of Hatboro'; Howells attacks the very idea of sympathetic identification as a tool for reform. We can see this if we compare one of Stowe's many scenes of sympathetic identification with a similar scene in *Annie Kilburn*. For Stowe, sympathetic identification doesn't just galvanize people to oppose racial injustice; it foments political, religious, and moral conversion in general—and often all three at once, as it does in a scene from Stowe's novel *The Minister's Wooing*. The protagonist, Mary Scudder, is talking earnestly with her friend Madame Frontignac, who, already on tenuous moral ground because of her Frenchness and Catholicism, is on the brink of having an affair with Aaron Burr, another character in this historical novel. Mary tries to reform her friend by reading her a verse from the Bible. It works, and the novel meditates on why: "The greatest moral effects are like those of music,—not wrought out by sharp-sided intellectual propositions, but melted in by a divine fusion, by words that have mysterious, indefinite fulness of meaning, made living by sweet voices, which seem to be the out-throbbings of angelic hearts. . . . Virginie de Frontignac sat as one divinely enchanted, while that sweet voice read on" (396). Mary persuades by Christlike example rather than precept, becoming an embodiment of the goodness that Madame Frontignac realizes she now has the fortitude to find within herself because she has so strongly identified with Mary. Biblical words on a page have transformed into a living embodiment, Mary, so Virginie's conversion isn't really brought about by her reading; it's brought about by a personal encounter.

Let's look at a similar reform-aimed personal interaction in *Annie Kilburn*. Annie wants to reform her friend Lyra, who is having, the novel suggests, an inappropriate relationship with her nephew, Jack. Annie is moved to intervene after she sees Lyra snub a young lady her nephew seems to be romantically interested in:

> "Lyra, may I—*may* I speak to you plainly, frankly—like a sister?" Annie's heart filled with tenderness for Lyra, with the wish to help her, to save a person who charmed her so much.
>
> "Well, like a *step*-sister, you may," said Lyra demurely.
>
> "It wasn't for her sake alone that I hated to see it. It was for your sake—for *his* sake."
>
> "Well, that's very kind of you, Annie," said Lyra, without the least resentment. "And I know what you mean. But it really doesn't hurt either Jack or me. (791)

After some further conversational attempts to set Lyra on the path to reform, Annie "felt that she was really gaining ground" (792). Annie continues:

> "And your husband; you ought to respect *him*—"
> Lyra laughed out with great relish. "Oh, now, Annie, you *are* joking! Why in the *world* should I respect Mr. Wilmington? An old man like him marrying a young girl like me!" She jumped up and laughed at the look in Annie's face. "Will you go round with me to the Putneys? . . . "
> "No, no. I can't go," said Annie, finding it impossible to recover at once from the quite unanswerable blow her sense of decorum—she thought it her moral sense—had received. (792)

Whereas Virginie is receptive, Lyra is ironic, her "step-sister" remark a clever rebuke to Annie's moral fervor, which Annie, in her excitement at inhabiting the role of moral savior, fails to register. Lyra is depicted as many times smarter and more cosmopolitan than Annie; Annie, with her plodding sincerity, can barely process the sensible and clever rejoinders Lyra makes to her clumsy attempts at proselytizing. But the reader can. The killing blow Howells deals to would-be sentimental reformers is contained in the last line I quoted: the idea that these lady reformers think they are acting out of moral impulses when in fact they are just enforcing conventional pieties. Another, less obvious blow comes from the pleasure the sophisticated reader, which is to say Howells's intended reader, gains from Lyra's ripostes, and with that pleasure, an awareness of the reader's own superior apprehension in contrast to Annie's obliviousness to nuance and humor. Lyra is in no danger of sympathetically identifying with Annie—and Annie only thinks she understands Lyra. Annie is a bad reader in this passage, and in recognizing that, the reader recognizes herself as a good one.

This passage suggests that Annie's reliance on sympathy ignores the particular in favor of the general and favors the black and white over the gray. Annie has character and story templates in her head. But she cannot grasp the mismatch between the type and the individual, the cherished cultural narrative and the way things unfold in the real world. Howells commits the realist novel to teaching the reader how to move beyond types, a plan that had long been percolating. In a famous analogy he used in an 1887 "Editor's Study" column for *Harper's*, an oft-cited passage later included in *Criticism and Fiction*, he compares the grasshoppers rendered in past novels to realist grasshoppers. He begins by adopting the voice of conventional wisdom:

> I see that you are looking at a grasshopper there which you have found in the grass, and I suppose you intend to describe it. Now don't waste your time and sin against culture in that way. I've got a grasshopper here, which has been evolved at considerable pains and expense out of the grasshopper in general; in fact, it's a type. It's made up of wire and card-board, very prettily painted in a conventional tint, and it's perfectly indestructible. It isn't very much like a real grasshopper, but it's a great deal nicer, and it's served to represent the notion of a grasshopper ever since man emerged from barbarism. You may say that it's artificial. Well, it is artificial; but then it's ideal too; and what you want to do is to cultivate the ideal. You'll find the books full of my kind of grasshopper, and scarcely a trace of yours in any of them. (*Criticism* 10–11)

Cardboard grasshoppers are the only kind that Annie knows. These grasshoppers include, but are not limited to, ideas Annie has concerning perfect and uninterrupted faithfulness in marriage and wives as self-sacrificing helpmeets. She cannot recognize the real grasshopper in front of her: a clever, beautiful young woman who sensibly holds that her elderly, foolish husband should not expect too much in the fealty department. Lyra is far from ideal, yet she is charming, clever, and, above all, distinctive. (That Howells engages in another cultural story of the cuckolded husband and the young, beautiful wife is something he encourages readers not to notice.)

Despite these attacks, *Annie Kilburn*'s ending at first seems to reward Annie's sentimental, reformist impulses. The dreamt-of social union has been established. Yet the victory is a realist rather than a sentimental one. The social union is not robust; it manages only to straggle on. In addition, the novel leads us to suspect that Annie's future husband, Dr. Morrill, will mock her out of any remaining vestiges of her sentimental ardor if the past is any guide.[20] The novel shows sympathy and the kind of sentimental reform it underwrites to be well past its sell-by date.

If I were doing only a thematic analysis, I might rest my case concerning the novel's attitude toward sentimental reform. But I make the argument in this book that we need to supplement thematic analysis with rhetorical narrative analysis to identify and understand sentimental writing. So instead of resting here, I consider how Howells bolsters his thematic arguments against sentimental reform through the unsentimental relationship he crafts between his intended readers and the characters in *Annie Kilburn*. He consistently rejects sympathetic reading in favor of critical distance, analysis, and judgment.

How does Howells cultivate his readers' critical distance? To explore this question, we have to reject a truism about what realism values. Critics of realism as well as Howells himself nurtured the idea of realism's commitment to objectivity,[21] by which, as I discussed in the introduction, they mean a view of the world that represents it as it really is and/or the depiction of the world without moral judgment (what enables them to represent kinds of people and situations that would have had the prim sentimentalists averting their eyes in horror). Many critics associate objectivity with omniscient narration. Let's look at a passage from *Annie Kilburn* that occurs in the early part of the novel while we are still getting to know Annie to see how the novel fosters the impression of objectivity:

> God made her, she thought, and He alone; He made everything that she was; but she would not have said that He made the evil in her. Yet her belief did not admit the existence of Creative Evil; and so she said to herself that she herself was that evil, and she must struggle against herself; she must question whatever she strongly wished because she strongly wished it. It was not logical; she did not push her postulates to their obvious conclusions; and there was apt to be the same kind of break between her conclusions and her actions as between her reasons and her conclusions. She acted impulsively, and from a force which she could not analyse. (647)

One can see why this passage suggests objectivity: a heterodiegetic (or "third-person") narrator tells us things about a character that the character does not know about herself. For example, Annie cannot analyze what motivates her actions even as the narrator can (even if the narrator chooses not to do so explicitly at this juncture). The narrator does not just know things the character doesn't; the narrator also has superior cognitive skills. For instance Annie can't follow to its logical conclusion the idea that God created evil although she believes that God created everything. Howells's syntactically needless "Yet" calls attention to this gap in her logic.

To see how this passage is not in fact objective, we need to remember that the opposite of "objective" is not just "subjective" but also "judgmental." And if we think of "objective" in the sense of withholding judgment, the passage starts to appear not very objective at all: it is quite, if subtly, judgmental. The narrator does not just know more than Annie; he points out her misapprehensions. She does not admit the existence of Creative Evil, but that is clearly a mistake on her part, as is the resulting conclusion she draws that the only evil she has to struggle against is within herself. Howells acknowledges the limits of an individual's power to do good, no matter how motivated that reformer might be. It's not just the narrator who sees Annie's failures of imagination; the reader does too. As Crane did in *Maggie*, Howells has designed this passage to position the reader above a character. One thing we have that Annie does not is an ability to do what she cannot: analyze. Howell gives us inducements to analyze in this passage, starting with our noticing the "she thoughts" in the passage, which indicate that the passage is being partially focalized through Annie. But he also ends things, if a bit on the nose, with the narrator's pointing out Annie's own shortcomings in the analysis department. We can liken it to when a person talks to a friend about the flaws of a different friend, implicitly acknowledging that the friend who is being currently addressed does not contain those flaws (or else challenging the friend not to exhibit them). Annie can't analyze worth a damn? But surely you, the reader, can.

Through passages like these, Howells acclimates readers to the technique that shapes the reader's relationship to Annie for the rest of the novel and that comes to shape the reader's relationship to so many characters in other realist novels: unreliable focalization, a concept that is key to the understanding of realism I advocate for in this book.[22] Unreliable focalization is the third-person version of unreliable narration, which can happen only if there is a first-person narrator. As would happen if Annie were an unreliable first-person narrator, the implied author leads the reader to understand that Annie's view of herself and the world is a limited and sometimes distorted one. The narrator leads us to infer that she's often wrong about things even if she herself does not know it. But she is not alone in her fallibility. Another character in *Annie Kilburn*, Mr. Putney, who is clever, ironic, and struggling with alcoholism, sums up this point about the fallibility of any one perspective toward the end of the novel: "I suppose the truth is a constitutional thing, and you can't separate it from the personal consciousness, and so you get it coloured and heated by personality when you get it fresh" (845). Putney is here articulating an idea that has been put in action throughout the novel, most often through the way Howells sets up Annie as an unreliable focalizer.

As we shall see happens in *The Bostonians*, the characters in *Annie Kilburn* need to be judged, the content of their dialogue sieved for truth, which will never equal the amount of truth claimed by the characters themselves. Characters don't misreport or get the facts wrong, but they almost always, to varying degrees, have problems connected to their interpretation or judgment of other people or events. One thing Howells does in *Annie Kilburn*, the work where he most explicitly distinguishes realism from sentimentality, is to set the reader the task of analysis: we are distant, in varying degrees, from his characters' view of themselves and the world. In other words, the characters in *Annie Kilburn* are unreliable to varying degrees, and we are meant to be critical of them, if never to dismiss them outright (realists do not have wholly bad characters).

How does realist characterization set readers up to judge its characters? I demonstrated in the passage quoted earlier how unreliable focalization sets up a reader to engage in judging a character. As the novel progresses, such judgment is ever more needed even as it becomes ever more complicated. At one point, for example, upon reuniting with acquaintances from her youth, Annie notes that "these old friends of hers seemed to have lost the sensitiveness of their girlhood without having gained tenderness in its place" (661). Are her friends lacking in tenderness? Annie's judgment might itself be somewhat unreliable; the passage ends with the narrator's commenting that "in the country and in small towns people come face to face with life, especially women. . . . But ever so much kindness goes with their disillusion; they are blunted, but not embittered" (661). So they're not unkind, the way Annie thinks they are. We have to evaluate not just the characters Annie judges but Annie herself, on the basis of what might be her own faulty judgment.

Melanie Dawson positions *Annie Kilburn* as Howells's *summa theologica* when it comes to embodying his problems with sentimentality, and I completely agree. In *Annie Kilburn*, Howells manages to align the thematic and the rhetorical aspects of his novel to produce a seamless whole. But as Dawson also notes, Howells's views were not themselves consistent. On the one hand, the realist project required him to problematize sentimental sympathy as unbefitting the emphasis the realists put on local context and individual histories; on the other, Howells wants realism to encourage the growth of fellow feeling and expose social injustice, tasks for which sympathetic reading is particularly well suited.

Howells, and as we shall see Twain, solve this problem by not following *Annie Kilburn*'s example: they will invite the reader's sentimental sympathy without admitting it. Instead, they will attack sentimental writing thematically while using it rhetorically. This strategy involves strewing throughout their novels red herring attacks on sympathy to divert readers from noticing they are also using it, a strategy that has had a long history of success. Yet the question remains: Why is sentimental writing and the sentimental sympathy it invites such a difficult narrative resource for Twain and Howells to give up? To answer that, I turn to the novel that directly followed *Annie Kilburn*, where the "no sentimentality" stricture Howells placed on himself proves incompatible with his reformist aims.

WHY W. D. HOWELLS IS NOT BASIL MARCH

In *Somebody Telling Somebody Else: A Rhetorical Poetics of Narrative*, James Phelan offers a powerful model, mentioned in the introduction, to capture the rhetorical nature of narratives: the "Authors-Resources-Audience" (ARA) model (25–29). Authors have at their disposal a range of narrative resources—from ambiguity to paratexts—to "connect with" (Phelan, *Somebody Telling* 25) their audience, although of course any actual reader can fail to feel the connection. This book puts the realists' use of one such resource, narrative unreliability, at the center of an analysis of their books because it is one of their most effective weapons against sympathetic reading. If we focus on narrative unreliability in addition to their explicit attacks against sentimentality, we can understand how Howells and Twain tried to solve the problems they saw sympathetic reading causing. By taking advantage of this narrative resource, realists sought to correct the sins of the immersed, uncritical consumers of sentimental fiction of the previous generation.

But I'd like to add a point derived from my study of Howells and Twain to Phelan's ARA model: the resources that authors deploy are better suited for some purposes than others. In fact, in some contexts, a resource an author chooses is more a liability than an affordance. Just as the sentimentalists' use of the narrative resource of sympathetic identification solved a central problem for them, namely, the problem of disingenuous eloquence, it opened up others.[23] So it is with the realists' use of unreliable focalization: effective at disabling sympathetic identification between reader and character, it nevertheless limits the effectiveness of the ethical fiction Howells wanted realist authors to produce.

In "William Dean Howells' Theory of Critical Realism," published in 1949, in a period in which critics like Lionel Trilling were disparaging realist fiction, Everett Carter lays out a description and defense of Howells's sense of what I think we might call the ethical nature of realist fiction or what Carter calls "critical realism." Critical realism for Howells must, as Howells declared in an essay on Henrik Ibsen, use its "power of dispersing the conventional acceptations by which men live on easy terms with themselves, and obliging them to examine the grounds of their social and moral opinions" (qtd. in Carter 164). Howells wants his fiction to induce his readers to challenge the social pieties they have unthinkingly accepted. As summed up by Carter, Howells believed that "realistic fiction must achieve its goals of human betterment by painting the victims of society in their true colors, and not in the sentimental pastels of the romantics" (162).

All of this likely sounds familiar: we think of the realists as aiming to instill in readers a more probing attitude toward conventional truths, especially those promulgated by sentimental authors. But Howells's idea of realism's purpose goes beyond this—and shows that the simple dismissal of sentimentality Carter attributes to Howells is inaccurate. Howells did not see the challenge realist writing offers to social pieties as an end, just as Stowe did not want *Uncle Tom's Cabin* simply to make her readers *feel right* in the sense that later critics understand that phrase: feeling as opposed to doing.[24] Realist writing should become an instrument of reform: "Words, words, words! How to make them things, deeds!" (Howells qtd. in Carter 163). If you didn't know this was written by Howells, you might think it was penned by Stowe. Yet unlike Stowe, Howells does not press a particular reform. Instead, he wants his fiction to produce in his readers an orientation *toward* reform, a will to act rather than just a propensity to problematize. It is this desire—to induce readers to take a step beyond the purely intellectual task of analysis—that leads Howells to the narrative resource of sentimentality.

A Hazard of New Fortunes was published in 1889, one year after *Annie Kilburn*. *Hazard* follows the move of the March family from Boston to New York City so that its patriarch, Basil March, can take on the editorship of a new literary magazine, *Every Other Week*. Critics have noted its thick description of Manhattan—Sidney H. Bremer calls it "Howells's breakthrough New York novel" (299)—but it is as concerned with meditating on and training readers to read properly as *Annie Kilburn* is.[25] Also as in *Annie Kilburn*, the question of how to read turns into a question of how much we owe others, specifically the ethical obligations the privileged have to the poor. This is a question that attains great urgency in a city like Gilded Age New York, whose most salient characteristic as depicted in *Hazard* is the proximity in the city of clashing features.[26] One of these involves people of different nationalities and socioeconomic circumstances commingling promiscuously. At different points, the novel is focalized through Basil March, who, in flâneur-like fashion, strolls around different neighborhoods and thus allows the reader to meet the variegated population of New York. These trips slow the forward momentum of the plot even as they illuminate Howells's overarching vision of New York as a place of dizzying variation.

This vision extends beyond Basil's strolls. Even within the horizontal slice of New York society that the novel focuses on, Howells takes pains to depict heterogeneity. For example, at a musicale hosted by Mrs. Horn, a grande dame of society, the narrator foregrounds the differences among this moneyed crowd by focusing on the arrival of a set of arrivistes, the vulgar daughters of Dryfoos, the owner of *Every Other Week*. This focus allows Howells to attend to the differences not just between them and Mrs. Horn but between them and the people they interact with during the fête. Howells's habitual focus on different kinds of people has resulted in contemporary literary critics' thematic assertion of his commitment to democracy, supported by Howells's own comments about realism's commitment to populations that had not previously received much representation.[27] It also leads to Melanie Dawson's own wonderful account of Howells's rejection of character types, evidence for which abounds in *Hazard*, for example, when he has Basil remark, "I suppose the typical Southerner, like the typical anything else, is pretty difficult to find" (289). New York becomes the perfect medium in which to practice the realist method. We can see clearly in *Hazard* that Howells's vision of New York as a place where different sorts of people with different backgrounds, values, foibles, and preoccupations reside, coupled with the novel's penchant for focalizing the narrative through a cross-section of different characters, allows the novel to offer a myriad of perspectives.

But to say the narration is focalized through a cross-section of characters is to say too little. In fact, the narration, like that in *Annie Kilburn*, is *unreliably* focalized through them. In *Hazard*, one has to filter characters' words through their values and beliefs, which might be ones the novel leads us to question. This is a process the narrator models for the reader in demonstrating how his characters perceive one another. For example, after meeting with Berthold Lindau, Basil's former German tutor, a disabled veteran and socialist firebrand, the narrator notes that "March went away thinking of what Lindau had said, but not for the impersonal significance of his words so much as for the light they cast upon Lindau himself" (194). (How much this sentiment is itself focalized through Basil is ambiguous.) But it's not just Basil performing this process with Lindau; the novel is preoccupied with showing characters working through their impressions of other characters, perhaps most charmingly in the conversations between Basil and his wife, Isabel, where they share their impressions of the people they are meeting and use the other's impressions to refine their own. To assess the merits of a character's idea, we have to consider not just what they say in relation to what we have gleaned about their personal character from the narrator and their own unreliable focalizations but also what other characters have said about them in relation to what we know about their character in an endless *mise en abyme* of analysis.

Sentimental novels teach through example in the sense that they translate principles of ethical living in the real world into the interactions of characters toward one another in the fictional one. Realist novels, however, place an array of examples before the reader and invite the reader to try to form conclusions about them. When reading a sentimental novel, readers must translate characters and their actions back into ethical principles, and these principles aren't meant to be questioned. In contrast, *Hazard* asks readers to acknowledge the complexity of an issue by exposing them to many different but imperfect perspectives on it and then suspends them in the state of adjudicating between these perspectives, placing a definitive answer just out of reach.[28]

Unreliable focalization prevents the reader from forming ethical conclusions, let alone translating them into the real world. Instead of forming the conclusions that would orient us toward reform, the novel occupies readers in assessing a character's unreliable judgment or attempting to distinguish the objective narrator's own judgment from that of a character.[29] In my discussion of *Annie Kilburn*, I described how the novel invites judgment, critical distance, and analysis. I'm returning to that claim to suggest the problem it engenders in its refusal to let those things come to an end.

From this refusal to stop the play of judgment, a tension arises in *Hazard* between its aim to train the reader to think discerningly about middle-class reactions to suffering and its aim to make its middle-class readers do more than think about it. Almost all the middle-class characters in *Hazard* aestheticize suffering, and the narrator invites us to judge this propensity harshly. For example, although he has many good qualities, Basil, whose name might be telling, has a habit of turning poverty into a piquant seasoning that makes New York's frantic panorama endlessly delectable. We can see this, for instance, in the narrator's revelation of Basil's thoughts as he views the poorer neighborhoods of New York from the window of a streetcar: "March never entered a car without encountering some *interesting shape* of shabby adversity" (183; emphasis added); Basil turns scenes of poverty into paintings. Although he tries to imagine what the immigrants whom he gazes on are "thinking, hoping, fearing, enjoying, suffering," these empathetic imaginings (formed at a safe distance) fuel his appreciation of "the shapeless, graceless, reckless, picturesqueness of the Bowery" rather than leading to any sustained thoughts about reforming the poverty he sees around him (183).[30]

In another, even more egregious example of aestheticizing suffering, the artistic director of *Every Other Week*, Mr. Beaton, gazes at Dryfoos, who has just lost his son:

> [Beaton] noticed, as the old man sank tremulously into it [his chair], that his movement was like that of his own father, and also that he looked very much like Christine [Dryfoos's daughter]. Dryfoos folded his hands tremulously on the top of his horn-handled stick, and he was rather finely haggard, with the dark hollows round his black eyes and the fall of the muscles on either side of his chin. He had forgotten to take his soft, wide-brimmed hat off; and Beaton felt a desire to sketch him just as he sat. (460)

The novel describes Dryfoos in terms of decline, most saliently with the perhaps inadvertent repetition of "tremulously": this vigorous and active businessman has turned into a vulnerable old man overnight. Even his manhood has been put in question, as evidenced by Beaton's observation that his suffering has made his resemblance to his daughter striking and the allusions to various forms of drooping. But Beaton sees this decline only as picturesque. This is not just neutral description; the novel has been inviting the reader to view Beaton as morally deficient for some time before this scene. The novel thus suggests that Beaton's is not the correct response to suffering, to merely turn it into art. But the problem for *Hazard* is that it is interested in depicting suffering and reactions to suffering as an artistic end in itself, just as Beaton and the other characters do even as it criticizes them for doing so.

The criticism I am directing at this realist novel is one that has often been lobbed against sentimental novels, starting with attacks made by the realists but continuing through the present: that they profit off scenes of suffering without actually doing any political good. Sentimental novels shrink the distance between readers and characters so there is no space of judgment between them. In this situation, sympathy ignites. But as I've been attempting to show, in *Hazard* there is always a space of judgment between readers and characters: the reader is meant to be aware of Basil's unreliable perspective in his visits to different New York City neighborhoods as well as the way that Beaton's narcissism renders him unable to sympathize with Dryfoos. Yet because it is not just Basil and Beaton but all of the characters whose perspectives are meant to be recognized as more or less faulty and because the perspectives the different characters represent are from what Howells wants us to think is a wide (albeit mostly white, male) sample of society, the reader is left in an infinite loop of judgment without ever feeling intimately connected to a character. Yes, Basil and Beaton are wrong to aestheticize suffering, to feel such distance from the people they witness suffering, but does the novel offer an alternative?

To answer that question, let me zoom out a moment to consider a central thematic aim in *Hazard*: to pit the values of the new against those of the old. As William Morgan puts it, Basil and Isabel March are "in the process of moving from Boston to New York City and from the nineteenth century toward the twentieth" (1), just as Howells himself seems to be in the process of moving from the realism practiced by Henry James in *The Bostonians* to a less rarefied, more democratic sort of realism.[31] The novel gives narrative shape to this conflict in different ways: in its depiction of New York's ordering of people and spaces against the more old-fashioned architecture of Boston that Howells brings to the reader's attention via Basil and Isabel's discussions of their life before the move; in its depiction of the rise of what sociologists have called personality against an older idea of "character," given dramatic life in characters like the entrepreneur Fulkerson (who is full of personality) and Lindau and Colonel Woodburn (who, different as they are, are rich in character); in its depiction of new forms of political thought and wealth accumulation that readers are introduced to as they follow the ideas and movements of the characters against older, more familiar (to the intended if not the actual audience) models. One could say that the novel is structured as a thought experiment: it brings to dramatic life the new choices that the modern era makes possible; yet unlike a philosophical thought experiment, this realist thought experiment does not clarify what the answer should be. The thematic and rhetorical are often in tension in this novel. If the novel wants to provide even a provisional answer to the thematic questions it has been meditating on, it requires a certain kind of rhetorical relationship between readers and characters. This necessity brings to a crisis the novel's own struggles to get us to do more than judge the characters' judgments of the social problems that they encounter.[32]

Despite its propensity to defer ethical judgments, the novel insists on the need to form them. Add to the critique of Basil's and Beaton's aestheticization a critique that the novel makes of Fulkerson, who has recruited Basil to work at *Every Other Week*. The novel asks us to judge Fulkerson's inability to come down on either side in the trolley workers' strike, which has brought the novel's action to a climax. Fulkerson "rejoice[s]" first at "the splendid courage of the police" (407) while at the same time "he believed what the strikers said, and that the trouble was not made by them" (407). Such dithering promises to come to an end with the newspapers' announcement of the "arrival of the State Board of Arbitration, which took up its quarters, with a great many scare-heads, at one of the principal hotels" (407). Yet even the State Board of Arbitration ends up unable to resolve the dispute, a parallel to Fulkerson's inability to take a stand. This passage suggests Fulkerson is too swayed by the conflicting opinions of the newspapers, which care more about selling papers than providing moral clarity. But the novel's mocking judgment of Fulkerson's dithering invites a skeptical reader to wonder how the novel, in depicting the strike, is better than the newspapers that it mocks. Basil teases Fulkerson a little later in the scene by recommending that *Every Other Week* should feature "a symposium of strikers and presidents" (409). Unfortunately for the novel, this kind of symposium, if taken only a little metaphorically, seems an apt way to describe the aim of Howells's ideal realist novel and its supposedly democratic nature in representing a range of different characters' inner and outer lives.

I hope I have shown that there's a tension in this novel between what it wants to do—and assumes it can do—and what its own rhetorical realist commitments prevent: the kind of rhetorical relationship that can induce its readers to take a stand against political injustice. Sentimental novels are good at inducing political outrage in their readers. But it's difficult for *Hazard* even to represent political outrage in an unironic way. But let no one say that Howells avoids trouble for himself: *Hazard*'s plot climaxes in the increasingly violent labor strike I mentioned earlier, a strike whose depiction was modeled on the Chicago Haymarket riot of 1886 and the resulting execution of four anarchists. The real-life events incensed the flesh-and-blood Howells, who referred to them as "an atrocious piece of frenzy and cruelty, for which we must stand ashamed forever before history" (qtd. in Avrich 403).[33] Howells sets himself a challenge in this novel: Could he depict a similar event and its aftermath in a way that would apparently stay true to both his political commitments and his realist principles?

Yes, but only by subterfuge—by smuggling in sentimental narrative techniques and hoping no one, including perhaps himself, noticed. But they're there to see if only we stop taking his word that sentimental writing has no place in realist texts. In *Hazard*'s version of the Haymarket Affair, a streetcar strike (which did actually take place in New York), two radicals die instead of four. One of them is Conrad Dryfoos, the son of the stubborn, abusive man we met earlier. Conrad's father wants him to be a businessman, but Conrad wants to be a reformer, and his allegiance to Social Gospel beliefs puts him at odds with his father's commitment to capitalism and personal enrichment. Yet beyond the way that Conrad and his father embody a contemporaneous religio-cultural conflict,[34] they also embody a literary one: the tension between sentimental and realist modes of persuasion. Conrad is a sentimental character. I make this diagnosis of Conrad by looking not at the thematics of his desire to help the unfortunate but at the rhetorical relationship the novel establishes between him and the reader.

Anomalously for this novel, we are not positioned to endlessly try to form a judgment of Conrad; we can decide on his character and his ethical standing with ease. Unlike the other characters, he seems made up less of a jumble of conflicting characteristics than of a scant handful of peacefully coexisting ones. The narrator early on dubs him "the gentle Conrad" (263), and nothing in later descriptions counters this unmixed impression of goodness. The narrator's one extended discussion of him does little to complicate him:

> His ideals were of a virginal vagueness.... The brutal experiences of the world make us forget that there are such natures in it, and that they seem to come up out of the lowly earth as well as down from the high heaven. In the heart of this man well on toward thirty there had never been left the stain of a base thought; not that suggestion and conjecture had not visited him, but that he had not entertained them, or in anywise made them his. (279–80)

Gentle, virginal, pure—there is no admixture of surprising qualities to make him three-dimensional according to Forster's understanding. He's more type than otherwise: the errant son who resists his father's attempts to make him worldly; the innocent who dies as if by the hand of social injustice itself. He's intensely sympathetic.

Sometimes authors do away with characters who present narrative problems for them, as when Stowe kills off Augustine St. Clare, whose irony threatens

Stowe's sentimental earnestness. Sometimes, however, it's the opposite, as when a realist author stages a character's death to introduce a narrative mode they could not achieve otherwise. Conrad's death should not be taken as Howells's dramatic renunciation of the sentimental. Instead, it's an implicit admission that Howells requires a sentimental mode of writing to register the tragedy of things like the Haymarket riot: for readers to feel political outrage, the novel has to kill this innocent. Starting from Conrad's death, readers are no longer invited to take up a stance of critical distance from him and other characters in the novel; the other characters lose their irony after Conrad's death. It is also no coincidence that the novel's harsh critique of Beaton's tendency to turn suffering into art happens after Conrad's death.

Conrad dies as a by-product of the Haymarket riot, a man in the wrong place at the wrong time: "[Conrad] heard a shot in that turmoil beside the [street]car, and something seemed to strike him in the breast" (422). Conrad's senseless death tilts the book off its realist axis; it becomes, for a little while, more sentimental not only in the way that it produces outrage in the intended reader via accessing the cherished cultural narrative of saintlike sacrifice of the one who least deserves it but in the other sentimental methods it uses, for a time, to close the distance between characters and readers.

After Conrad's death, other characters, heretofore complexly characterized, become more familiar and hence more vivid. I alluded earlier to Dryfoos's change from master of the universe to tremulous old man, but his character changes not just in kind but in complexity. Before his son's death, he was a man who encompassed many conflicting characteristics: a Pennsylvania Dutch farmer "old-fashioned in his ideas" (87), but also the most vulgar kind of arriviste; the sharpest and most heartless of traders yet with "large mild eyes" (137); a country bumpkin who wears his lack of learning with pride ("I don't want no present of Longfellow's Works, illustrated," he says to Fulkerson [90]), who nonetheless becomes "the financial angel" (365) of *Every Other Week*. After Conrad's death, Dryfoos loses these irreconcilable qualities; his contours are much easier for the reader to limn. We feel his guilt over his treatment of Conrad right before he died, when he had struck his son. The narrative invites us to imagine what he is feeling, gazing at his dead son with the mark he himself made on his son's cheek, issuing "a low, wavering cry, . . . like a soul's in the anguish of remorse" (427). Other characters also become less filled with contradictory characteristics, perhaps none more so than one of the novel's heretofore most jarring, Margaret Vance, at once a society girl and an on-the-ground worker among the poor. After Conrad's death, she gives up her first identity to become a Sister of Charity.

Even the novel's most salient narrative technique shifts. Unreliable focalization gives way, in the wake of Conrad's death, to a few occasions of mask narration, wherein a character functions as a spokesperson for the author, a favored technique of sentimental novelists.[35] For once this novel wants not just to consider a question from different angles but to settle on an answer, in this case the import of Conrad's death. Discussing Miss Vance's conversion, Basil addresses his wife:

> Isabel, we can't throw aside that old doctrine of the Atonement yet. The life of Christ, it wasn't only in healing the sick and going about to do good; it was suffering for the sins of others. That's as great a mystery as the mystery of death. . . . If we love mankind, pity them, we even *wish* to suffer for them. That's what has created the religious orders in all times. . . . That's what is driving a girl like Margaret Vance, who has everything that the world can offer her young beauty, on to the work of a Sister of Charity among the poor and the dying. (452)

Here Basil alludes to the timeless role of sentimental sympathy in shaping mankind (the movement from loving to pitying to feeling another person's pain), a counter to what has until this point been the novel's previous dismissal of it. Unlike other instances of commentary by the characters, we are not invited to question Basil's remarks. For one thing, absent is the usual disagreement by the other characters in the scene. Mrs. March, who normally takes great pleasure in dissenting from her husband (as he does from her), replies in the double affirmative to his sentiment: "Yes, yes!" she says after he has spoken his piece (452). Furthermore, to those who might still object that the final judgment Basil offers here is not mask narration but yet another somewhat faulty perspective, another deferral, I'd respond by saying that such a view ignores the novel's own adherence to a trajectory in which some characters grow in wisdom as do his intended readers, a trajectory Howells favors even in *Annie Kilburn*.

To discover how far the novel has both traveled and, at the end of its journey, chosen a sentimental path, we need to compare what I see as Howells's mask narration to a scene from early in the novel that is its thematic and rhetorical inverse in its invocation of the mystery of suffering. Early in the novel, on their way to the theater, the Marches encounter a "decent-looking man"

(70) searching the gutters for something to eat. Basil goes to him and gives him a coin, upon which action the man "caught the hand of this alms-giver in both of his and clung to it. 'Monsieur! monsieur!' he gasped, and the tears rained down his face" (70). Basil, or "the benefactor" as the narrator calls him in this scene, "pulled himself away, shocked and ashamed, as one is by such a chance, and got back to his wife; and the man lapsed back into the mystery of misery out of which he had emerged" (70–71). It's not that Basil doesn't identify with the man: Basil's and his wife's shock at what he is doing seems to be a result of their thinking he is similar to them. Basil also seems to continue to identify with him as the scene progresses. I'd hazard that the shame he feels at the man's outburst results from Basil's putting himself in the man's place. Basil is ashamed that this man would so abase himself before another man, an abasement that is deepened by the man's gush of unmanly tears. Howells calls attention to the sentimentally scripted quality of such a scene: Basil loses his individuality and becomes the "benefactor" and "alms-giver." So the passage seems as much a comment on the failures of sympathy as it is a development of the Marches' complex characters, for example, kind but pleasure-seeking. The problem with sentimental sympathy, Howells seems to be saying here, is not so much the impossibility of identifying with the poor, as it is in *Annie Kilburn*, but rather the variety of other emotions that arise in the wake of the initial feeling of identification, emotions that cut short the sympathetic process. If this were a sentimental story in which this scene took place, Basil and the sufferer he helps would be bonded and have a subsequent relationship; perhaps the sufferer would later be revealed as being related to Basil in some way. Instead, Basil is mortified and rushes off to make it to the theater on time.

The conversation between Isabel and Basil that follows this incident is an even closer echo of the one that comes at the end of the novel. Isabel responds to this scene of desperation by saying they must refuse to settle in New York because "I shall not come to a place where such things are possible" (71).

> "Yes? And what part of Christendom will you live in? Such things are possible everywhere in our conditions."
> "Then we must change the conditions—"
> "Oh no; we must go to the theatre and forget them. We can stop at Brentano's for our tickets as we pass through Union Square." (71)

Before we reach the novel's ending, it might appear that Howells is merely describing how middle-class people react to suffering rather than orienting readers to ameliorate it. But the end of the novel enables us to revisit this scene and see it as a rebuke of Basil's earlier attitude. The novel, it turns out, offers a conclusion about Basil's early reaction to suffering, as it does to other examples in which Basil aestheticizes suffering: it makes us feel that it's an inadequate response because it did not incline readers to follow a new path. The novel does not prescribe exactly what pro-social actions the reader should take in the real world; realists don't, as a rule, do that. But the novel enjoins us that it is ethically right to do *something*. That is, it doesn't want its intended middle-class readers simply to throw up their hands on their way to indulging in purely aesthetic experiences. Through the way he compels strong emotion from his intended readers both via his depiction of Conrad's death and from the model he offers of how his other characters act, Howells suggests that people adopt this inclination when they are suffused with strong emotion. The novel ultimately teaches Basil and the reader that one cannot stand apart from suffering. (The novel has also tried to prove this through its plot point of nearly killing Basil when he goes to the strike with the purpose of merely witnessing it rather than intervening.) The novel rebukes Basil's turn away from the starving man toward the theater, rebukes the move from ethics toward aesthetics by having Howells voice via Basil, at the end of the novel, an alternative that isn't there to be undermined or reach us merely intellectually. And it does this by resorting to a sentimental mode of writing.

I don't want to overstate the novel's turn to the sentimental; by its very end, the novel has largely returned to its accustomed mode. In fact, the novel tries to cover its tracks, with Basil reverting to his mocking, epigrammatic ways: "Yes, people that have convictions are difficult. Fortunately, they're rare" (441). Basil also offers a way of thinking about what might otherwise seem to be Dryfoos's sentimental conversion: "I suppose I should have to say that we didn't change at all. We develop. There's the making of several characters in each of us" (485–86). In addition, what seemed like the characters' sentimental conversions might not be as radical or long-lasting as they initially promised to be. True, Dryfoos had offered, in what would have seemed like an anomalously selfless gesture before his son's death, to give up control of *Every Other Week*; but as Basil points out, "He *can* sell it to us for *all* it's cost him; and four per cent. is not bad interest on his money till we can pay it back" (486). The final transfer, "arranged with a hardness on Dryfoos's side," leaves Mrs. March "with a sense of his incomplete regeneration" (492). Yet the next sentence begins with "Yet": "Yet when she saw him [Dryfoos] there on the steamer, she pitied him; he looked wearied and bewildered; even his wife, with her twitching head, and her prophecies of evil, croaked hoarsely out, while she clung to Mrs. March's hand where they sat together till the leave-takers were ordered ashore, was less pathetic" (492). Here there is sympathy that does not result in embarrassment and a turning away from the sufferer; instead, Mrs. March's sympathy for this elderly couple becomes part of the glue that holds the Marches and the Dryfooses in a continued relationship. Rhetorically, by its very end, the novel has returned readers to their habitual posture of judging fine distinctions and assessing different points of view. Yet its brief relaxation of its otherwise rigorously unreliable focalization and realist characterization has enabled readers to settle on the truth of some things and engage in their own acts of sympathetic identification.

How to explain the difference between *Annie Kilburn* and *Hazard*? I suggested when introducing *Annie Kilburn* that here Howells was at his most successful in avoiding sentimentality because in so directly addressing the problem of charity and sympathy thematically, he couldn't resort to sentimental writing without appearing inconsistent. My analysis of *Hazard* has revealed another possibility, however: a difference in stakes. As Annie points out repeatedly, there is no very great need for charity in Hatboro'. This is not the case in New York, where the suffering has become a matter of life and death. In this case Howells forsakes, at crucial points, the distance between characters and readers that he insisted on in *Annie Kilburn*. Howells provides the opportunity, via his sentimental scenes and characters, to abandon our critical distance and care deeply about this social problem.

It turns out that a lack of critical distance is not an obstacle to ethical acts but a way to position readers to engage in them. As a *New York Times* reviewer commented about *Hazard* in 1889, "The reader, still intellectually amused, is morally quickened" (qtd. in Abeln 27). C. Daniel Batson, the social psychologist who discusses the many things empathy (and sympathy) can mean, mentions that "to feel for another, one must think one knows the other's internal state . . . [b]ecause feeling *for* is based on a perception of the other's welfare. . . . To feel for someone does not, however, require that perception be accurate" (10). In other words, one can be wrong about what another person is feeling or suffering. Professional readers worry that such inaccuracy leads to a myriad of ethical harms or might even be an ethical harm itself. Better not to try at all. Batson illuminates how projection ("a [possibly inaccurate] perception of the other's welfare") might be less an unforgivable sin than the price of admission for feeling for another—and potentially acting on their behalf. We can return now to the curious fact that Conrad is the rare character whose thoughts Howells doesn't attempt to penetrate; instead, Conrad offers a blank canvas for the reader. I like to think that Howells knows at some level that sympathetic identification always involves at least an element of projection and knows, too, that projection is acceptable because of the possible ethical benefits (and narrative affordances) it provides.

As in *Hazard*, Twain's novel *A Connecticut Yankee in King Arthur's Court* (1889) shows how sentimentality can engage readers in the social problems a fictional text depicts in a way that the realist repertoire of techniques cannot. It also allows us to explore other narrative affordances of sentimentality. Superficially a meditation on Arthurian England, *A Connecticut Yankee* also meditates on Gilded Age wealth inequality, US imperialism, nineteenth-century bourgeois perversions (see Elizabeth Freeman for the juicy details), and the problem of reform. How do you persuade a populace to change? The novel offers readers a chance to witness the playing out of different methods of persuasion used by Hank Morgan, the first-person narrator of the novel. Self-described as "practical" and "nearly barren of sentiment" (4), Hank tries to persuade the populace of Arthurian England to adopt both postbellum humanitarian ideals and postbellum advances in technology and capitalist forms of trade. (To demonstrate that these aims inevitably come into conflict seems to be one of Twain's thematic aims.) Amanda Claybaugh also sees the novel as preoccupied with persuasion. She considers it a sustained attack on the sentimental variety: "It . . . expands Twain's critique of sentimentalism" (176). I think that claim is right, but we can take it further. The novel offers not just a sustained attack on sentimentality but also places where Twain uses it. When seen this way, the novel becomes more contradictory, and thus, I'd argue, illustrative of Twain's and Howells's red herring relationship to sentimentality.

Here is perhaps the one contradiction in *A Connecticut Yankee* that rules them all: Twain's simultaneous desire to tell jokes on the one hand and to develop his characters on the other. (A closely related tension is one between Twain's adeptness at the sketch and his commitment to the more financially lucrative novel.) Claybaugh analyzes a moment that offers a clear demonstration of this tension. At one point in his adventures, Hank, who otherwise has quite humane ideas about how to treat the lower classes, meets Morgan le Fay and bemoans her cruelty, an example of which is her order to hang the composer of a band of musicians who come equipped with "cymbals, horns, harps and other horrors" (150). Hank countermands the order, but upon hearing the band play again, he changes his mind: "I saw that she was right, and gave her permission to hang the whole band" (152). Claybaugh sees this moment as demonstrating Twain's contention that "sympathy itself is fleeting" (176). But I see it as more of a joke with unfortunate narrative consequences. This turn to cruelty on Hank's part is completely antithetical to his beliefs on other occasions. Here the joke trumps Hank's integrity as a character.[36] In contrast, there are a scattering of scenes that deepen him as a character by making him vivid in a way that lets Twain's intended readers forget he's a character at all. I turn now to one such scene. The scene evokes sentimentality thematically in the way it's modeled on the nineteenth-century "investigative visit," as Claybaugh refers to it (7), wherein a middle-class person visits a scene of poverty. But the scene also summons it rhetorically, in the intimate, caring relationships it instantiates between characters and readers.

The scene takes place during the part of the novel that features Hank and King Arthur traveling together after Hank has persuaded the king to make a tour of the kingdom disguised as a commoner. One day they visit the hut of a family of peasants. The family has been stricken by smallpox, except for the sons, who have been imprisoned in their lord's dungeon. Hank and the king find that half the family has already died, and the other half is dying. Previously, Twain's account of Hank and the king's incognito journey has centered on a particular joke that also makes a thematic point—that the king cannot be taught to impersonate a commoner: "But it was an obstinate pair of shoulders; they could not seem to learn the trick of stooping with any sort of deceptive naturalness" (277). But that changes upon their arrival at the smallpox hut. The scene is the inverse of the moment when Hank orders the band of musicians to be executed: in this case, a joke is largely suspended but the characters are made more vivid. Upon seeing the mother caress her dying daughter, Hank notes: "I saw tears well from the king's eyes, and trickle down his face. The woman noticed them, too, and said: 'Ah, I know that sign: thou'st a wife at home, poor soul, and you and she have gone hungry to bed, many's the time, that the little ones might have your crust; you know what poverty is, and the daily insults of your betters, and the heavy hand of the Church and the king'" (286). The woman is of course wrong about the grounds of the king's sympathy. Yet his tears show that he does feel sympathy toward this woman and her family, as does Hank himself. Furthermore, her assumption, though false, is nonetheless effective: "The king winced under this accidental home-shot" (286).

Sympathy does what Hank could not: makes the king into a convincing peasant. The king's sign of sympathy—his tears—provides the (false) clue that allows the wife and mother to read him as belonging to her class. Yet in this scene, unlike the scene in *Adventures of Huckleberry Finn* of Pap's very temporary conversion to teetotaling, tears are not the mark of the scoundrel or a way for a scoundrel to find a mark but the sign of a real moment of sympathy. Even if sympathy does not make everyone transparent to everyone else in this scene, it lifts the scales from the king's eyes—if only briefly. By the next scene, he has resumed his kingly ways, questioning whether they ought to turn in the woman's sons, who have escaped from their imprisonment. One could see how we might take this turnaround as evidence for Claybaugh's argument about Twain's critique of sympathy as fleeting, but there are two points that might make us reconsider. First, the king's inability to extend sympathy to the sons does not necessarily mean that the king's sympathy toward the mother was transient, only that he cannot, unlike Hank, extend that sympathy to a situation he sees as unconnected to it (rather like the struggles of students to make connections between ideas they learn in different classes).

Second, we'd do well not to think that the novel's meditations on sympathy begin and end with the king's reactions to it. We should not view sympathy as only a matter of what happens between characters in a narrative. Accounts of a novel's attitudes toward sympathy can be enriched if we look not just at intradiegetic relationships—that is, relationships between characters—but at the relationship between characters and *readers*. Beyond the question of how much sympathy the king feels and for how long, the reader's engagement with the injustice of wealth inequality is strengthened in this scene to the extent that she feels sympathy herself toward this blighted family. The king's heartlessness when it comes to the sons is used by Hank in order to sarcastically make a contrary point to the reader: "To imprison these men without proof, and starve their kindred, was no harm, for they were merely peasants and subject to the will and pleasure of their lord, no matter what fearful form it might take; but for these men to break out of unjust captivity was insult and outrage, and a thing not to be countenanced by any conscientious person who knew his duty to his sacred caste" (292). The king's heartlessness is rendered all the more palpable because the narration follows the sons' return to the hut after their escape from prison and their expectation of a happy reunion with their family. Hank does not narrate this ghastly reunion with the dead bodies of their mother, father, and sisters. Twain makes the choice to have Hank refer to rather than narrate the sons' discovery ("Come, my liege!" Hank says to the king "in a moment they will strike a light, and then will follow that which it would break your heart to hear" [291]), a choice that makes the reunion something the reader is left to imagine on their own. Thus, it's a particular affront when we read of the king's impulse to report the sons to the lord. Readers are meant to act better than the king, which means holding on to their sympathetic reaction to this family longer and connecting it to more things than the king does, in the intended reader's case not just Arthurian-era serfs but Gilded Age workers, who are themselves oppressed by the owning class.

Just as in *Uncle Tom's Cabin*, *A Connecticut Yankee* makes injustice vivid to readers not only from the depiction of the breakup of families but also from the sympathetic reactions of characters who witness the breakup. In addition to making vivid Hank's arguments about the inhumanity attendant on wealth inequality, this sentimental scene makes Hank and the king, who both have sympathetic reactions to this family (Hank more so than the king), vivid as characters.[37] The connection we feel to Hank and the king in the "Small-Pox Hut" chapter deepens the ethical import of the novel, not just in the chapter itself but in what follows. For example, the ending, which puts to death much of the populace of Arthurian England, is made more troubling to the extent that we really do care about the fate of at least one member of this populace: Hank. Even if the thematic meaning of this final scene is not exactly clear—is it a critique of reform efforts in general or only of Hank's methods of pursuing reform?[38]—readers will be impelled to grapple with its ethical import more if they care about Hank's fate, especially the permanent separation it effects between Hank and his wife and daughter.

But some readers might be left cold by the "Small-Pox Hut" chapter, especially readers who are literary critics. That many contemporary critics might not have the sympathetic reaction intended by the text is not proof that Twain did not turn to sentimentality as a mode in which to deepen his thematic critique and his intended readers' connection to his characters. Instead, it's proof that critics have inoculated themselves against having such a reaction or at least acknowledging it in their criticism. It's a truism that good novels make us care about their characters, a truism that contemporary literary critics often reject, at least in their pedagogy, when they caution students to ignore their own readerly identifications and sympathetic reactions. Yet Twain forges just such a readerly identification with Hank and other characters through the sentimental scenes that dot the novel and demonstrate that Twain believes, despite his attacks on sentimentality, that a reader's ethical engagement is not stymied but furthered by sentimental modes of writing.

THE SENTIMENTALITY CURE: HOW HOWELLS AND TWAIN BECAME BELOVED

What does it look like when contemporary literary critics accept Twain's and Howells's charges against sentimentality? Here is an assessment of Basil March from Paul Abeln: "Rather than imagining himself as a functioning member of the American polity, [Basil March] becomes a sociologist, an anthropologist, and at his worst, a sentimental reader" (33). Like me, Abeln sees critical distance, or what he calls "detachment," the stance required of sociologists and anthropologists, as pulling against involvement in social issues, yet he also sees sentimental reading practices as in tension with involvement. For Abeln, sentimental reading becomes the final destination on the path of bad interpretive practices, defined here as practices that disable one from accurately assessing what's going on and hence being able to weigh what one should do.

Against this view, I have been suggesting that we see critical detachment not as existing on the same continuum as sentimental reading practices but as antithetical to them. As evidence of that contention, I've shown how Howells and Twain use sentimental characters and scenes as a corrective to the critical detachment that they elsewhere train their readers to adopt. But the realists get to have their cake and eat it too because they simultaneously offer flamboyant thematic attacks on sentimentality that hide from detection their own use of it. In light of contemporary literary scholars' dismissal of sentimentality as leading to bad art and political impotence (charges originally laid by the realists themselves), I suggest it's no coincidence that two of Howells's and Twain's most famous novels, *The Rise of Silas Lapham* and *Adventures of Huckleberry Finn*, are both explicit in their intertextual denunciations of sentimentality and effective because of their covert use of it.[39]

Daniel T. O'Hara has pointed out that at the same time that *The Rise of*

Silas Lapham is so strenuously pointing out the folly of Penelope's proposed self-sacrifice via its mockery of the sentimental novel *Tears, Idle Tears*, Lapham makes his own needless self-sacrifice by repeatedly renouncing an opportunity to sell some land that will allow him to escape financial ruin. Lapham spurns this opportunity even after the proposed buyers reveal that they don't care that the land might be worthless. Furthermore, Lapham's sacrifice, unlike Penelope's, is carried through rather than merely contemplated. In O'Hara's words, "*The Rise of Silas Lapham* is a novel radically at odds with itself" (97). We can build on O'Hara's point by naming one of the novel's central contradictions: between its explicit thematic denunciation of sentimentality and its covert rhetorical use of it. Lapham's renunciation makes him much more sympathetic than he has been up to this point in the novel by placing him in two related cherished cultural narratives: the idea that masters of the universe can be reformed and the idea that wealth occludes the most important things in life. Toward the end of the novel, the narrator confirms Lapham's regeneration through adversity: "Adversity had . . . restored him, through failure and doubt and heartache, the manhood which his prosperity had so nearly stolen from him. Neither he nor his wife thought now that their daughter was marrying a Corey; they thought only that she was giving herself to the man who loved her" (315). Here we can see how adversity also allows Lapham and his wife to adopt a wiser view of their daughter's marriage into a Boston Brahmin family, a changed perspective that intended readers find immensely satisfying. *The Rise of Silas Lapham* thus contains one of Howells's most explicit and memorable denunciations of sentimentality as well as a most satisfying use of it, inviting us to feel sympathy for them and put us in intimate, uncritical relation with them.

As I discussed earlier, *Adventures of Huckleberry Finn* joyously mocks Emmeline's sentimental effusions. That is easy to notice. It is also easy to notice how Jim's characterization deepens as the novel progresses, minus the final, disastrous ten chapters, wherein Huck loses the ethical standing he had gained in the novel by dehumanizing Jim, under the guidance of the hateful Tom Sawyer (or at least I hate him by the end of the novel). That Jim has become a more vivid character before this ending, one whose humanity the novel foregrounds, forms the basis on which many critics' continuing commitment to teaching and writing about the novel depends.[40] Even Brook Thomas, who comes to a very different conclusion from the one I do about the reason for the novel's continuing pull on readers and critics, puts Jim's humanity at the center of his explanation: "Jim's 'humanity' is undeniable" ("*Adventures*" 17). Thomas's scare quotes are presumably the result of his contention that the novel "did not challenge many of its readers' racial beliefs as much as some of its champions today claim" (17). Thomas makes a convincing case for his contention, but the question remains as to why critics continue to care so much about what the novel is saying about race, especially in light of the final chapters' cruelty toward Jim. I contend that we care so much because we have come to care so much about Jim, and, by extension, care so much about the thematic import of how the novel unfolds his fate and depicts his relationship with Huck.

I'm going to remain agnostic here on what the thematic import of the novel on the issue of race ultimately is, but I want to focus on why it continues to matter so much to readers to find out. Having done his realist due diligence in *Adventures of Huckleberry Finn* by explicitly trashing sentimentality, Twain is free to use it as a narrative resource to ensure a powerful bond between Jim and the readers of the novel. I think the novel does this via a scene that comes in the middle of the novel, which Gene Jarrett calls the "homesick episode," in which Jim reveals to Huck how much Jim misses his family. This scene contains a particularly vivid memory: Jim describes a moment when he had treated his daughter badly. Jim has asked her to close a door, and when she doesn't obey him, Jim strikes her, at which point she starts crying. He leaves, but upon returning he realizes that she couldn't obey his command. Jim explains to Huck: "Oh, Huck, I bust out a-cryin' en grab her up in my arms, en say, 'Oh, de po' little thing! de Lord God Amighty fogive po' ole Jim, kaze he never gwyne to fogive hisself as long's he live!' Oh, she was plumb deef en dumb, Huck, plumb deef en dumb—en I'd ben a-treat'n her so!" (155). Jim's cruelty toward a blameless victim, his deaf daughter, which results in her tears; his subsequent identification with her, which results in his tears—here's a moment when tears, previously the mark of Pap's perfidy, become a mark of Jim's humanity. Jim's homesickness allows Huck to see that Jim "cared as much for his people as white folks does for their'n. It don't seem natural, but I reckon it's so" (154). But if Jim's longing and regret as a husband and father act on Huck, they act even more so on the reader.[41] Camfield describes how in this scene "not only does Twain use sentimentalism to elevate the character of Jim, he reciprocally uses Jim to elevate the value of sentimentalism in the face of his own skepticism about [its] worth" (11). And Toni Morrison has called Jim's remembrance of his daughter "one of the most moving remembrances in American literature" (389). It leads to a new, sympathetic relation between the reader and Jim, one that is *not* critiqued by the implied author.

To show that Black people cared for their children as much as white people do—this was, in fact, exactly Stowe's purpose in writing *Uncle Tom's Cabin*. Jim's tears in this anecdote are a sign of his humanity but not simply in the bankrupt sense that James Cox and Claybaugh have identified—the sense that the novel is certifying the humanity of enslaved people only after it was safe to do so. Instead, Jim's act of sympathy allows Huck to sympathize with him and the reader to sympathize with both: it helps to establish a new, deeper relationship between Huck and Jim as well as between these characters and the novel's readers. This chain of sympathy also has formal ramifications, which result in new preferences on the part of the reader. It allows Jim to transcend the various demeaning and flat roles that Twain forced him to inhabit earlier in the novel and makes it all the more upsetting when the novel imprisons Jim in them once again. Jarrett, in fact, sees the homesick episode as the pinnacle of Jim's humanization and the novel's "evasion" not as taking place just in the last ten chapters but as beginning right after this episode. Jim's sentimental humanization is what enables *Adventures of Huckleberry Finn* to become more than a clever deployment of an unreliable narrator capable of hilarious inadvertent unmaskings of other people's pretensions, duplicity, and self-interest. It makes the novel moving, painful, and ethically potent, for good or ill depending on the critic's interpretation of the ending and, by extension, the novel's racial politics. Emmeline's dreadful poetry, so strongly marked as sentimental, is the prophylactic that protects critics from acknowledging how its sentimentality makes urgent for readers the fate of the characters and the ethical questions their relations to one another raise.

CHAPTER 3

The Unmastering of Henry James, or, Searching for Sentimentality in *The Bostonians*

WHEN HENRY JAMES was twenty years old, he attended a talk by the medium and trance lecturer Mrs. Cora L. V. Hatch, who was discoursing, at the behest of the audience, on "the Evidence of the continued existence of the Spirit after death" (James, *Selected Letters* 8). James concluded in a letter he wrote to Thomas Sergeant Perry "that the whole thing was a string of such arrant platitudes, that after about an hour of it, when there seemed to be no signs of a let-up we turned and fled" (*Selected Letters* 8). Basil Ransom, in *The Bostonians*, serialized in *Century Illustrated Magazine* in 1885–86, also spends an evening listening to an inspired female orator, Verena Tarrant, whose words produce in him a similar feeling of contempt. He concludes that "she had been stuffed with this trash by her father," a known charlatan (49). Yet even though Basil has contempt for Verena's words, he does not have contempt for Verena herself: he finds her "as innocent as she was lovely" (49).

It seems a remarkable fact that the novel's treatment of Verena differs so sharply from the young James's personal reaction to Mrs. Hatch. Basil is not James's mouthpiece in the novel, but I shall endeavor to demonstrate how James's novel shares some of Basil's wonder at and all of his curiosity about this sentimental orator. This is an attitude at odds with the identity that critics have constructed for James as a literary master whose mastery derives at least partly from his familiarity with and distaste for sentimentality. Alfred Habegger, for example, documents James's immersion in the sentimental novels produced by antebellum women writers, as evidenced in James's biography

(*Uncle Tom's Cabin* was one of the first adult novels he read) and his many reviews of them (*Henry James*). Habegger finds James's stance toward this sentimental fiction to be both "masterly and distorting" (*Henry James* 4). Yet I do not think this is the stance toward sentimentality that James assumes in *The Bostonians*. In this novel, rather than "distorting" sentimentality, I find James to be curious about it; instead of acting "masterly," I see him as evincing humility in the face of its power.

Because James's stance in this novel differs from the contemptuous stance that so many contemporary literary critics have assumed when analyzing sentimental literature,[1] *pace* Habegger, I want to isolate it and hold it up as a potentially productive alternative. Isolating it also advances my efforts to map the different ways that realist writers approach sentimentality. James's approach is not just an alternative to the contemptuous stance taken by contemporary critics; it's also an alternative to the contradictory response I delineated in the last chapter. Howells and Twain express contempt toward sentimentality, but they cannot give up the narrative affordances that come from constructing sentimental characters and scenes. In *The Bostonians*, James gives up those affordances—he does not try to evoke sentimental sympathy in his readers—while still giving his readers a sense of sentimentality's immense power. Indeed, we might think of his approach in *The Bostonians* as the opposite of Twain's and Howells's: James assesses sentimentality generously even though he does not rely on it himself. Thus, his stance strikes me as an especially intriguing one for professional readers, who will likely choose not to write sentimentally themselves (as I myself have chosen not to do in this book) but might still want to approach sentimental literature without the armor of their mastery.

Admittedly, it is difficult for professional readers to give up that armor when confronted with sentimental writing. I would wager that no set of novels has appeared as easy (and pleasurable) to master for critics as the antebellum sentimental ones. As mentioned in the previous chapter, Hawthorne was a founding father of the contempt so many readers have felt toward sentimentality with his endlessly quoted 1855 comment to his publisher about the "damned mob of scribbling women." In the postbellum period the contempt hardened, aided, as we have seen, by the disparagement of realist writers like Twain, Howells, Wharton, and even James himself on occasion.[2] So successful has this disparagement been that since the 1980s, critics interested in the actual reception of these sentimental novels have published satisfyingly counterintuitive works that document their original reception and try to explain it to their mystified colleagues.[3]

As I discussed in the previous chapter, Twain and Howells explicitly referred to real and fictional sentimental works in ways that would distinguish their own works and provide cover for their own use of sentimentality. At the same time, the narrative techniques they and other realist authors use inculcate in their intended readers a critically distanced analytic stance that is still prized among professional readers. As Nancy Bentley writes of the realists, "In their faith in and fondness for analysis, these nineteenth-century literary authorities are our critical ancestors" (13). It is much easier for modern professional readers to discern and approve realists' attacks against sentimentality than to acknowledge their strategic use of it.

James can help us escape the well-worn groove of contempt. As a foretaste of how he does this, we can turn to "The Art of Fiction," which he published while finishing the last chapters of *The Bostonians* (Johnson 295). In it, James recommends that novelists not be imprisoned by the idea that there is a definitive way to produce a novel; authors ought to discover a way for themselves. James discounts the attitude "that a novel is a novel, as a pudding is a pudding" ("Art of Fiction" 29). He believes that "art lives upon discussion, upon experiment, upon curiosity, upon variety of attempt, upon the exchange of views and the comparison of standpoints" (29). Although James might be targeting novelists with this observation, it can apply just as well to critics. Through his own commitment to "the comparison of standpoints"—or what I shall identify as shifting, unreliable focalization—James encourages the reader of novels to adopt a humbler, more self-reflective consideration of novels and what they can contain, which, in the case of *The Bostonians*, is a sentimental character.

VERENA AS SENTIMENTAL CHARACTER/ORATOR/OBJECT

Let me return to a central claim of this book: sentimentality is best identified not via the existence of a certain kind of plot or set of themes but in the intimate relationship that authors sometimes choose to cultivate between their characters and readers by making their readers forget they are reading a fiction at all. Sentimental authors want their writing to be experienced as a living reality, as if their characters were real people. As I mentioned in the first chapter, Peter J. Rabinowitz has argued that all fictional narratives invite readers to assume, in part, just such a credulous stance toward what they're reading, but he also observes that readers never, even if they are lost in the storyworld of a narrative, lose their belief that what they're reading is fiction. Sentimental authors ask us to do just that—to suspend our belief. We have seen that one way they do this is to make their characters register as vividly real to the reader. And one way they make their characters register this way is to embed them in cultural narratives that are cherished by the author's intended audience.

Instead of critical distance, a novel like Harriet Beecher Stowe's *Uncle Tom's Cabin* encourages sympathetic identification. Instead of presenting interpretive difficulty, *Uncle Tom's Cabin* assures its readers that what they see is what they get. Furthermore, many of the most morally advanced characters in *Uncle Tom's Cabin* function as sentimental orators; they spend a lot of their time engaged in the work of persuasion. These sentimental orators have a double audience for their persuasive rhetoric: the people around them, within the storyworld of the novel, and Stowe's intended readers. The efforts of these sentimental orator-characters to persuade other characters mirror the techniques of sentimental writing more generally. Distrustful of mere words, they rely on the strong feelings that they elicit in their audience(s), often through recourse to the suffering they have both experienced. Elizabeth Barnes notes the double communicative function of the fugitive slave mother Eliza's request for help from Mrs. Bird—a storyworld appeal that also serves as an extradiegetic appeal from Stowe to her white readers. Barnes sees this scene as "offer[ing] a glimpse of the methodological crux of sentimental fiction" (94). Stowe forges a chain of sentimental sympathy uniting author (Stowe was partially inspired to write *Uncle Tom's Cabin* because of the loss of her son Charley), characters, and readers. According to David Reynolds, this strategy was extremely successful at turning Stowe's white readers against slavery.

While I read Verena as just such a sentimental character and orator, I do not contend that *The Bostonians* should be counted alongside *Uncle Tom's Cabin* as a sentimental novel. Instead, it is a sustained meditation on sentimental novels and their persuasive techniques. James will not—cannot, I would claim, because of his simultaneous commitment to critical distance and his disinclination to offer a political message—offer his readers the emotional experience that would explain why Verena exercises such power over her storyworld audience by having her produce such an effect on them. Nevertheless, he does show how a reader's sense of distance from a sentimental object does not have to result in that reader's feeling of superiority.

I propose we see Verena Tarrant as just such a sentimental object: *sentimental* because she is an effective practitioner, within her storyworld, of the sentimental techniques deployed by Stowe and other sentimental authors; *object* because not only does she function as the object of the desire of the two other main characters in this novel, Olive Chancellor and Basil Ransom, but also she comes to be treated as a "thing" by them and others—a commodity to be circulated or taken out of circulation, for profit. The "celebrated magazinist" (41) Matthias Pardon is only one of the characters who want to use Verena.[4] Pardon suggests to Olive, "Couldn't they run Miss Verena together?" adding, "I want to make history!" (111). A horrified Olive rejects Matthias and his designs on Verena, which are not, however, the novel suggests, completely unlike those of Olive, who also plans to put Verena on the lecture circuit as a means, in Pardon's words, to "help the ladies" (111).

There is another, less obvious way that Verena is made an object in the novel: James, that connoisseur of consciousness, declines to make her into a distinct subject the way that Olive and Basil are made subjects in the novel;[5] instead, Verena reflects these subjects back at themselves, should they choose to notice (they do not). Verena remains a figure very hard to make out. James's ambiguity has, of course, been seen as one of his most salient formal qualities. *The Bostonians* suggests that James's characteristic practice might derive, at least in part, from his response to a genre that appears nothing if not transparent, both in its own self-report and to many of the contemporary critics who have analyzed it. In a sentimental novel, we no sooner meet a character than we can form a judgment about them: good or bad, to be sympathized with or to be cast into the reader's emotional outer darkness. As mentioned earlier, even Jane Tompkins concedes that *Uncle Tom's Cabin* lacks "stylistic intricacy [and] psychological subtlety" (126).[6]

James's novel, by contrast, has no dearth of intricacy and psychological subtlety. Yet James's tenacious ambiguity around Verena can give us insight into the sentimental object, specifically how that object can be more obscured than illuminated by literary critical analysis. *The Bostonians* stands as a warning to the modern critic of the nineteenth-century American sentimental novel, always in danger of inhabiting one of two extremes. She may find herself denigrating sentimentality so much as to make it seem impossible that anyone would ever have fallen for it, as the critic Ann Douglas does, or, conversely and much more rarely, she may find herself making it seem so accurate, so trustworthy, as to make an interest in its synthetic aspects seem beside the point, as does Joanne Dobson.[7] Yet these opposing reactions have something in common: the assumption that sentimental writing is transparent to analysis, that is, that one can master it.

More recent criticism of sentimentality has moved away from these earlier, more Manichean critical responses. For example, Cindy Weinstein's influential and insightful work on sentimentality demonstrates "the ideological complexities of sympathy" (67) and discusses the very different rhetorical and political purposes sentimental rhetoric was put to by different antebellum writers, a nuanced approach that is shared by Lora Romero and Susan M. Ryan. Ryan similarly characterizes her work as employing an approach that "allows us to move beyond the question of whether benevolence [an overlapping category with sentimentality] was progressive or retrograde" (5). The analytical perspective that these critics bring is one they take up without doubting the ability it affords to identify its object of scrutiny. In these more recent critical accounts, sentimentality can still be nailed down even though what is getting nailed down is sentimentality's complex political effects.[8]

The sentimental novel's assumed straightforwardness differs from the way that James's texts have been discussed. We can see this difference if we look at an article on James's debt to sentimental literature, which juxtaposes James's ambiguity to sentimentality's transparency. In his excellent "Overhearing Testimony: James in the Shadow of Sentimentalism," Brian Artese illuminates James's complex handling of the confessional mode. Artese juxtaposes this complexity to sentimental literature's "demand for confessional transparency" (119). The word "transparency" shows up again and again in Artese's treatment of the sentimental (104, 105, 109, 114, 119). According to Artese, Henry James's novels adhere to no such demand, only to the careful consideration of the implications stemming from their simultaneous use of confession and testimony. This comparison makes sentimental writing seem easily analyzed.

THE SENTIMENTAL FIGURE OF VERENA

In 1960 the critic John Bayley called Henry James "the *least* sentimental of writers" (235; emphasis added).[9] Presumably Bayley meant this as a compliment. When Bayley was writing, about a decade before the feminist rescue of the antebellum sentimental women writers began, to distance an author from sentimentality was simultaneously to praise them as an artist.[10] But how should we assess Bayley's judgment in light of more recent scholarship on

James? Recent scholars have demonstrated James's debt to the sentimental tradition, from William Veeder's analysis of how James transformed the stylistic techniques of the "scribblers" to Habegger's exploration of James's implicit acknowledgment of the contradictions in the sentimental novel (*Gender; Henry James*) to Bonita Rhoads's claim that the modernist novel owes a great debt to the sentimental novel's focus on domestic interiors and Artese's analysis, described earlier. I share these critics' interest in exploring how the connection between James and sentimentality might entail more than documenting his disparagement of it. *The Bostonians* is a place where we can explore what lies beyond it.

The Bostonians follows a conventional sentimental plotline, as defined by the extremely contemptuous critic Henry Nash Smith: after many hardships, the orphaned heroine "finally attains economic security and high social status through marriage" (49). *The Bostonians* ends with Verena betrothed to the genteel southerner Basil Ransom. But this outline does not do justice to the changes that James rings on this ur-plot. Verena is not exactly orphaned; instead, Olive spends time wishing she were; Basil might be from a genteel family, but it has slipped into poverty, and the novel points out his lack of financial acumen. There are other differences too. Sentimental novels generally delay the marriage of their heroine until the close of the narrative, and these delays are caused by the need for the protagonist to grow into an adult and to learn lessons in self-abnegation or self-determination (depending on whether you follow Smith or Nina Baym). *The Bostonians* indeed ends in the marriage of Verena to Basil. But although young, Verena is already an adult at the novel's opening, and her schooling in "true womanhood" takes the form of a Boston marriage to Olive Chancellor, who extracts a promise from Verena to "renounce heterosexual attraction" (Thomas, "The Construction" 731). As I hope even this brief description of the revisions James makes to the sentimental plotline suggests, James borrows elements of sentimental plotlines and critiques these novels thematically. But he also spends time meditating, much more generously, on their powerful effects.

James's thematic critique has been easier to see because it dovetails with the tendency to view sentimental novels as defined by the ideas they convey or the plots they construct. One plot often featured in antebellum sentimental novels is the marriage plot. Here's how James takes it up in *Washington Square* (1880): James mocks the sentimental view of how the engagement of Catherine Sloper, daughter of a wealthy doctor, to the penurious Morris Townsend should proceed. This view comes from Mrs. Penniman, Catherine's aunt, who holds the conventional romantic idea that marriage should be about love rather than money. Mrs. Penniman queries Morris on his motives in asking Catherine to marry him: "'Ah, you know what it is, then?' said Mrs. Penniman, shaking her finger at him. 'He [Catherine's father] pretends that you like—you like the money.' Morris hesitated a moment; and then, as if he spoke advisedly. 'I *do* like the money!'" (122). And why not, the reader wonders. Isn't it awfully naïve to think that money doesn't matter? James is adept at making readers conclude that sentimental authors are out of touch with reality.

Yet it is James's meditation on sentimentality seen *not* as a set of themes or kind of plot but as a collection of distinctive narrative resources that I would like to explore. Although it's hard not to conclude that James mocks Verena's political views about women, he refuses to settle for an easy or dismissive interpretation of Verena herself. James suggests that Verena can be read as a figure for sentimentality. He constructs Verena as a tremendously successful female orator, consistently bringing many in her audience to tears. As with the earlier sentimental authors, she is a reformer. In Verena's case, she wants to educate her auditors about the plight and potential of women. Even when a sentimental novel does not have one of the great social reforms of its time as its topic (*The Lamplighter*, for example, does not; James has noted his "absorbed perusal" of this novel in his memoir *A Small Boy and Others* [77]), it still seeks to reform the character of those who populate—and read—its pages. Of course, *Uncle Tom's Cabin* did engage with the great political issue of its day. There is, as has been generally acknowledged, a straight line connecting slavery and the issue that preoccupies Olive and Verena: many white nineteenth-century female reformers (the Grimké sisters being two of the most famous) first found their voices in support of abolition, "a seedbed of women's public speaking" (Sells 339), before raising them on behalf of women's rights.[11] This was the course that the nineteenth-century reformer and actress Anna Dickinson, who is supposed to have been the model on which James based Verena, followed.

James has Verena use an array of sentimental techniques of persuasion in her role as a reformer. For one thing, he highlights how her efforts at reform rely on her voice. James describes the reaction of Basil to one of Verena's orations: "After he had stood there a quarter of an hour he became conscious that he should not be able to repeat a word she had said; he had not definitely heeded it, and yet he had not lost a vibration of her voice" (206). As in the case of Verena's other orations, the narrator spends little time transcribing Verena's words. Verena conforms to the hierarchy of persuasion that *Uncle Tom's Cabin* lays out. As the narrator of that novel notes of the New England spinster, Miss Ophelia, who manages to reform the enslaved child Topsy consigned to her care (and who shares not a little in common with Olive Chancellor), "Miss Ophelia's voice was more than her words, and more than that were the honest tears that fell down her face" (273). Words, then voice, and then tears—this is also the hierarchy that shapes Verena's rhetorical performances.

Verena's effect on her audience is—and the narrator could be describing Stowe's original reception—one of "extraordinary artless vividness" (*The Bostonians* 86). Sentimental novels strive to present pictures to their audience. To repeat a quotation that I used in the first chapter, Stowe wrote to her publishers regarding *Uncle Tom's Cabin*: "My vocation is simply that of a *painter*, and my object will be to hold up in the most lifelike and graphic manner possible slavery. There is no arguing with *pictures*, and everybody is impressed by them, whether they mean to be or not" ("Letter"). Verena also acts on her audience through not only her voice but also the pictures, full of pathos, she presents.

When Verena speaks, her audience does not focus on her words. By "audience" I mean both her extradiegetic audience (because the novel mostly declines to transcribe Verena's words) as well as her storyworld one (because they can't stop fixating on the picture Verena presents). Here is a representative example of how the novel avoids transcribing what Verena says; it is, in fact, the very first time Verena orates in the novel. The stage is set when the appointed speaker, the famous Mrs. Farrinder, refuses to speak. Verena's father, the "mesmeric healer" (27), offers up his daughter to say a few words on the subject of the woman question. Basil seems about to report on what she has to say, but instead we get this:

> It was not what she said; he didn't care for that, he scarcely understood it; he could only see that it was all about the gentleness and goodness of women, and how, during the long ages of history, they had been trampled under the iron heel of man.... The effect was not in what she said, though she said some such pretty things, but in the picture and figure of the half-bedizened damsel (playing, now again, with her red fan), the visible freshness and purity of the little effort. (48)

What matters are much less the words Verena utters than the qualities Verena evinces; her essence is, in some sense, the content of her oration. In fact, "essence" plays a double role in this speech: Verena's own essence, her "freshness and purity," carries her rather slim argument, which itself relies on a notion of women's essence, "their gentleness and goodness," to show how unjustly they have been treated. It is quite possible that Verena's speech is not nearly as cliché-ridden as Basil makes it out to be. Assuming it is, these clichés merely allow the audience to turn their attention to the picture that she presents. And while Basil's mention of Verena's "figure" suggests Basil's sexual interest in Verena, it also suggests James's use of Verena as a "figure" for sentimental rhetoric.

At one point Olive herself thinks that "she might have been satisfied that the girl was a mass of fluent catch-words and yet scarcely have liked her the less" (63). Olive's response illuminates another aspect of sentimental rhetoric: its love of "fluent catch-words" and reliance on clichés. Ann Douglas, that supremely contemptuous critic of antebellum sentimental novels, whose 1977 work *The Feminization of American Culture* shaped a generation of critics' responses to them, quotes what she takes to be a hideous poem from Lydia Sigourney: "Beautiful boy, with the sunny hair / What wouldst thou do with that birdling rare? / It belongs to the sky—it hath wings, you know, / Loosen your clasping, and let him go" (256). Though Douglas does not specify exactly what makes this poem so dreadful, she does, as I mentioned in the previous chapter, call it "rancid." "Rancid" implies language that has been left out too long, handled by too many different people.[12] Douglas seems to object to the triteness of the central metaphor, the way it, unlike a live metaphor, presents us with absolutely no frisson of the unexpected or strange. Douglas accuses Sigourney of being a bad artist.

It is an unfair accusation: Sigourney does not want to seem highly trained in the arts of rhetoric. A review of her poetry from 1835 shows the extent to which she was successful in this effort: "Such writings [a collection of her poetry] do not ask nor admit of the display of some of the very highest attributes of poetry, and to these Mrs. Sigourney presents no claim. The excellence of all her poems is quiet and unassuming. They are full of the sweet images and bright associations of domestic life; its unobtrusive happiness, its unchanging affections, and its cares and sorrows" ("Mrs. Sigourney and Miss Gould" 447). Sigourney wants the language of her poem to be so familiar that it can seamlessly convey the feelings that author and reader share. Sentimental persuasion takes place when all textual barriers—including the originality of the author's figures, which catch the reader's attention in their defamiliarizing effect—have been removed. Verena, like other sentimental orators, is filled with catchwords, with banal expressions. James is of course mocking her and other female reformers by pointing them out, but there's something beyond this mockery. Her banal words highlight her essence. Her character suffuses the scene and allows her to form a connection with her interdiegetic audience in a way it could not if people were caught by her words, the content of what she is saying.

HOW NOT TO JUDGE VERENA

If Verena *is* a sentimental object, then we should be able to read back from her to at least the narrator's, and possibly James's, judgment of sentimentality. After all, one could say that the business of this novel, as with many of James's novels, is to involve readers in the evaluation of its characters. Unlike in the sentimental novel, this evaluation is a drawn-out process, the "content" of the novel perhaps.[13] In James, almost every character is caught up in what I will refer to as a "web of judgment."[14] The reader's involvement in a "web of judgment" is the process I alluded to in the previous chapter with my claim that unreliable focalization leads to critical distance, but looking at how it functions in James provides a demonstration of how this process works.

The task of reading back from Verena to the narrator is complicated because, unlike in *Uncle Tom's Cabin*, much of the narration is focalized through one or another character whose self-interest and perceptual limitations (which we know in part from how they, in turn, have been evaluated by other characters and the narrator) infuse their impressions of Verena. Take, for example, the passage about Verena's first oration. We are getting not an objective picture of what is going on but an interpretation focalized through the anti-feminist Basil, who denigrates Verena's message. He is struck by the clichés of her speech: "long ages of history" and "iron heel of man." His inability to hear her in favor of gazing at her "figure" might say as much about his tendency to objectify women as about a characteristic of the sentimental orator.

For more evidence of the way this focalization reveals more about Basil than Verena, let us turn to his mental summing-up of her speech:

> The necessity of her nature was not to make converts to a ridiculous cause, but to emit those charming notes of her voice . . . to please every one who came near her, and to be happy that she pleased. I know not whether Ransom was aware of the bearings of this interpretation, which attributed to Miss Tarrant a singular hollowness of character; he contented himself with believing that she was as innocent as she was lovely,

and with regarding her as a vocalist of exquisite faculty, condemned to sing bad music. How prettily, indeed, she made some of it sound! (49)

On the one hand, we seem to have further proof that Verena is a sentimental object, whose voice carries much more persuasive weight than her words. (As Basil says at the end of the novel, "I don't listen to your ideas; I listen to your voice" [258].) Yet on the other hand, our overwhelming impression is of Basil's misogyny. Basil sees her as a pretty, brainless bird, emitting "charming notes," beguiling him with her vivid plumage. Even the narrator seems to cast aspersions on the objectivity of Basil's view of Verena through his own interjection "I know not whether."

Some readers, however, have assumed that the narrator is complicit in this misogynist view. It is, after all, not only Basil who describes Verena as slight but also the narrator himself: "Her ideas of enjoyment were very simple; she enjoyed putting on her new hat, with its redundancy of feather, and twenty cents appeared to her a very large sum" (61). Here the narrator reveals not just Verena's innocence but her inanity. Not surprisingly, many critics have argued that the narrator (and also James) dismisses not merely women but their public voice,[15] especially if one considers how the narrator seems to sympathize with Basil, how Basil seems to be his mouthpiece in the novel. They are both men, after all, and they are both authors. (Toward the end of the book, Basil publishes a story in a journal.) This is exactly how Sandra Gilbert and Susan Gubar have influentially read the novel, pointing out James's complicity with Basil. They go on to say that "Basil's rescue of Verena from the diseased clutches of Olive and her band of fanatical acolytes reflects James's desire to tell women that 'Woman has failed you utterly—try Man'" (26–27). Thus, they neatly sum up the novel. For them, Basil is pure villain; Verena and those whom Basil/James can see only as "fanatical acolytes" are pure heroines. On this view, the veil thrown around Verena's particular words seems the effect of a patriarchal conspiracy rather than a characteristic feature of sentimentality.

I second the critic Wendy Lesser, who says that this reading is actually a misreading of the novel. Let us grant for the sake of argument that James and his narrator are equivalent. As Lesser points out, James does not choose Basil as his stand-in. The narrator appears as distanced from Basil as he does from his other characters. He leads us to doubt Basil's perceptions of the world. Basil appears ridiculous at certain points, nowhere more so than in his attempts at authorship. As one editor comments on Basil's writing, "His doctrines were about three hundred years behind the age; doubtless some magazine of the sixteenth century would have been very happy to print them" (148). And it does seem rather strange to propose the fastidious and sexuality-complex Henry James as a kind of patriarchal he-man. When once asked who the greatest American female novelist was, Elizabeth Hardwick responded, "Henry James" (qtd. in Lesser 99).[16]

Gilbert and Gubar simplify this novel in order to make it serve a particular political purpose. To accomplish this simplified reading, they must conflate Basil's and the novel's treatment of Verena, and this conflation turns her into a lamentable figure, neither trifling nor disingenuous. This is not to say that they make Verena into an active heroine: they highlight her complicity. "Submissive Verena" they call her (25). They see her as a victim of Basil's and James's patriarchal designs. Gilbert and Gubar solve the mystery of Verena, and they do this by making Verena into a victim. Yet this does not reflect the feel of the novel, where Verena exerts a fascination for everyone who stands in her presence and hears her voice. Gilbert and Gubar deny Verena's and the novel's real strangeness, a strangeness that can be summed up in a question that Lesser poses: "Verena Tarrant is possibly the darkest of James's deep wells of desire, in that it is almost impossible to understand why two intelligent people are so wildly attracted to her" (109). Gilbert and Gubar foreclose the mystery. They might respond that men often are wildly attracted to women they can dominate. Yet James suggests Verena's attractiveness—and, by extension, the attractiveness of the sentimental object—is not so easily mastered, especially as we explore the difficulties in evaluating Verena that James puts in our way with his commitment to "the comparison of standpoints," in this case the shifting, unreliable focalization that structures this novel.

Verena does present a puzzle, yet it is not one to be solved by recourse to a story of patriarchal oppression, as can happen if we focus exclusively on Basil's judgment of Verena. After all, it is not only men whom Verena attracts. She attracts Olive, Basil's blue-blooded cousin. Olive is a social reformer with mixed motives. She wants to use Verena to advance the cause of women, but she also wants to keep Verena for herself. Olive certainly does not see Verena as a victim. She sees her as powerful in her eloquence; she finds Verena "very remarkable" (62). Unlike Basil, Olive does not judge Verena's discourse to be meaningless or false. And nowhere is Verena's power over Olive more confirmed than by Olive's own suspicion that Verena's eloquence might have something suspect about it.

It is easy to dismiss Olive's fascination with Verena as simply the result of Olive's personal desire for her—a position the novel gives us ample evidence to adopt. (Olive believes that "if they were all in all to each other, what more could they want?" [127].) If that is true, then what remains of Olive's assessment of Verena is the impression of Verena's intellectual insubstantiality and possible disingenuousness (and I could just as well be describing realist-inflected assessments of sentimental authors more generally).[17] An alternative characterization of Verena emerges, one that I imagine Douglas, the eviscerator of Sigourney, might offer: instead of giving Verena the status of a victim, as Gilbert and Gubar do, readers can instead discount her as a charlatan. The narrator seems to provide us with more than enough clues that this is the proper reading. For one thing, the narrator makes much of Verena's crass huckster of a father, Mr. Tarrant, the mesmeric healer, who cares more than anything else for "receipts" (81). How far can the apple fall from the tree? Here is how *he* speaks: "He looked like the priest of a religion that was passing through the stage of miracles; he carried his responsibility in the general elongation of his person, of his gestures (his hands were now always in the air, as if he were being photographed in postures), of his words and sentences as well as in his smile, as noiseless as a patent hinge" (79). In his association with "patent hinges" and his hunger for having his picture taken, Mr. Tarrant is a modern mountebank. He also seems to be the endpoint toward which Verena is tending. She is described as having "a new style [of speaking], quite original" (41). This can hardly be taken as a compliment, uttered as it is by Matthias Pardon, whom James makes us understand to be a fool. Verena, too, enjoys her publicity, a penchant for vulgarity we can see even in her choice of dress, for example, "her little jacket (the buttons were immense and gilt)" (56), which she dons for her first meeting with her future patroness, the celebrity-shunning Olive. We should be able to dismiss her as we can her disingenuous father.

If Gilbert and Gubar's reading dignifies Verena as a victim, this reading cuts her down to size. And both readings demystify the mystery of Verena's attractiveness. In the former case, it is because she is deliciously submissive; in the latter, it is because she has fooled the people around her. Both readings make Verena fully intelligible. Gilbert and Gubar do not use the term "sentimental" to discuss *The Bostonians*, and we can assume they would not consider it a sentimental novel, but their technique of reading—of deciding whether the characters are to be wholly embraced or wholly rejected and to be absolutely certain of our decision—is one invited by sentimental novels.

These focalized characterizations tempt us either to pity Verena or to discount her. Pursuing either of these readings, readers find in Verena an antidote to the frustrating position *The Bostonians* puts us in. Where is the foundation on which we can judge her? *The Bostonians* does not always focalize its narration through its characters; there exists in this novel a narrator who seems to be of the classic omniscient variety.[18] If we could finally know whether this narrator either condemns or sympathizes with Verena, we could solve the mystery that she poses. The novel would *share* characteristics of Verena's sentimental style of persuasion. As it is, Verena's own style of persuasion stands in marked contrast to James's, which is not particularly persuasive, in Verena's sense, at all. Verena aims to make her audience feel strongly about a cause, but as Barbara Hochman notes, "James's fiction is especially difficult to reduce to a political message" ("Reading Historically" 275).[19] If the sentimental novel wants to reform the world through its "political message," it still does so by first immersing readers in the vivid lives of its characters. Yet Verena's life, especially her inner life, remains opaque to readers. The performance of her speeches—the content of which the reader never quite hears—immerses the characters who *do* hear them in Verena. Yet it is hard for the *reader* to become immersed in her. We never directly see or hear her; instead, we observe the other characters' immersion. Rather than enlist the reader in the cause of women's rights, the novel addresses the question of whence Verena's—and sentimentality's—attractiveness. Who exactly is she?

As I mentioned earlier, there are moments when the narrator does comment directly on Verena, without the lens provided by another, shaping consciousness, for example, when the narrator comments on how large a sum twenty cents appeared to her. And here is how the narrator describes Verena toward the end of the novel: "All her artlessly artful facilities . . . were not a part of her essence, an expression of her innermost preferences. What *was* a part of her essence was the extraordinary generosity with which she could expose herself, give herself away, turn herself inside out, for the satisfaction of a person who made demands of her" (296).

"Artlessly artful"—the import of this phrase is echoed early in the novel when Basil wonders if another character, Mrs. Farrinder, finds Verena a "parrot or a genius" (52). Even when the narrator describes Verena directly, the narrator still seems to forestall a clear view of her. The passage just quoted balances itself between criticism and praise. On the one hand, it highlights Verena's essential emptiness: she becomes what other people want her to be.

On the other hand, there is the narrator's tender tone produced by words like "generosity" and the sense the narrator conveys of her disregard for her own ease. Verena is neither wholly believable as an ingenuous speaker nor wholly discountable as a charlatan. In fact, Verena remains a paradox. On first introducing Verena, the narrator describes her in a flurry of similarly paradoxical terms: she "gave almost the impression of a lesson rehearsed in advance. And yet there was a strange spontaneity in her manner" (42); she is "naturally theatrical" (42). Lesser does not extend her analysis of Verena to include her identity as a sentimental orator, but the mystery that Lesser refers to, Verena's attractiveness despite her obvious limitations, remains.

We are never allowed to see Verena clearly. This blurriness differs from the way James depicts the other characters in the novel. Olive is portrayed in direct contrast to Verena. For example, Basil is impelled to correct Olive's sister's characterization of Olive as a "dear old thing" (74). Basil thinks to himself that "least of all was she a 'thing'; she was intensely, fearfully, a person" (74). Here and elsewhere Basil identifies Olive by her distinctive sharpness—she is "sharply young" (74). Basil's perception is picked up by the narrator when he comments on Olive's desire to have her era "feel and speak more sharply" (98). In fact, almost every character is rendered sharply in this novel, and in almost all cases, the reader can draw conclusions about the character in question, even if it is often a complex process to do so.

I have been describing how judging different characters requires us to take account of the novel's technique of shifting, unreliable focalization. For example, the first time we really meet Mrs. Tarrant, we become acquainted with her by being let into her own perceptions about herself and her world: "She supposed Verena would marry some one, some day, and she hoped the personage would be connected with public life—which meant, for Mrs. Tarrant, that his name would be visible, in the lamplight, on a coloured poster, in the doorway of Tremont Temple" (77). The narrator does not share in either Mrs. Tarrant's estimation of the desirability of publicity or what she thinks represents its pinnacle. We both inhabit Mrs. Tarrant's thoughts and gain distance from them. James creates unreliable characters, whose judgments about the world the reader accepts not as trustworthy observations but as the means to judge (often harshly) these characters' own character. We know where Mrs. Tarrant stands and where we stand in relation to her.

In this single passage, James gives us evidence enough to judge Mrs. Tarrant, which is unusual. Elsewhere in the novel, evaluation depends on a web of judgment. These judgments are often secondhand and reveal as much about the judger as the judged. When Basil wonders if Mrs. Farrinder finds Verena a "parrot or a genius," this question derives not from Basil himself but from Basil's perception of what Mrs. Farrinder might be wondering. Thus we can use this question of parrot or genius not just as a further invitation to wonder about Verena but as an insight into Basil: that he might be projecting his own question onto Mrs. Farrinder or that, alternatively, he has drawn a bead on Mrs. Farrinder (the narrator leads us also to suspect that Mrs. Farrinder might, in fact, be wondering this) and that Basil may be on occasion a good judge of character.

These webs of judgment appear everywhere. Verena's mother, Mrs. Tarrant, observes with satisfaction how Olive "seemed to think her young friend's [Verena's] gift *was* inspirational, or at any rate, as Selah [Verena's father] had so often said, quite unique" (78). Here we can judge not only Mrs. Tarrant's overinvestment in her daughter's oratorical power but also Selah's pompous verbosity. "Quite unique"—surely James intends his readers to catch the revealingly needless "quite." Yet Olive's judgment of Verena that Mrs. Tarrant considers—that she is inspirational—is not undermined, unlike her estimation of her husband, by either the narrator or the other characters. They too are inspired by Verena's orations. But because we readers have gotten in the habit of imagining there should be a distance between Mrs. Tarrant's thoughts about the world and our own, we are left with a frisson of unease about this judgment. We know that Olive has thought Verena to be inspirational, so does it mean that Olive has gotten it wrong? But the narrator, too, has narrated how she has inspired people. It is difficult to know what to think about Verena.

But Verena is an exception. Though all of the other major characters (and many of the minor ones) are enveloped in judgments, with regard to most of them, readers can formulate a final evaluation with some assurance that they have gotten it right. Many times the reader's evaluation will turn out to match ones that either Olive or Basil has made without the same kind of effort (a resonance that might explain why so many critics conclude that James identifies with Olive or Basil or both). I don't mean to suggest that the reader's judgment-forming process is easy or quick in this novel—just that it is possible. For the reader to make these final judgments, she must involve herself in a complex reading process: toggling between the narrator's descriptions (often embedded in passages focalized by one of the characters) and the judgments one character will make of another, which are often conveyed indirectly or hypothetically, as in the Basil–Mrs. Farrinder example. The reader's final judgments are rarely as easily arrived at as the judgment we make of those two wholly unreliable characters in the novel, Verena's parents. (If I have come too quickly to judgments about them, that is the fault of my own reading practice, not evidence, I hope, of faultiness of the point I'm trying to make.) But when it comes to Verena, the narrator's and reader's powers of judgment are stymied. Verena remains blurry.

There is another character, Miss Birdseye, said to be modeled on Nathaniel Hawthorne's sister-in-law Elizabeth Peabody, who remains indistinct, but the way the narrative produces an impression of her indistinct character is instructive. As with Olive, Miss Birdseye's primary quality is directly alluded to in the novel: Basil sees Miss Birdseye's face "as if it had been soaked, blurred, and made vague by exposure to some slow dissolvent" (22), a judgment picked up by the narrator, who comments on what a "confused, entangled, inconsequent, discursive old woman" she is (23). But this impression of indistinctness is produced much more directly than in Verena's case. The narrator gives us a definite, non-focalized idea of Miss Birdseye's character, which is also affirmed through the perceptions of the other characters. We know what Miss Birdseye is like. Verena's blurriness is the product of the conflicting impressions she produces in the other characters and the paradoxical one the narrator offers of her.

The reader's inability to form a final judgment of Verena departs from the characters' own often lightning-quick evaluations of her, which result in definite judgments on their part. Olive doesn't doubt her judgment of Verena, nor does Basil doubt his. But the narrator does not tell us which of these conflicting judgments is correct or if either of them is. (The same goes for the judgments formed of Verena by the more minor characters.) The novel leads us to the idea that Olive and Basil and all the other characters who judge Verena with such certainty are involved less in discrimination than in projection. We have seen how Basil's assessment of Verena's oration reveals his misogyny.

Here is a common syntax in *The Bostonians*: "This narrative [of Verena's childhood, told by Verena], tremendously fascinating to Miss Chancellor, made her feel in all sorts of ways—prompted her to ask herself whether the girl was also destitute of the perception of right and wrong. No, she was only supremely innocent; she didn't understand, she didn't interpret nor see the *portée* of what she described" (86). The reader infers that this is Olive's judgment of Verena (the *"portée,"* for one, alerts us that this is from the cultured Olive's perspective) more than the truth of the matter. It is Olive's answer to the question she herself posed (can Verena distinguish between right and wrong?), but the question lingers for the reader since the answer has the status not of truth but of a judgment focalized through a character whose ulterior motives regarding Verena are known. The reader is led to suspect Olive is projecting Verena's innocence rather than discovering it. Let's call this syntax the focalized subjunctive, a syntax that can sound, if one is not attentive to the focalization, as if it's simply relating facts rather than psychological projection. It is a kind of wish fulfillment on the part of the focalizing character. This syntax appears throughout the novel, especially when characters think about Verena.

It is easy to miss the tenuousness of Olive's judgment of Verena or that of the many other instances of focalized subjunctive judgments. As I detailed earlier, most critics do not hesitate to form their own conclusions about Verena. But how, the novel invites us to ask, can we be sure that it is not projection on our part, for do we not have ulterior motives concerning Verena as well? Perhaps our critical project is not as polemical as Gilbert and Gubar's, but don't we all want to use Verena to advance our own reading of the novel?

As I noted earlier in the chapter, polemical does not describe the tone of the recent work on sentimentality that acknowledges its ideological complexity. Melissa Homestead explicitly calls attention to the critical aporia that prevents modern commentators on sentimental novels from recalling how contemporaneous readers like John DeForest thought of *Uncle Tom's Cabin* as an aesthetic triumph (Homestead 453). Homestead and other critics who come to nuanced conclusions about sentimentality allow us to develop a renewed appreciation for sentimentality but one that differs from the purely celebratory tone of early rescuers like Tompkins and Dobson. In this regard, more recent work has something in common with James's simultaneously skeptical and generous view of sentimentality. Also like James, these critics retain their critical distance from it: they remain able to analyze it and not from on high.

Yet I think *The Bostonians* can add something even to these capacious readings. Although Homestead asks us to acknowledge that contemporaneous readers of *Uncle Tom's Cabin* were able to feel its power, she does not discuss what enabled them to do so—and what makes it difficult for us later critics to register it, at least in our criticism. Here is a clue: discussing James's fiction "The Figure in the Carpet" as a response to Constance Fenimore Woolson's "'Miss Grief,'" Dorri Beam suggests that each text in its way "mock[s] certain textual approaches" (143). I would suggest that one of the textual approaches "The Figure in the Carpet" mocks and *The Bostonians* holds up for scrutiny is the critically distanced one that James himself develops and encourages, the approach that Bentley enjoins us to recognize as our own critical inheritance from James and other realists. This approach, which forms the bedrock of how we modern professional critics operate, encourages us to find a thematic meaning to attach to Verena rather than see in her unresisting malleability an invitation to become aware of our own critical reading protocols and their distinctive effects on sentimental objects. Other reading practices, like the uncritical ones that many antebellum readers possessed and that Dobson and Tompkins catch hold of at moments in their criticism, have their own distinctive effects. *The Bostonians* asks us to notice what we critics do and how we do it, to become aware of this process and how it impels us to ignore or explain away the power of the sentimental object by, on the occasions we are not unmasking it, feeling as if we can master it, thematically, by accounting for its political complexity.

I want to return to two details I mentioned in the opening of this chapter: Bayley's remark, which I'll come to in a moment, and my characterization of Verena as both a "sentimental object" and a sentimental character. I hope we can now see how Verena is *not* a sentimental character in the way that Stowe's Eliza, the escaped fugitive, or Howells's Conrad, the innocent killed in the streetcar riots, is. Conrad especially seems to bear a salient resemblance to Verena in his blank slate–ness, his being "content-free," as Victoria Coulson has characterized Verena (*Henry James* 63). Here's the difference: Conrad and Eliza are vivid both to other characters in the novel *and* to Stowe's and Howells's intended readers. In contrast, Verena is vivid only to the people in her storyworld; she's vivid to them because, among other reasons, she seems to fulfill cherished cultural narratives they hold. (Basil's cherished narrative apparently involves the snuffing out of women's public voice once they enter the domestic sphere, Olive's the freeing of such a voice.) Basil and Olive and the audiences that Verena addresses during her speaking engagements eagerly fill in the blank slate she offers. That is not the case with James's intended readers. James scrupulously maintains and holds up to our view Verena's status as a cipher. She does not feel vivid or immediate to us.

The distinction between Conrad/Eliza and Verena allows James to invite his intended readers to see her as a sentimental character without feeling the emotional force of attraction. If you want to help a professional reader free herself from the force of a (sentimental) character, just make it clear that the character is sentimental. It makes her embarrassed about the strong feelings this character evoked in her, even to the extent of forgetting she ever experienced them; it's a shaming tactic. But James enables us to label Verena "sentimental" without shame because we don't feel her force. Yet he still doesn't want us to unmask or master her.

Now, to return to Bayley's remark about James being the least sentimental of authors. For me, it is not just the fact that James does not ask us to feel strong emotions in the presence of Verena and the other characters in *The Bostonians* (however interesting we find them) that makes him the least sentimental of authors. Instead, it's his sustaining of Verena's mystery. Sentimental novels want, above all, their orator-characters to be intelligible; they want you to be able to *decide* whether the orator is being disingenuous or not. Contemporary critics have been happy to oblige them in their invitations to form judgments about their characters. James recognizes this compulsion, but instead of simply disavowing it, he allows it to linger as a possibility, but one that his own work never realizes. Reading James, we know Verena is a sentimental character, but beyond that, it is impossible to *decide* about Verena. (This is not the same as saying that Verena is a charlatan: we *can* decide about charlatans once we recognize them as such.) James refuses his readers a definite judgment about sentimentality; he refuses to let us rest easy because we have finally pinned it down.

Why does James treat sentimentality with this generosity? Why would James hesitate to deride a narrative technique that differs so much from his own? James's narrative technique does not induce in its readers the kind of transformative tears that works like *Uncle Tom's Cabin* or *The Lamplighter*—or speakers like Verena—seek to induce. James cannot produce in his readers the effect that Verena's orations produce in her audience; the narrator can only describe how Verena's audience were all "exceedingly affected" (50) and record in detail the reactions she produces in some of the individual characters. The narrator takes an analytical approach. Though Verena's persuasion moves beyond words, toward voice and then tears, James never eschews words for voice. Most of his characters do not persuade other characters or the reader through their sentimental speeches, nor do his own works strive to sound as if they were spoken (and when he tried in his dramatic productions to turn his words into voice, it was not a success). Further, one does not encounter clichés in *The Bostonians* unless they are attributed to others: the words matter supremely. I am willing to bet that never has a "scribbling woman" cast aspersions on a character for the use of a redundant "quite."

James's novel differs from a sentimental novel in another way as well—in the nature of its vividness. As I discussed in the introduction, literary realism has been associated with vividness, a fidelity to reality that eluded previous genres. "Realism is nothing more and nothing less than the truthful treatment of material" (966), as Howells wrote in his November 1889 "Editor's Study" column for *Harper's*, implicitly insulting sentimental literature with the statement. *The Bostonians'* vividness differs from sentimental vividness. This difference can be explained by returning to Stowe's association of her novel with a series of paintings. Stowe thinks about paintings as though they contain an emotional force that the reader cannot resist. Furthermore, Stowe believes that what they represent is self-evident: it is not available for interpretation. The realists did not think much of such an "immersive" form of literature or of art, one that swept up the reader headlong, ignoring (or undermining) her capacity for interpretation.[20] In *The Bostonians*, insights about the characters are slowly wrought by the author and hard won by the reader. Its vividness derives, in part, from creating psychologically subtle characters, but this way of depicting characters, I would claim, gains traction through its distinction from sentimental methods of characterization. That is, the vividness of realism could not arise without, at the same time, a reappraisal of earlier characters as "flat," a characterization that I dispute in the introduction. James's marriage plots are not realistic until they are compared with earlier ones. Realistic complexity attains meaning in relation to sentimental simplification.

James demonstrates via *The Bostonians*, however, that this simplification does not prevent a reader from registering a character's vividness; instead, it provides a different path to this effect (perhaps one whose endpoint might be an even stronger sense of vividness because it adds the tints of the reader's strong emotion). The reading practice required for a work like *The Bostonians* has come to be viewed not just as different from but as more sophisticated than that required by the sentimental novels. When sentimentality works, it does not seem sentimental at all. It just seems "realistic." But realism would later take on the mantle of "realistic" for itself. When sentimental fiction does not work on a particular reader, it seems as if it is a disingenuous attempt to manipulate her, to shut down her brain and drain her will, just as Douglas portrays it and just as we might have expected James to as well.

Despite all these inducements to debunk Verena's sentimental persuasion, so different from his own writing technique, James refrains. He does not want to reproduce sentimental rhetoric but still chooses to sustain its mystery. This is an extraordinarily rare position. In not choosing, James has something to teach the modern critic of the sentimental novel. James manages to stand outside sentimentality, to register its strange, fragile, overwhelming powers without experiencing contempt or reaching for mastery. James offers this unusual perspective on the sentimental object in his generous choice to keep Verena's true character veiled, or, even more radically, by suggesting the possibility that she has no "true" character, for example, that her ethical effects might depend on perspective or context.

I'm intrigued by James's position because it offers to the professional reader a way to respond to the sentimental object that is quite unique. James suggests that we cannot master the sentimental object even if we think we can. But we *can* use the sentimental object to gain insight into our own reading practices, if we're willing to read ourselves according to the ways that James trains us to read Olive's and Basil's readings of Verena. Verena remains largely unchanged by the fact that she is an object constantly being read and read into by the characters around her, but their reading practices (and very character) are illuminated by their judgments of her. We can use James's depiction of Verena not to pass a final judgment about her own character but to gain insights into the character of her readers—not just the ones within her storyworld but the ones without. Modern critics have chosen not to use the sentimental object this way; instead, many of us have chosen to believe in Howells's and Twain's characterization of sentimentality as something that proves our own superiority as readers (without accounting for their inability to give it up). Instead of accepting this affirmation, I am asking critics to attend to how James declines to let us dismiss either Verena or any doubts we have about the superiority of our own reading practices.

CHAPTER 4

Constance Fenimore Woolson's Rhetorical Passing

THE FEMINIST RESCUE of Constance Fenimore Woolson from literary obscurity seems finally to have succeeded. We now have an authoritative biography and two new collections of her short stories, including a 2020 Library of America edition.[1] Yet there has been a cost: the downplaying of Woolson's use of sentimentality. In this chapter I illuminate her reliance on sentimentality and ask not just why Woolson uses it but why it has been so difficult for the critics who admire her to acknowledge it.

At this point I want to make explicit something I've suggested in earlier chapters: that authors are not either sentimental or unsentimental. To insist on such a Manichean distinction derives, I think, from viewing sentimental rhetoric as something abject. By this logic, if an author is identified as even briefly deploying sentimental rhetoric in their text, they must be a sentimentalist.[2] Instead, I suggest that authors in the postbellum period use sentimentality more like a spotlight than a light switch. People discuss it as a literary mode or genre, but we should also see it as a narrative resource, and as the latter, it allows realist authors to highlight a particular scene or character, the better to persuade readers to take on certain political and ethical commitments.

Thus, even though I explore Woolson's use of sentimentality, it's still true that Woolson is a realist author. Accordingly, I contend that like Twain and Howells, she is also an author who sometimes writes sentimentally. Woolson, however, uses sentimentality differently from the way they do. She uses sentimentality as a tool of critique. That claim might come as a surprise because sentimentality is usually seen as stifling critique. In fact, sentimentality is often the very thing that the literary critic's wielding of critique is meant to dispassionately neutralize. Nonetheless, Woolson's depiction of what I claim to be the sentimental characters and objects in her stories reverses the usual directions of critique. Instead of using realism to critique sentimentality, Woolson uses sentimentality to critique realism. She especially critiques its cultivation and valorization of the discriminating reader, the reader who can make discerning judgments about everything from whether the decor of a particular home is to be considered tasteful to whether a given character is to be trusted in their judgments of another character.[3] As a woman realist author always in danger of marginalization by the literary and critical establishment, Woolson had good reason to critique discriminating readers. In identifying how she does so, we can further illuminate sentimentality's narrative affordances.

THE RESCUE OF CONSTANCE FENIMORE WOOLSON

Despite Woolson's having been one of the best-known writers in America during her lifetime, discriminating male readers have often been unkind to her.[4] In addition to promulgating the enduring portrait of Woolson as the poor talentless lady who loved Henry James unrequitedly, Leon Edel, James's most famous biographer, describes her as a writer of popular fiction.[5] This characterization feeds into a long-standing and misogynist bias against women authors who are too popular. Edel's claim about Woolson as a writer of popular fiction evoked an enduring view of her as a sentimentalist. Who, after all, had been more popular than the antebellum sentimentalists? Edward J. O'Brien, writing in 1931, noted that Woolson "does not always avoid the reproach of sentimentality" (qtd. in Torsney, *Critical Essays* 89). As Victoria Coulson observes, James himself characterized Woolson's writing "as [belonging to] an essentially feminine genre" ("Teacups" 91). In *Partial Portraits* (1894), in which he profiles a range of American and European authors, James opines that in one of Woolson's novels, *East Angels*, "the famous 'tender sentiment' usurps . . . a place even greater perhaps than that which it holds in life" (188). The step from being considered a sentimental writer to a writer lacking in artistry is both short and inevitable. No surprise, then, that in a 1910 "Editor's Study" column for *Harper's*, George Harvey writes that Woolson, like other of "our women," is "not eminent in constructive art" (961).[6]

Nineteenth-century American women writers were rescued in a way that countered the specific charges that had been laid against them: that they were trivial and sentimental. The earliest rescue critics insisted that nineteenth-century women writers were major artists, and this characterization shaped the form that the post-rescue criticism of particular women artists would take.[7] Cheryl B. Torsney, Ann Boyd Rioux, Sharon L. Dean, and Victoria Brehm characterize Woolson as an artist, as does Colm Tóibín, who wrote the foreword to one of the many recent reissues of Woolson's writings, *Miss Grief and Other Stories*: "It is Constance Fenimore Woolson's great gift that [her artistry] is done without any obvious effort or display, but with much subtlety, controlled sympathy, and writerly skill" (Tóibín xvi). Or to take another example, when asked in an interview how she came to write about Woolson, Rioux, author of the wonderful biography of Woolson I mentioned at the beginning of this chapter, responds: "I was interested in finding out when and how women writers had first committed themselves to the pursuit of serious literary artistry. . . . [T]here had been popular women writers who wrote for moral reasons rather than the pursuit of artistry, such as Harriet Beecher Stowe. But where were the artists?" (qtd. in Wolff).

Although these critics have mounted a brilliant defense against the earlier dismissal of Woolson, I want to highlight one way that they may have accepted the terms laid out by the disparagers of Woolson: that women authors become artists by turning away from sentimentality. If sentimentality is mentioned at all by these defenders of Woolson, they see her as rejecting it. This rejection gives her work its critical edge. For example, Torsney debunks the myth that Woolson committed suicide because her love for James was unreciprocated, "a myth that turns Woolson into a sentimental heroine herself and precludes serious study of her work" ("Castle Somewhere" 7); Brehm contends that Woolson "outstripped the possibilities offered by the sentimental genre she had inherited" (100); and Grace McEntee mention Woolson's "disdain of the 'sweet' fiction produced by many women writers" (154). For these admiring critics, to appreciate Woolson requires distancing her from the popular antebellum sentimental writers who preceded her—and who can blame them?

Both the male disparagers and the feminist rescuers share a view of the art-mangling power of sentimentality, and this view, as I discuss in chapter 2, resembles the view of sentimentality established by Howells and Twain. But what happens if we change our assumptions about sentimentality? What if we cease to see sentimentality as art's antithesis and instead see it as a powerful narrative resource for artists to take advantage of, its power achieved, paradoxically, through its own disavowal of artfulness? Sentimental writing allows readers to form profound attachments to what they read by closing the distance between authors, narrators, characters, and readers.[8] A focus on sentimentality's power rather than its deficiencies resonates with the way Woolson represents it in her own work.

To recognize Woolson's appreciation for and strategic use of sentimentality, we need to jettison two long-held beliefs about realist artistry that I've challenged in previous chapters: that realist artists never write sentimentally and that realist artists employ objective and impersonal narration (what is often called "omniscient narration," that is, third-person, unfocalized narration). Woolson's sentimentality can be perceived only if we're willing to recognize her employment of what is in fact a fundamental component of realist artistry: unreliable narration and unreliable focalization.[9] If we uncover the workings of narrative unreliability in Woolson's writings, we can acknowledge that she had both a much closer relationship to sentimentality than her recent defenders lead us to believe and a much more strategic relationship to it than her earlier detractors assert.

Past critics have not emphasized Woolson's habitual use of unreliable narration however much her celebrators tend to admire the subtlety of her writing. But the characterization of subtlety does not go far enough. Woolson was not just a subtle writer but one whose unreliable narrators allowed her to be strategically secretive. She could choose to reveal different things to different readers. There have been some inroads in recognizing her penchant for secrecy. For example, Brehm and Dean claim that Woolson does much of her work subtextually (xvii). Coulson directs us to a notebook entry where Woolson relates a conversation in which a character exclaims: "Give me a calm, composed, *in*expressive face to the public; a quiet mask. That is like the necessary clothes for the body; we do not go about the streets naked, do we?" ("Teacups" 90). Subtlety, secrecy—these qualities suggest but do not precisely name the narrative unreliability of her stories. Until we explicitly recognize unreliability, we will have a hard time detecting Woolson's sentimentality, which depends on it.

Yet it is not surprising that critics have not seen Woolson as habitually using unreliable narration.[10] She engages in narrative unreliability at the same time that she makes it difficult for many of her readers, especially contemporary literary critics, to detect it. Woolson crafts her narrators in such a way as to ensure that readers who are attached to discerning reading practices—those who have been trained in the practice of what Rita Felski calls critique—will be unlikely to recognize their unreliability.

FINDING THE SENTIMENTALITY IN "SOLOMON" AND "'MISS GRIEF'"

Woolson knew that the literary influencers of the postbellum era celebrated critical distance. She wrote in a review of James's novel *The Europeans* that "in this American nineteenth century . . . everything is taken lightly, and . . . ridicule is by far the most potent influence" (qtd. in Torsney, *Critical Essays* 71). Woolson contrasts this habit with that of the characters in *The Europeans*, who she says can now be considered "mastodons, . . . objects of amusement to the lighter-footed modern animals" because of their "tremendous earnestness" (qtd. in Torsney, *Critical Essays* 71). Woolson's desire to find both a large audience and critical approbation led her to construct stories that also seem to celebrate critical distance and literary discrimination. According to Rioux, she wanted to distance herself from critics' unwavering and dismissive efforts to categorize her solely as a woman writer (Wolff), a desire that led her to disavow connections to fellow women writers. In other words, Woolson embraced a conception of realist artistry that entailed a concomitant rejection of sentimentality. Yet I'll argue for an additional dimension to her stories: if on one view they seem to celebrate realist distance, they also register problems with it. Woolson mounts this critique by constructing narratives that document the cruelty this conception of realist artistry unleashes on those least able to withstand it. She positions sentimental art as a refuge from this cruelty and an antidote to the problems of critical distance.

To do this, Woolson employs the particularly subtle and sophisticated version of narrative unreliability that has been named and elucidated by Peter Rabinowitz in his theoretically groundbreaking but under-cited article on Nella Larsen's *Passing* (1929). In "'Betraying the Sender': The Rhetoric and Ethics of Fragile Texts," Rabinowitz calls this strategy "rhetorical passing." According to Rabinowitz, rhetorical passing requires that the author have two intended audiences, one of which he calls the "gullible authorial audience," which "is ignorant of the subtext"; the other is the "'discerning authorial audience' who both understands the subtext and appreciates the existence of an audience who is ignorant of it" (203). I'm going to rename what Rabinowitz calls the "discerning audience" the "masterful audience" to differentiate it from my own use of "discerning audience" as well as to nod to the previous chapter's discussion of the mastery of professional readers.[11]

In the case of *Passing*, gullible readers interpret the narrative as unfolding a story of racial passing, but masterful readers, although they register the story of racial passing, *also* recognize the narrative as unfolding an additional story of sexual passing, of lesbian desire.[12] Authors who construct narratives that rhetorically pass split their readers into these two different camps, and it's usual for gullible readers to make up the larger one. I'd like to point out that Rabinowitz uses "gullible" and "discerning" (what I will call "masterful") in reference to whether or not the reader apprehends the subtext of rhetorically passing texts. This means that "gullible readers" in some contexts can in fact be quite sophisticated readers, who employ close reading techniques and have an appropriate amount of distance from a text. To deploy a strategy of rhetorical passing, the author uses a first-person narrator whose unreliability will be recognized by only some of her readers. I also want to make explicit a point that lies implicit in Rabinowitz's conception of rhetorical passing. To be able to rhetorically pass, the author has to know her actual readers intimately: their values and beliefs, their self-conceptions, and their illusions.

The recognition of Woolson's strategy of rhetorical passing hinges on the reader's assessment of narrative reliability in her stories. In "Solomon" (1873) and "'Miss Grief'" (1880) the reader chooses whether to accept the reliability of Woolson's first-person narrators. If readers notice Woolson's subtle clues about their unreliability, then they can access a more masterful interpretation of the story: Woolson's depiction of the deep ethical experience that sentimental art offers, something that these narrators cannot access themselves. Yet to access this masterful interpretation, readers must be willing to give up their own treasured ability to read critically and to lose the considerable rewards such cultivation makes available. They must give up the mastery their training as professional readers has armored them with.

"Solomon" follows the pattern that characterizes what we might call Woolson's "failed artist" stories, many of which conform to the conventions of the regionalist sketch. Donna Campbell has identified how regionalist sketches often feature a narrator with whom the sophisticated northeastern reader, who consumed these stories in prestigious monthlies like *Harper's* and the *Atlantic Monthly*, could identify. The narrator of the regionalist sketch is usually a first-person narrator, and it is this feature that allows Woolson such freedom in appealing to both gullible and masterful readers since character narrators are required for unreliable narration, and unreliable narration is required for rhetorical passing.

First published in the *Atlantic Monthly*, "Solomon" is both a conventional regionalist sketch and its subversion. The story makes divergent interpretations available to different sets of readers. The first interpretation is made by readers who have learned to consume regionalist fiction the way Richard Brodhead describes such consumption, as "experiential imperialism" (*Cultures* 134), a desire on the part of readers to "appropriate experience vicariously" (133). They do not recognize the sentimentality in the story. The second interpretation is made by those who do not take Brodhead's approach and who recognize the story's sentimental elements. Each interpretation hinges on the extent of the reader's identification with the character-narrator, a well-off urbanite who has come to the remote Ohio village of Zoar.[13]

To pursue this first interpretation, which assumes a strong identification between reader and narrator, I'll proceed with a plausible way of summarizing the plot of the story. Two women go on a trip; one is a woman of a certain age, the narrator of the story. Accompanying her is her fashionable cousin Erminia, with whom the narrator lives. They are frequent travelers, entertaining themselves on their trips with a lively repartee, characterized by their differences in opinion, "the argumentum nonsensicum with which we were accustomed to enliven our conversation" (Woolson, "Solomon" 47). On this trip they have come to Zoar to consume the local culture: "We stayed among the simple people and played at shepherdesses and pastorellas. . . . [W]e went to church on Sunday and sang German chorals as old as Luther. We even played at work to the extent of helping gather apples, eating the best" (46). They find sustenance, both literal and otherwise, in their sojourn. Describing what they ate, the narrator reveals at least one of the intended audiences of her account: "Let not the hasty city imagination turn to the hard, salty, saw-dust cake in the shape of a broken-down figure eight. . . . The Community bretzel was of a delicate flaky white in the inside, shading away into a golden-brown crust of crisp involutions" (46). What better way to entice the "city imagination"—the gullible realist readers of the elite northeastern magazines—than with literal tasty morsels of regionalism? And what better way for the narrator to underline her own and Erminia's sophistication than by identifying those with whom they sojourn as "simple folk"?

Lured by a "new diversion" (46), the narrator and her cousin travel to an even more out-of-the-way place beyond the borders of Zoar. They do so to experience a "sulphur-spring," which can be accessed only from inside the house of a couple with the unfortunate last name of "Bangs," Dorcas and her husband, Sol. Dorcas turns out to be a faded, incongruously fashion-hungry woman who recounts the piteous story of her life: her marriage to Sol, a would-be artist, who has taken her as his muse but cannot sell a painting to save his life. The narrator and her cousin are aghast at his "barbarous pictures" (54), which bear "no likeness to anything earthly" (51). They are paintings of the wife as various famous personages. Taking pity on Sol, Erminia gives him a lesson on perspective, and Sol completes one final portrait of his wife, what he takes to be his masterpiece. It is left incomplete, however, by his sudden death, followed by the death of his wife a few months later. Dorcas leaves the narrator and Erminia this final picture, "a mere outline, but grand in conception and expression" (67), which allows the narrator and her cousin yet another opportunity to express their divergent opinions (in this case, on whether Dorcas was ever beautiful). The story seems to end where it began. Their trip has not altered the contours of these two women's lives but merely brought some fresh diversions to it, in which the urban reader can share.

Howells himself greatly admired this story (likely also its Ohio locale), and his admiring review of it allows us to see how it can so easily be interpreted as a typical, though accomplished, example of regionalist fiction and realist artistry:

> Her story of Solomon is really a triumph of its kind—a novel kind, as simple as it is fresh. The Zoar community, with its manners and customs, and that quaint mingling of earthy good-feeling and mild, coarse kindliness with forms of austere religious and social discipline . . . has had the fortune to find an artist in the first who introduces us to its life. Solomon's character is studied with a delicate and courageous sympathy, which spares us nothing of his grotesqueness, and yet keenly touches us with his pathetic history. . . . His death, after the first instruction has revealed his powers to himself, is affectingly portrayed, without a touch of sentimentalistic insistence. ("Recent Literature" [1875] 737)

I quote Howells's review at length to highlight how many opportunities for cosmopolitan discrimination he finds in this story. The inhabitants of Zoar are "earthy" and "coarse." In recognizing these qualities, the reader is assured that he himself is the opposite. Further, Howells's somewhat qualified praise of Woolson evokes the virtues of the local colorist: her depiction of some curious folk and her ability to convey their eccentricities—eccentricities the discerning reader can identify and leverage to assure himself of his own benign superiority. Yet these characters also touch the reader with their pathos.

The story offers readers a rich broth of emotions, but it's a delicate one, and the waitress is polite. The sympathy this story evokes is free from "sentimentalistic insistence," as if *Uncle Tom's Cabin* were pushy as well as artistically deficient. Howells is often remembered as championing realism's bravery in confronting life straight on, its aim to depict kinds of people and aspects of modern life that previous sentimental or romantic authors had shied away from. But in this review we see that however democratic Howells's impulse was to represent not just the wealthy but the impoverished, the forgotten as well as the movers and shakers, Howells believed that the stance realist authors take toward their characters ought to reflect their own bourgeois refinement. It's not that he eschews Woolson's "delicate and courageous sympathy" in portraying Sol, but he thinks that the relationship between a narrative's tellers and their sympathetic objects should be distanced and polite. In "Solomon," any intimacy between Sol and the narrator or Sol and the reader is tempered by an awareness of Sol's "grotesqueness." We can assume Howells counts Sol's art as contributing in large part to his "grotesqueness," and we can assume it is this grotesqueness that guards against any possible "sentimentalistic insistence"; that is, readers will be saved from doing or feeling what Sol's art wants from them by their awareness of its grotesqueness. Howells describes a complex emotional mixture that Melanie Dawson in her work on realist emotions has led us to predict. For Howells, Woolson's artistry enables her readers to be touched by this folk artist without becoming too close; their powers of evaluation remain intact. (For the realists, a lack of distance between viewers and the object of their scrutiny is a problem endemic to sentimental artifacts.)

My summary of the story augmented by Howells's evaluation offers what I hope is one highly plausible reading of it: it's a shining exemplar of realist artistry. In this reading, the narrator of the story is reliable. Woolson does a lot to ensure this reading, using broad strokes like matching the narrator's characteristics to the profile of her imagined *Atlantic* readers: well-off, sophisticated, and generally well-disposed to people worse off than she is. (A pattern in the story is the narrator's defense of Dorcas, Sol's ridiculously dressed wife.)

But she also ensures this reading of narrative reliability in smaller ways, like its reliance on seemingly objective geographical description. The story opens by painting a closely observed picture of the Ohio landscape: "Midway in the

Eastern part of Ohio lies the coal country; round-topped hills there begin to show themselves in the level plane" (43). The description goes on for a very long paragraph. It has at least two purposes, an obvious and a more subtle one. It fulfills the charge laid on regionalist fiction to satisfy its readers' appetite to learn about regional, generally rural, geographies different from their own, in other words, its tour guide function. But more subtly, this opening testifies, however deceptively, that this is an objective account offered by a trustworthy narrator because what's more objective than physical description?

Yet however the story gulls its sophisticated readers into assuming the objectivity of the narration and hence the reliability of the narrator, there's another interpretation possible, one that notices the openings, once we're past the story's own opening, that the story gives readers to find the narrator unreliable and to feel differently about the endless discriminations performed by her and her cousin. One way to access this alternative reading is to notice clues that the narrator is not as happy or as superior as she makes out. "Why should we come masquerading out among the Ohio hills at this late season? And then I remembered that it was because Ermine would come; ... [F]rom childhood I had always followed her lead" (63–64). With its connotation of the fake and the superficial, "masquerading" suggests both the narrator's melancholy and the emptiness of what at the beginning of the story she characterized as rejuvenating ("we played at shepherdesses and pastorellas"). There's the suggestion of empty artfulness here, and if we go back and start reading with that theme in mind, we can see that it's initiated in the first exchange the reader witnesses between the narrator and her cousin. The narrator remarks: "I do not believe we are all masked, Erminia. I can read my friends like a printed page" (45). This is the kind of hubristic statement that unreliable narrators make (it also echoes Woolson's interest in masks); it sets the narrator up for a fall. The tenor of the narrator's simile, however—"printed pages" an interesting variant on "books," which appears in the form the cliché more often takes ("I can read my friends like an open book")—suggests that Woolson wants to associate this character with the printed word. Similarly, the narrator habitually describes the natural world in terms of (man-made) art—at one point she describes a real forest as "painted woods" (56)—but the story allows us to see the problems with this kind of enforced artfulness: loneliness and ethical disengagement.

Erminia, the narrator's leader since youth, is hardly a moral polestar, as we judge from the narrator's casually dropped observation "that my beautiful cousin enjoyed the company of several poets, painters, musicians, and other of that ilk, without concerning herself about their stay-at-home wives" (56). Erminia's coquetry, her substitution of art for life, of flings for intimacy, is contrasted with the devotion of Sol to his wife, who in turn, "strange as it may seem, . . . pined for her artist husband" (69) and dies three months after he does. If we pursue this reading, we see Erminia and her cousin's local color journeys less as diversions than as attempted escapes, their witty repartee not shorthand for their closeness but the irritated exchanges of two relatives forced to spend too much time with each other.

Once we pierce the seeming complacency of the narrator, we can see that this story contains two central couples, one authentic and one fake. But which is which? Howells and Brodhead's audience of regionalist readers—the consumers of regionalist tales and marginalized lives offered in elite northeastern magazines—would see Sol and his wife as the wannabes rather than the real thing: Sol's art as "nothing earthly," his wife's getup a pitiful attempt at fashion ("The delaine [a dress made of light woolen fabric] was there; but how altered! Flounces it had, skimped, but still flounces. . . . the hair, too, was braided in imitation of Ermine's sunny coronet" [58]). But the story suggests an alternative reading: it asks us to compare Erminia's coquetry to the deep intimacy between Sol and his wife; the masquerades of these travelers to the real activities of the farmers; and, finally, the drawings produced by Erminia to those made by Sol. "Ermine had taken lessons all her life, but she had never produced an original picture, only copies" (64). Sol's art expresses a depth of feeling that Erminia's cannot begin to match.

In fact, Sol's art is sentimental art, just as in their earnest devotion to each other, Sol and Dorcas are sentimental characters. Sol's last picture, produced after Erminia has taught him perspective, is described by the narrator thus: "Upon [the easel] stood a sketch in charcoal wonderful to behold,—the same face, the face of the faded wife, but so noble in its idealized beauty that it might have been a portrait of her glorified face in Paradise. It was a profile, with the eyes upturned,—a mere outline, but grand in conception and expression. I gazed in silent astonishment" (67).[14] Note how much this passage resembles Stowe's initial description of Eva: "The shape of her head and the turn of her neck and bust was peculiarly noble, and the long golden-brown hair that floated like a cloud around it, the deep spiritual gravity of her violet blue eyes, shaded by heavy fringes of golden brown—all marked her out from other children" (*Uncle Tom's Cabin* 132–33). These passages are similar in their depiction of the spiritualizing power of certain images, and they are also similar in their use of the word "noble." In fact, "noble" is an adjective beloved by Stowe: she uses it to describe many of her favored characters. Furthermore, these descriptions do not just ennoble what is being described but also ennoble their witnesses, both the narrator and Woolson's and Stowe's extradiegetic readers. Sol's painting and Eva's visage are powerful machines of transformation. Just as Eva's spiritual gaze will transform those around her, Sol's painting also, briefly, transports the narrator: "I gazed in silent astonishment." For the moment, her endless talk, her endless judgments, have ceased.

Woolson's description of the painting suggests it's a sentimental object, one that can act on its audience in powerful ways. It suggests that contained within "Solomon" is a recipe for a relationship to art distinct from the one that Brodhead's model of regionalist consumption produces. This alternative relationship to art is not based on discrimination in the sense of endless evaluation and critical distance; it is based on immersion. Art is not a matter of multiple copies, of endless hunts for the eccentric and charming. If art is seen this way, consumers of art are engaged in a futile, exhausting series of never-ending journeys. How can such consumers ever stop to find true, transformative art, since what's on brief acquaintance charming and authentic will inevitably dull upon familiarity? We might recall at this point that in this story Zoar is not itself enough; the two travelers must find an even more remote locale.

If we read the story masterfully, rather than with discrimination, we can see that the story posits that there might exist a kind of art that is singular, spiritual, and of course completely vulnerable to the contempt of Woolson's contemporaneous audience, who chose to interpret Woolson's own art as espousing only realist precepts. The narrator too is trapped by her critical distance, unable to recognize the similarities she has with Dorcas: "Looking back we saw the outline of the woman's head at the upper window, and the dog's head at the bars, both watching us out of sight" (53). On one reading, the narrator simply observes Dorcas's melancholy at their leaving—and why wouldn't she be sad, considering the excitement and sophistication these two cosmopolitan women brought to her house? But Woolson suggests another way to interpret the narrator's description, one that the narrator seems at best only dimly aware of: that Dorcas is a prisoner of her own house. And there's an even deeper possible interpretation of this image. If we have been tracing the narrator's inadvertent revelations of her melancholy at her artful existence, then we might further notice that Dorcas and the narrator are doubled in their imprisonment. The narrator is imprisoned by her search for diversions and employment of discriminations, the very qualities that she thinks Dorcas envies her for.

Yet the narrator's realization of the prison house of discrimination is, if it takes place at all, fleeting. The story ends with Sol's picture bequeathed to the narrator and Erminia, where, at least on Erminia's part, it will go unappreciated, occasionally taken out, perhaps, as a souvenir to augment her recounting to a crowd of sophisticated painters and writers the out-of-the-way place that she once visited (aren't you jealous?) and the amusing eccentricities of its inhabitants. Will the narrator have a different relationship to it? That is a question the story leaves with its readers.

To read the story the second, masterful way opens the door to a sustained reaction of sympathy. For one thing, sympathy is not confined to Dorcas and Sol (who, on this reading, is not particularly grotesque) but extended to the narrator, who is unable to go deeper than her own superficial relationships or venture outside her prison house of discrimination. Howells and other discerning readers might see nothing but a little bit of humor in the last few lines of the story, where the narrator and her cousin argue once again about who is more deserving of pity, Dorcas or her husband. "Even then we could not give up our preferences" (70), the narrator notes. But this line reveals the unending cycle of regionalist consumption in store for the narrator—cycles of diversionary travel that give the narrator, this sophisticated urbanite, the chance to play at but never really experience sympathy.

I mentioned earlier that "Solomon" belongs in the category of Woolson's "failed artist stories." But who exactly fails in these stories? The gullible audience assumes that failure is suffered by the untrained artist whom the sophisticated narrator happens upon. The descriptions of this impoverished artist and his or her work furnish the narrator with those opportunities to discriminate that are so sweet both to him or her and to the story's readers. Yet because a story like "Solomon" allows readers the opportunity to see the narrator as unreliable, it offers a counter-narrative, visible to a masterful audience, wherein these sweet tidbits of discrimination can be seen to be less sweet than bitter: in consuming them, the sophisticated narrator loses the opportunity for a certain immersive, ethically significant experience of art.

Critics have often interpreted Woolson's failed artists psychologically, as embodying Woolson's own fears or desires.[15] But I'd like to offer an additional way to read them: these supposedly failed artists can also be seen as formally untrained or barely trained *sentimental* artists, whose work lacks artifice. Instead, their work offers an immersive and transcendent experience of existential and ineffable truth. But this is not apparent to the narrator, who serves as the point of identification for the realist reader. For a different kind of reader, however, who reads with an awareness of the narrator's unreliability, the narrator's dismissal of this failed art becomes a warning against believing that discrimination and critical distance are the be-all and end-all of reading. In this interpretation, "Solomon" becomes not a diversionary bonbon but a painful story that asks, pushily perhaps, for readers to feel for and with the main character by recognizing some of the narrator's own self-destructive qualities *in the readers themselves*. For these masterful readers, the failed artist reveals not just the narrator's own limitations but their own. In fact, these become stories not just of a failed artist but of failed sympathy and the damage to another person's life that a failure of sympathy inflicts. These stories offer the narrator the chance to engage in self-critique, which the narrator inevitably fails to do. The reader, by contrast, has the chance to do what the narrator cannot.

I realize that in presenting these two interpretations of "Solomon" the way I have, I've made the second one look like the better one because the more hidden and hence the more valuable according to modern literary critical protocols. Yet each of these readings is as hidden or as self-evident as the other, depending on the audience. Some audiences recognize unreliability more easily than others. One obstacle to recognizing unreliability is the extent to which the reader shares the values of the narrator. Contemporary literary critics, attuned to the ethical problems that arise from regionalist authors' depictions of regionalist Others, would seem to be primed to reject the values of the narrator in this story, her "experiential imperialism" and belief in the superiority of the metropole. These same critics, however, are often also invested in distancing Woolson from sentimentality, which depends on seeing the narrator as reliable. Furthermore, this judgment of reliability may be reinforced by their acceptance of the narrator's discerning ways of determining what constitutes worthwhile art. So although the masterful reading is not more valuable in general, it does have particular value in uncovering how literary critics like to read—and how they like to read is not just un- but anti-sentimentally.

Making a similar diagnosis of narrative unreliability can also open up new understandings of Woolson's best-known short story, "'Miss Grief.'"

Depicting the relationship between a "shabby, unattractive" ("'Miss Grief'" 158) woman author and a successful male writer who is also the first-person narrator, the story has become a touchstone in Woolson's recovery because it affords a terrific opportunity for feminist critics to overturn previous, sexist characterizations of Woolson. Earlier male critics read the story both as a rather simple roman à clef (with the narrator as Henry James and Miss Grief as Woolson) and as revealing Woolson's inferior literary talents. Feminist critics have put paid to that interpretation. Torsney, who brought the story back into contemporary circulation by having it reprinted in *Legacy* in 1987, notes that Woolson was a well-known, successful author when it was originally published, and subsequent critics, like Rioux, have noted that the story was published (in *Lippincott's*, in 1880) before Woolson had even met Henry James ("Anticipating James" 192).

"'Miss Grief'" tells the story of the unfolding relationship between the character-narrator, an author who is successful in both his literary and social life, and a woman whom he persists in calling "Miss Grief" even after he learns her actual last name. Aaronna Moncrief is a writer herself, a woman writer, but an unsuccessful one. Readers gradually realize she is so poor that she is starving to death. Nonetheless, she has begun visiting the narrator at his home to implore him for his opinion of her work, especially a drama she has titled "Armor." Expecting to hate it, the narrator instead recognizes its "earnestness, passion, and power" (168); he even decides to ask his friends in the publishing business (the story implies the existence of a well-developed old boy network) to accept it, yet they decline to do so. Recognizing the same "faults of expression and structure" (171) in it that the publishers do, he determines to fix it: "I amended, altered, left out, put in, pieced, condensed, lengthened; I did my best, and all to no avail. . . . [T]he obstinate drama refused to be corrected" (179). Summoned by her aunt, he finds Miss Grief on her deathbed, whereupon he lies to her about her work's rejection by his publisher friends. She dies happy. After her death, he keeps the drama for himself in a "locked case" (185).

As with "Solomon," the key to unlocking Woolson's intimate relationship to sentimentality depends on recognizing the unreliability of the narrator. Though feminist critics have only sometimes called him unreliable, they have almost always seen him as a heel. Torsney gives a list of the ways the narrator tries to dominate Miss Grief: "by refusing to grant her access to him; by renaming her; by acting as her intermediary in such a way as to pretend to champion her efforts while actually undermining her; by taking control of her production" ("Introduction to 'Miss Grief'" 12). So heel-ish does he seem that it's hard to recognize that many of Woolson's contemporaneous male readers, as Woolson knew, would not see him as unreliable, instead agreeing with him about Miss Grief's inferiority (even to the extent of ignoring the narrator's own concessions about her talent).

But let me build on feminist analyses of the narrator by focusing on his unreliability. He has a habit of seeing the world through misogynistic cultural scripts, a habit that prevents him from interpreting or judging things around him accurately. This affects all of his relationships with women. For example, it affects his views of a fiancée whom he feels he understands perfectly and so is shocked when she temporarily rejects him. But it affects his relationship with Miss Grief most of all: he is an inveterate misreader of her. Here are some of his misreadings, in order: Miss Grief as interested in selling him worthless antiquities, as talentless, as socially inept, as socially oblivious, as not starving. As to the last, he laughs at the picture she presents when she smokes, but she reveals at the end of the story that she and her aunt had begun to smoke to relieve their hunger pangs; they "had heard ... that one was no longer tired and hungry—with a cigar" (185).

As James Phelan has shown, unreliable narration works much more subtly than has commonly been supposed. Phelan has demonstrated that unreliable narrators are not unreliable all the time or along all axes; even if we are meant to reject their interpretations or judgments of people or events, we are not normally meant to reject the facts that they relate.[16] I would argue that although the narrator of "'Miss Grief'" is unreliable when it comes to his views of women, it does not mean the reader should see unreliability in his assessments of the literary merit of Miss Grief's writings. The reader is not given a reason to dispute his judgment that Miss Grief's "Armor" is powerful and emotional. Yet even as we are meant to accept his judgment, it should lead us to wonder just why the drama is so "armored" against what he sees as his efforts to improve it.

The answer, I would suggest, is that it's not a realist work but a sentimental one. Miss Grief herself shares much in common with both sentimental writers and sentimental characters: a failure to fit into feminine gender norms with her strange appearance and her forthrightness (antebellum woman authors frequently ran into accusations of "unsexing" themselves), an impatience with social hierarchy when it gets in the way of existential emergencies, and an ability to reform reprobate characters via her voice, as so many sentimental characters are able to do.[17] The oral is often associated with regionalism and its salient presentation of dialect, but we should not forget that it is also a crucial feature of sentimental novels. As I discuss in previous chapters, *Uncle Tom's Cabin* favors voice over the printed word for the former's immediacy and perceived naturalness. Note how at one point in "'Miss Grief,'" the narrator commands Miss Grief to read her story so that she can finally see the errors of her writing. "I will not read it, but recite it" (171), Miss Grief responds. Print is dead; the voice is alive.[18] Miss Grief's preference for the oral stands in contrast to the narrator's reliance on print, even to the point of seeing death as merely a literary artifact. Commenting on Miss Grief's claim that she would have ended her life had the narrator not thought well of her work, the narrator comments: "Then you would have been a weak as well as wicked woman. . . . I do hate sensationalism" (170). In this line we can hear an echo of the "Solomon" narrator's comparing friends to the printed page. Both narrators empty out what should be emotionally resonant aspects of existence by thinking of them in terms of print or performance—a cognitive analogue to St. Clare's lamentable habit of hiding his eyes from the injustice of slavery by blocking his sight of it with the daily paper. Under the pitiless critical gaze, sentimentality seems artificial and manipulative, but for the receptive, it appears artless and true, as when, in *Uncle Tom's Cabin*, the names printed in a newspaper transform, a few scenes later, into real (within the storyworld of the novel) enslaved men and women.

Miss Grief's own antipathy to print and to reading can be seen in our first introduction to her in the story, with her choice of her favorite of the narrator's works. She initially wins over the resistant narrator by *reciting* this work, which no other reader had ever made much of. As the narrator notes, it is "secretly my favorite among all the sketches. . . . I had always felt a wondering annoyance that the aforesaid public, while kindly praising beyond their worth other attempts of mine, had never noticed the higher purpose of this little shaft, aimed not at the balconies and lighted windows of society, but straight up toward the distant stars" (162–63). This is a spiritual work, not a secular one, even if the narrator substitutes the more secular "distant stars" for the expected "heavens." Miss Grief herself has no truck with such fancy discriminations or the social niceties and hierarchies that the narrator insists on, ones that insulate him from the basic existential facts around him, like the fact that Miss Grief is dying. Readers, by contrast, if they can look past the narrator's obliviousness, should be able to descry Woolson's sentimental appeal in the choice she shares with Miss Grief to foreground pain and survival over etiquette and social hierarchies.[19] But we can also see, if we *don't* look past the narrator's obliviousness and instead focus on its ramifications, the way that realist protocols of reading, including its celebration of the artfully wrought over the earnestly expressed, of the dispassionate over the immersive, condemn their wielders to miss the ethical import of the suffering experienced by marginalized figures like Miss Grief.

If Miss Grief shares features with sentimental authors and characters, her magnum opus, "Armor," shares features with a sentimental work. It's a drama, first of all. Rioux explains this feature as contributing to the generic variety of Miss Grief's output, which in turn mirrors Woolson's own ("Anticipating James" 194). We might also see its generic identity as recalling both the sentimental insistence on the living voice and the fact that *Uncle Tom's Cabin* itself reached more readers as a drama than in its original serial or novel form. But of course there are many unsentimental plays (Henry James's own *Guy Domville* comes to mind). Another clue is its imperviousness to revision. Sentimental art, as described by its practitioners, is not a product of wordsmithery. Nineteenth-century readers found resonant the idea of a work of art that would resist any amendment, as we can see from the ending of Hawthorne's tale "The Birth-Mark."[20] But the sentimentalists took this trope for their own, as when Stowe claimed *Uncle Tom's Cabin* arrived to her in visions rather than revisions.[21]

But perhaps the strongest piece of evidence for recognizing "Armor" as a sentimental work is its effect on its audience. The narrator reports that he had "sat up half the night over her drama, and had felt thrilled through and through more than once by its earnestness, passion, and power" (168). This reaction by the narrator evokes the sleep-resistant immersiveness, as I described in chapter 1, experienced by both Georgiana May and Henry Ward Beecher upon reading *Uncle Tom's Cabin*. Furthermore, the three adjectives the narrator uses evoke qualities associated with sentimental works much more than realist ones: although the touters of realism would view their works as powerful and honest, they would not describe them as earnest, let alone as evoking passion. Twain and Howells see themselves as members of Team Dispassion, even as they sometimes write sentimentally.[22] Finally, it's notable what this description lacks: we do not learn about the content of "Armor"; instead we learn about its effect on its listeners. This is exactly how Henry James presents Verena Tarrant's sentimental speeches, suggesting that what is notable about them is not so much what they say as the effect they have on their audience.

From the narrative audience's point of view,[23] sentimental utterances are not artful; they are unscripted, spontaneous outpourings, spoken in a time of emergency. They dissolve boundaries between author and narrator as well as character and reader.[24] Yet the literary critic has no way of analyzing the sentimental without falsifying its own claims. We know that sentimental authors wrote drafts; that characters are not real people;[25] that authors and narrators are not the same. Concerning this last, it is instructive that the narrator of "'Miss Grief'" admits his failure to amend Miss Grief's literary output: "One afternoon, about the time when I was beginning to see that I could not 'improve' Miss Grief . . ." (181). The narrator conflates Miss Grief and her works in this description. Certainly, one way we can read this conflation is as a bit of clever wordplay characteristic of this narrator and his cosmopolitan and rather Melvillean wit (as well as his desire to make Miss Grief more attractive and less plangent than she is). But another way to read it—the masterful way—is as another clue that Miss Grief's works are sentimental: they have worked on the narrator as sentimental works seek to do by rendering him unable to disentangle the author from what she has produced.

Yet when it comes to this narrator, the sentimental "Armor" can work only so far. As in "Solomon," the narrator yearns for a sentimentally transformative kind of art even as his own commitment to critical distance prevents him from undergoing actual transformation.[26] As in "Solomon," the sign of the narrator's rejection lies in the refusal to do more than play fitfully at sympathy. In "'Miss Grief,'" the narrator refuses, for most of the story, to recognize Miss Grief as a fellow human in need even as he admits (jealously) her superiority as an artist, though, he would hasten to add, a seriously flawed one. He must continually emphasize his difference from her: well off rather than impoverished; polished rather than awkward; male rather than female. Yet, as in "Solomon," the story provides clues that the narrator and the object of his pity are not as different as he would believe. Miss Grief too is refined even if poverty-stricken, and she too is socially perspicacious. (In fact, she's better at interpreting people than he is, as he proves when he initially mistakes her for a figure only to be pitied.) Furthermore, the story often codes her as masculine.

If Miss Grief and the narrator are twinned in some ways, does that mean, as it does in "Solomon," that the story sets him up as an object of sympathy for the reader? I don't think so. The narrator's situation, unlike that of the narrator of "Solomon," is just too privileged. Although the narrators of both stories are wealthy, the narrator of "'Miss Grief'" is free to choose his own companions and to marry. His choice of mate, a socialite named Isabel Abercrombie, reveals not his own metaphoric imprisonment but his approval of the social imprisonment of women: "Isabel was bounded on all sides, like a violet in a garden-bed. And I liked her so" (180). She is the antidote to the "vast" nature of Miss Grief's works, a vastness that he recognizes, attempts to modify, and covets for himself.

The complex relationship between the narrator and Miss Grief enables Woolson to offer an allegory of the relationship between realism and sentimentality. In the reading I've offered, we can see that the story castigates critical distance and valorizes sympathetic reading even as it reveals how difficult it is for realist readers to admit that they admire it themselves. The narrator sympathizes with Miss Grief most after she is dead, when her threat to him can be controlled. And yet . . . In both stories, the realist character, who survives and seemingly triumphs over the sentimental ones, cannot just leave the sentimental work to die with its author. In "Solomon," the painting is left to Erminia and her cousin; in "'Miss Grief,'" the narrator chooses very deliberately to keep her drama in a locked case. He will hoard it for himself but keep his possession of it a secret, exactly as Howells and Twain do.

But can Woolson reveal her dependence on sentimentality in a way that the narrator of "'Miss Grief'" cannot? Ironically, what might make my own reading of "'Miss Grief'" interesting—the idiosyncrasy of reading Miss Grief as a sentimental writer and "Armor" as a sentimental work—attests to Woolson's hesitation to reveal the identity of Miss Grief's "Armor" to any but a small group of readers. I've been emphasizing the way that Woolson's strategy of rhetorical passing allows certain readers to access a particularly radical message in her stories: a yearning for stories that dispense with artfulness and that try to dissolve not just gender discrimination but realist discrimination. These stories associate artlessness in the sense of directness and honesty not with realism but with sentimentality. A sentimental story can open powerful channels of sympathy between readers, characters, and narrators but not if it's recognized as sentimental. If it is, Woolson justifiably fears, that recognition will likely cause it to be dismissed. Rhetorical passing is compelling to marginalized realist authors who want to be popular but can achieve popularity only because of this strategy's masking effect. Most readers of Woolson's stories would not have, and in fact have not, registered the sentimental aspect of her stories. Woolson wanted recognition as a realist artist. Supported by the work of a group of committed feminist critics,

Woolson is finally being recognized as one. Yet touting her realist artistry has meant downplaying her attachment to sentimental art.

BEYOND SUBVERSION

I close this chapter by revisiting the feminist rescue of nineteenth-century women writers. I contend that even as this rescue led to invaluable advances in how we have come to understand the literary works of nineteenth-century women authors, it has also led to a limitation that has lingered on in our criticism, one that Woolson and her strategy of rhetorical passing can expose and thus help rectify.

The feminist rescue of nineteenth-century American women writers, which began in the 1970s, was built on claims of subversion. These forgotten women writers were worthy of critical interest because they subverted the patriarchy or current paradigms of American literary history.[27] The patriarchy and a woman author–averse model of American literary history were things that the feminist critics who rescued these writers had to contend with themselves. The subversion these critics found manifested itself in a particular way: it was there if the reader could dig below the status quo–affirming surface of the author's works. Critics had to look beyond the "coverplot," to use Susan K. Harris's resonant term.

Although contemporary critics who write about these women writers have moved well beyond analyzing them along a single axis of subversiveness, one still sees traces of this link between subversiveness and literary value in contemporary criticism of American women writers, not least in Woolson criticism. For example, McEntee has demonstrated how Woolson challenges colonial ideology in her short story "Jeannette," and both Christine Healey and Rioux have revealed Woolson's uncovering of prejudices against women writers among the male realist literary establishment. How does my own claim about Woolson's rhetorical passing line up with this impulse? On the one hand, it supports it. I am expanding the list of things that Woolson critiques—not just the realist publishing establishment but realist reading practices themselves. But my claim also allows us to identify a limitation the searcher for subversion might unwittingly possess. It's easy for her to overlook critiques by marginalized authors that are aimed at the critic herself. To identify that limitation, I need to articulate just how the ascription of rhetorical passing differs from the feminist interpretive strategy of digging below the coverplot to find subversion.

Even though my identification of Woolson's strategy of rhetorical passing expands the purview of her subversiveness, it also acknowledges how hard it is for readers to register all of her targets. Rhetorical passing obscures for many readers the extent of a marginalized writer's subversiveness because it works in combination with the author's deliberate misdirection: the seeming embrace of a dominant group's favored reading practices. In Woolson's case, her strategy of rhetorical passing requires her to stud her stories with regionalist bonbons—all the delicious descriptions of places and people so different from those encountered by metropolitan readers—to distract realist readers from her critique of how they read. The *point* of rhetorical passing is to enable an author to be subversive without detection by the bulk of her readers.

This can sound a lot like a "coverplot"—the conventional surface that masks the subversiveness that lies underneath—but there's a subtle yet crucial difference. Harris describes the coverplot less as a structural feature immanent in these women writers' texts than as an interpretive strategy that readers should engage in when they read these women authors' works. Harris explains "that women's novels written during the midcentury [i.e., the mid-nineteenth century] embed radical possibilities within their thematic and rhetorical frameworks, [and] that those 'deviations' were accessible to contemporary readers and that those readers were capable of 'configuring,' or realizing, the texts differently than the cover story indicated" (13). Harris avoids saying that it is authors who are doing this work; instead, it is the "novels" themselves that embed the radical possibilities that readers can realize. The recognition of a coverplot initiates a reading strategy rather than highlights these authors' encoding practices. It empowers readers and removes the author as a figure of any utility in interpreting a literary work. In this discounting of the author, Harris follows larger disciplinary protocols that derive from the intentional fallacy and claims about the death of the author.[28]

The concept of rhetorical passing has a different emphasis than "coverplot": it emphasizes *authorial* agency rather than the agency of the reader or critic. Although it is implicit in the idea of the coverplot that women writers embed coverplots in their works, Harris wants the emphasis to fall on readers; she wants to motivate them to read beneath this coverplot. Yet rhetorical passing, unlike the coverplot, calls attention to the *author's* efforts to encode two different interpretations into their works, which depend in turn on these authors' thorough knowledge of their readers. (Charles Chesnutt, as we'll see in the next chapter, had his contemporaneous white readers down cold.) In other words, a coverplot makes a noise in the forest only if a literary critic is around to hear it, but a strategy of rhetorical passing in a text exists even if critics never register the quiet sound of its stealthy, hidden critique. The sound its critique makes will be particularly difficult to hear if it goes against a critic's own theoretical and critical allegiances. When it comes to women writers whom literary critics want to rescue, critics are much more likely to register a hidden story of lesbian desire than one of sentimental attachment because the field remains wary of sentimentalism. Rhetorical passing exposes the biases of its readers. Thus, it is useful not just in illuminating Woolson's stories but in illuminating the possible problem with an interpretive technique that bets everything on a reader's ingenuity rather than an author's strategy. This problem comes to the fore when an author has embedded in a text a critique of the reader's ingenuity itself. In that case, the critics' favored techniques of interpretation are precisely what might prevent them from recognizing the author's strategy and hence the author's critique.

When theorizing about how to interpret an author's work, we might not want to rely solely on the reader. Instead, we might think of interpretation as depending on a dynamic between an author's strategizing and a reader's ingenuity. What makes Woolson's rhetorical passing so effective is that it's precisely the adoption of realist interpretive practices that renders a reader unable to recognize it. Or maybe that's what makes her rhetorical passing so ineffective: modern literary critics, who are committed to realist reading practices, have not been able to recognize it.

When we ignore the existence of a strategizing author of a text by, for instance, talking about "novels" embedding something rather than "authors," a common locution not just in discussions of the coverplot but in literary criticism in general, we assume that our own powers of ingenuity are enough to uncover all the meanings a text has to offer. But a rhetorical narratological approach raises the possibility of interpretations existing in a text that are difficult for the literary critic to see. Strategizing postbellum authors might embed in their texts precisely what they know most of their contemporaneous readers will have difficulty registering: the limitations of their powers of discernment. To be a masterful reader of Woolson requires us to shed the armor of our mastery as professional readers.

Women writers and Black writers have a long history of having their agency ignored. Stowe fed into this idea when she claimed that she did not write *Uncle Tom's Cabin*, God did. An otherwise secular, male-dominated critical establishment was happy to accept this view, as we can see from George Whicher's head-scratching mid-twentieth-century critical assessment of *Uncle Tom's Cabin*. According to Whicher, Stowe's explanation that God wrote *Uncle Tom's Cabin*'s "solved the paradox" of her novel's popularity, considering that "obviously Harriet Beecher Stowe was neither a great personality nor a great artist" (586). Woolson's characterization as regionalist or, even worse, sentimentalist puts her in double jeopardy, because regionalists and sentimentalists have often been seen as transcribers of their cultures rather than artful depicters of it. Even as Howells and Twain called for realists to transcribe more accurately what they saw around them, they believed that the realist author needed to transform the raw data of experience into art, or as Daniel H. Borus puts it, "The 'simple, direct, and honest' account [how Howells characterized realist writing] was art that appeared artless" (78).

The more recent characterization of Woolson as a realist artist counters the way previous critics dismissed her. In this chapter, though, I've tried to expand that characterization to show how Woolson was also, through her rhetorical passing, a skeptic of realist artistry as well as a defender of sentimentality and occasional wielder of it. To be able to be all these things at once, Woolson was a consummate strategist. She knew her readers intimately—their values as well as their illusions—and she was able to use them to her own advantage. She would have been hard-pressed to recognize the rise of a discipline that sidelines the figure of the author in its interpretive practices, but she was quite familiar with a readership that coalesced around its fancied powers of literary discrimination. One reason literary critics haven't recognized Woolson's strategy of rhetorical passing might be because it targets their own favored practices of reading. Although the narrators of "Solomon" and "'Miss Grief'" don't get very far in their own self-critique, Woolson—and, as we shall shortly see, Chesnutt—challenge us to do better.

CHAPTER 5

Weaponizing Sympathy

Charles Chesnutt's Narrative Experiments

How can Charles Chesnutt be responsible for both the conjure tales and *The Marrow of Tradition*? The conjure tales, fantastical sketches about life on a grape plantation before the war, were consumed with delight; *The Marrow of Tradition* (1901), a grimly realistic novel depicting the race riot that took place in Wilmington, North Carolina, in 1898, met with lukewarm reviews and poor sales. Published in elite northeastern magazines like the *Atlantic Monthly* and *Harper's* before being collected in *The Conjure Woman* (1899), the conjure tales are, according to an 1899 review in the *New Orleans Daily Picayune*, "well written, showing familiarity with the whimsicalities and comicalities of negro character, and a subtle perception of the poetry and romance often hidden in their hearts" (qtd. in Ashton and Hardwig 6). By contrast, *The Marrow of Tradition* was seen as a "purpose novel" in the words of a 1901 *Brooklyn Daily Eagle* review, an attempt to make its white readers confront the racial oppression they were hell-bent on maintaining in the post-Reconstruction South. Although a supporter of Chesnutt's promotion of Black equality, the reviewer goes on to point out the novel's "obvious literary defects, its faults of construction and its extravagancies." The reviewer was not alone in seeing it as a seriously flawed literary effort. Even Howells, an early champion of Chesnutt, described *The Marrow of Tradition* as "bitter, bitter," further commenting, "Though . . . of the same strong material as his earlier books, it is less simple throughout" ("A Psychological Counter-Current" 882).[1]

This varied reception correlates to the different levels of political engagement Chesnutt's contemporaneous audience registered in the tales and in the novel. In contrast to the fantastical and apolitical nature of the conjure tales, where characters turn into grapevines or trees and usually avoid killing one another, *Marrow* is obviously didactic. As I mentioned, *Marrow* tells a story based on the Wilmington race riot—or what Matthew Wilson calls Wilmington's "coup/pogrom" (*Whiteness*). The coup/pogrom was catalyzed by white rage at newly elected Black politicians and Black economic success during Reconstruction and resulted in the death of nineteen Black people, deaths that were justified in the contemporary media, including the northern media.[2] Chesnutt's novel gives the lie to such depictions. Another difference between these works arises if we turn from theme to form. The conjure tales differ not just in terms of length but in terms of narration: the conjure tales feature a first-person narrator, whereas *Marrow* features third-person narration.

Yet for contemporary literary critics, these works are not so different after all. There is now a critical consensus about the conjure tales' political-racial resonance.[3] In this chapter, I hope to build on this work by looking closely at the narrative methods Chesnutt uses to mount his critique of the postbellum racial order across his works. I do this in my effort to limn another way that realist authors use sentimentality: Chesnutt uses it as a weapon.

As I did with Woolson, I foreground these works' narrative unreliability, one of the neglected but salient features of realism that this book has tried to bring to light. Beyond their common thematic interests, another feature that unites the conjure tales and *Marrow* is their use of unreliability. We're more familiar with unreliable narrators, first-person narrators whose reports, perceptions, and/or judgments are meant to be questioned by the reader. But *Marrow* features third-person "objective" narration. As I've discussed in previous chapters, even if third-person narrators are not commonly unreliable, third-person narratives can feature, as *Marrow* does, unreliable focalization: narration that is filtered through the consciousness of characters (what many people call "free indirect discourse").[4] In other words, unreliable focalization in *Marrow* works the same way that unreliable narration does in the conjure tales. But also as in Woolson, Chesnutt does not just engage in narrative unreliability; he engages in rhetorical passing. Chesnutt constructs the unreliability of his white narrator and white characters so that it is apparent to only some of his readers. For other readers, it is not apparent at all. These gullible readers will not feel distant from these characters; instead, Chesnutt invites them to feel sentimental sympathy for them. He does this in *Marrow*, as we shall see, to make them acknowledge their own racism.

Why does establishing an even tighter connection between the conjure tales and what Craig Werner classifies as one of his "conventional" novels matter?[5] For one thing, tracing this connection can reconcile two conflicting portraits of Chesnutt. Chesnutt has been seen as an author either galvanized by his need to have white readers register the racial injustice that characterized the post-Reconstruction period or motivated by his quest for literary and professional success. Yet he delineates both aims in the journals he wrote as he was mulling over a career as an author:

> The negro's part is to prepare himself for social recognition and equality; and it is the province of literature to open the way for him to get it—to accustom the public mind to the idea; and while amusing them to lead them on imperceptibly, unconsciously step by step to the desired state of feeling. (*The Journals* 140)
>
> I want fame; I want money; I want to raise my children in a different rank of life from that I sprang from. . . . I shall strike for an entering wedge in the literary world, which I can drive in further afterwards. (*The Journals* 154–55)

These aims seem jarring, and critics who emphasize his commitment to racial justice do not, as a rule, consider his commitment to filthy lucre. The opposite obtains as well. Either Chesnutt was motivated by a quest for artistic or financial success or he was driven by his need to fight for racial justice.[6]

Chesnutt's rhetorical passing allows us to put these two portraits together. Because unreliability muted Chesnutt's racial critique for pro-realist, self-reflection-averse white readers, it enabled his success. Yet despite what it enabled, unreliability also posed a problem for Chesnutt, who wanted to reform his white readers. With few exceptions, the white readers who loved his conjure stories did not recognize the critique of white supremacist thinking embedded in them. To the contrary, the narrator of the conjure tales, John, is so unobjectionable to them as to be generally unremarked upon by contemporaneous reviewers except to point out what brought him to the South. In one review, from the *Philadelphia Press*, which reflects the general approbation with which these readers considered him, he is called a "Northern gentleman." How can you reform a reader who implicitly trusts the person whom the author knows to be a problem? Following this line of inquiry allows us to see that these two very different publications are tightly connected: they reveal Chesnutt's evolving attempts to solve the problem of making white readers identify their complicity in a racial order whose benefits they reaped and whose injustices they ignored.

Realist writers resist the apostrophes and other kinds of authorial intrusions that characterize antebellum sentimental novels. In favoring what seem like more subtle and objective narrative techniques, they flatter their readers by trusting them to make their own judgments—to become, in other words, critical readers (however guided these judgments still are). Yet Woolson and Chesnutt show how these realist/critical readers are also gullible ones. Like Woolson, Chesnutt uses sympathy to launch his critique. Yet unlike Woolson, Chesnutt weaponizes sympathy: his narrative experiments reveal a consistent reliance on sympathetic identification. What changes is how much he cares about his white readers' reeducation at the expense of his own success as an author. At the start of his writing career, he was content for only part of his audience to master his subtext; he evolves, however, into a writer who wants more and more of his audience to register their flawed beliefs and values concerning the racial order. If we focus on how Chesnutt wields sentimental sympathy, we realize that in addition to launching a critique of "white supremacist discourse" (Sampson 191), he has another object of critique in mind: his white readers' self-regard. He hopes to change their self-regard to self-critique by taking advantage of their capacity for sympathetic attachments.

In this chapter I turn to three of Chesnutt's works: the conjure tales; *The House Behind the Cedars* (1900), published a year after *The Conjure Woman* (where his conjure tales were first collected); and *The Marrow of Tradition* (1901), published a year after *The House Behind the Cedars*. I see them as a series of evolving experiments in persuasion. Chesnutt knew how discrimination worked—both the kind of literary discriminations realist authors had trained their readers to make and the kind of racial discriminations white people had trained themselves to make. As his career as an author takes off, Chesnutt takes increasing advantage of his white readers' fancied literary discrimination in an effort to make them repudiate their unacknowledged habits of racial discrimination. Chesnutt draws on both realist and sentimental narrative conventions, and instead of oscillating between these two modes as we've seen other realist authors do, he constructs passages that demonstrate both at the same time. Tracing the evolution of Chesnutt's narrative experiments allows us to register, along with him, the affordances and limitations of the narrative choices he makes in each of these texts.

An analysis of his evolving choices as an author allows me to demonstrate that one of the conventional distinctions we make between realism and sentimentality as narrative modes has gotten it backwards. Sentimental writing is, in fact, more objective than realism because it doesn't focalize through different characters' perspectives, let alone unreliably focalize. But the assumption that realist novels use objective narration, still alive and well in our own era, gives Chesnutt his chance with white readers. If he can use this assumption to induce readers to trust and sympathize with his white characters, then maybe he can also force them, in a moment of self-reckoning, to renounce their racist ways of seeing the world.

Throughout his works, as critics have recognized,[7] Chesnutt criticizes a binary way of conceptualizing race, which he believed led to such things as the Wilmington coup/pogrom. Yet what has remained obscure is how Chesnutt's racial critique can help us recognize a similar kind of binary logic that literary critics still hold about American literary realism. Howells and Twain led a successful campaign to characterize realism as a genre uncontaminated by the false notes of sentimentality. We can think of this as realism's Purity Principle: as soon as readers recognize a sentimental scene or character in a realist novel, it ceases to be considered either realist or well written. The evolution of Chesnutt's works demonstrates that realist authors do not slip into sentimentality in moments of inattention or bad artistry. Instead, they do so because realism's narrative limitations and sentimentality's narrative affordances complement each other. Chesnutt allows us to see that these limitations and affordances are not just aesthetic but ethical ones. Realism requires sentimentality to fulfill its ethical mandate.

THE CONJURE TALES AND THE PROBLEM OF POPULARITY

Chesnutt tries to solve the problem of how to write fiction with a purpose in a literary era that had rejected didacticism. He does so by relying on narrative unreliability, which in some configurations allows you to bite the hand that you also want to feed you. Chesnutt's and Woolson's writings both share the strategy of "rhetorical passing," Peter J. Rabinowitz's term for the technique that allows a work to be taken one way by a "gullible authorial audience," who miss the subtext, and another way by a "discerning authorial audience," who understand both the subtext and that other readers will remain ignorant of it ("Betraying" 203). (For more details, see the preceding chapter. Note that

I replace Rabinowitz's term "discerning reader" with "masterful reader.") Chesnutt's story "The Goophered Grapevine," first published in 1887 in the *Atlantic Monthly*, relates either the entertaining and absurd story of an enslaved man whose ingestion of some "conjured" or cursed grapes imbues him with the characteristics of a grapevine or a horrifying account of slavery's cruelty, which includes the quotidian practice of starving the enslaved and its foundational legal practice of turning Black people into things.

"The Goophered Grapevine" is narrated by a white northerner named John, who has come down south to scope out possible locations for a vineyard. At one derelict vineyard he meets a loquacious man named "Uncle Julius," who had formerly been enslaved there and who tells John a tale from that period. The story ends with John buying the vineyard and hiring Julius to work as his coachman. Different readers find different salient details and read similar details differently. For the gullible reader of "The Goophered Grapevine," aka readers of *The Atlantic*, who had been fed a steady diet of similar regionalist tales, what stands out are the charms of the dialect, Julius's own "venerable"[8] and "genial" character ("From the *Southern Workman*" 232)—an "old-issue negro" in the words of an 1899 review ("From the *News and Observer*" 233)—and, finally, the common element in all of these reviews, Julius's shrewdness in attending to his own interest in telling his tale, an observation that makes John the exploited figure, never mind the fact that John is contemplating taking away the vineyard as a source of income for Julius. In sum, gullible readers fasten on details that lead to the story's being read as belonging to plantation fiction, a genre with which *Atlantic* readers would be very familiar, featuring faithful, happy slaves and beneficent masters.

The stories provided a way for their most important gullible audience, white northern readers of elite magazines like *The Atlantic*, to escape confronting their prejudices. For gullible readers, these stories propose a foible-ridden humanity shared between white people and Black people. We see this idea in an 1899 review of *The Conjure Woman* that appeared in the *New York Times*. The reviewer observes that the stories "[suggest] that the black man is no more above making his superstitions profitable than his white brother" ("From the *New York Times*"). This consoling idea of shared humanity allows the reviewer to pass over the racial hierarchy that had defined the United States since its inception.

By contrast, what becomes salient to a masterful reader are the story's references to slavery's cruelty: among them, the near starvation the enslaved suffered from and the bloodhounds that hunted them.[9] Yet it's not just a matter of these two audiences focusing on different details; they also read the same details differently. The gullible reader takes the adjectives that John uses to describe Julius as simply accurate: John is the one who originally calls Julius "venerable" and "shrewd"—two adjectives that contemporaneous reviewers pick up unproblematically. The masterful reader, however, descries the prejudice contained in John's view of Julius: John is thinking in terms of Julius's shrewdness in financial matters, conveniently ignoring how whatever small allowances Julius manages to wrest from him pale in comparison to John's own material advantages. John is not thinking about Julius's actual shrewdness in dealing with white people, giving them—as Chesnutt himself does—just what they want. For example, soon after John and his wife, Annie, come upon Julius, John notes Julius's alacrity in moving off the log he had been sitting on: "[Julius] respectfully rose as we drew near, and was moving away, when I begged him to keep his seat" (5). To the gullible audience, John is simply making an observation about an expected bit of bodily deference from a Black man. But the discerning reader sees this either as an instance of misreporting (perhaps John invented the alacrity to sustain his sense of racial superiority) or a choice bit of playacting on the part of Julius, who tends to serve John just what John wants. Julius's mention of the love of the enslaved for watermelon ("Goophered" 7) functions similarly, as does his calling enslaved people "darkies" ("Goophered" 7). White readers can consume racist slurs as if they are local color details; that they are provided by a Black character makes them seem even more benign.

Let me loop back to the gullible reading of the story and note how much it conforms to John's view of the situation. Gullible readers take on John's point of view; in other words, he becomes not just reliable but their own point of sympathetic identification in the story. (Gullible readers assume he is also the author's spokesperson.) In fact, he tends to disappear from their account of the story: he is not an intrusive narrator but an invisible one. John has an absolute faith in the correctness of his view of Julius and Julius's stories. He is a role model for Chesnutt's real gullible readers, who acknowledge neither John's gullibility nor their own.

But masterful readers see a distance between their view of Julius's stories and John's, an alignment with the implied author, whom we assume holds the same dim opinion of John's view of the racial order as they do. In other words, John becomes, for the masterful reader, an unreliable narrator, whose unreliability clouds his seemingly objective observations. John becomes what

Benjamin Harshav would call a "junction," a detail in the text that is taken up differently depending on the reader's mental schemata.

"'Rhetorical passing'" Rabinowitz writes, "is not simply a disguise, but a virtuoso tightrope performance, a flirtation with risk by flaunting your disguise in a context in which you know that it will *fool only some people*, an act, in other words, that has built into it the exhilarating possibility of exposure and destruction" ("Betraying" 202). One might suspect Chesnutt's exhilaration at the often great subtlety with which he creates his junctions. In "Po' Sandy," published in *The Atlantic* in 1888, John, once again the frame narrator for one of Uncle Julius's tales, categorizes the tales his wife has been hearing from "the older colored people" (15) in the neighborhood. Here is his taxonomy: "Some of these stories are quaintly humorous; others wildly extravagant, revealing the Oriental cast of the negro's imagination: while others, poured freely into the sympathetic ear of a Northern-bred woman, disclose many a tragic incident of the darker side of slavery" (15). As the editors of *The Conjure Stories*, Robert B. Stepto and Jennifer Rae Greeson, tell us in a note, these are common categories of plantation stories that were circulating contemporaneously (15). Where we see Chesnutt's virtuosity is in the last category of plantation fiction that John mentions, the ones that describe the "darker side" of slavery. At first it can sound like Chesnutt has blown his cover, revealing, through John's comment, the way the conjure tales illuminate the horrifying nature of slavery if you read them masterfully. But if we look closely at John's wording, we can detect the ways in which John is still getting it wrong and hence still appealing to his gullible readers: he gets it wrong with his oddly jaunty "many a," as if these tragic incidents were equivalent to any other repeated activity. One can imagine it being used in a locution like this: "Many a day, Annie and I went on a picnic." Worse is the implication that slavery had a "light side"; but to the reader of plantation fiction (hello, *Atlantic* readers!), the existence of such a side is a given. So what seems, initially, to be Chesnutt's revelation of his hand is cloaked by John's particular locutions. Why wouldn't Chesnutt feel exhilarated by his own artistry?

Yet I doubt exhilaration was Chesnutt's only emotion. His subtlety was too successful. I've found evidence of only a very few masterful contemporaneous white readers of the conjure tales who could register his critique of white obliviousness.[10] Rabinowitz thinks of the two audiences for rhetorically passing texts synchronically: that they exist at the same time. Yet the two audiences for Woolson and Chesnutt exist, in a more meaningful way, diachronically:

first came their contemporary, gullible readers and much later came literary critics and readers who were finally able to register their critique (and in the case of Woolson, it's unclear if her critique of realist reading practices has been registered at all). On that note, I'd like to come back and think more about the overall tone of Rabinowitz's evaluation of these authors' rhetorical virtuosity. This failure to reach a white audience capable of masterfully reading his conjure tales most likely troubled Chesnutt—and for evidence, I offer my readings of the narrative changes made in the two novels published after the conjure tales. Chesnutt was likely not very happy with the cast of mind that allowed *Atlantic* readers to read John as a reliable narrator and even as a role model; Chesnutt's very success as an author was also, in a crucial way, a failure.

As evidence of Chesnutt's dissatisfaction with the subtlety he practiced as a newly minted author, I offer a brief analysis of the changes he made to the first section of "The Goophered Grapevine" between the time when it was first published in *The Atlantic*, in 1887, and when he republished it as one of the stories in *The Conjure Woman*, in 1899. Many of the changes make more obvious Chesnutt's critique of John—and make more obvious John's unreliability. For example, the original version includes this line: "[My cousin] assured me that no better place could be found in the South than the State and neighborhood in which he lived: climate and soil were all that could be asked for, and land could be bought for a mere song" ([1887] 254); the revised version inserts "labor was cheap" before the phrase "land could be bought for a mere song." This change indicates John's enthusiasm for exploiting his workers, including the soon-to-be-encountered Julius. Other additions to the version published in *The Conjure Woman* flesh out this evolving portrait of a complacent, ethically deficient white man of means (just like many of Chesnutt's *Atlantic* readers), as when Chesnutt has John comment, in the later version but not the original, *Atlantic* one, on the ease he feels in the company of the rich white man hosting Annie and him during their scouting trip to South Carolina: "Our host was a man of means and evidently regarded our visit as a pleasure, and we were therefore correspondingly at our ease, and in a position to act with the coolness of judgment desirable in making so radical a change in our lives" (4). Chesnutt thus signals to readers the way that the presence of Black people makes white people like John uncomfortable and unsettles them from what they take to be their habitual rationality. (The way Chesnutt frames the difference between white people in the presence of Black people versus white people in the presence of other white people is homologous to the way sentimental writing is said to unsettle readers versus realism's ability to produce cool-headed ones.) Finally, the long passage that reveals John's phrenological/anthropological gaze—"[Julius] was not entirely black. . . . There was a shrewdness in his eyes, too, which was not altogether African" (6)—is also a later addition. We can see Chesnutt coming much closer to lifting the veil from his gullible readers' eyes. But it was not nearly enough.

Instead of changing minds with the conjure tales, Chesnutt changed his status from an unknown author into a popular and lauded one, which may very well have been his primary aim when he was starting out as an author. Or perhaps it is not that Chesnutt developed a different aim but that he saw his popularity as the necessary first step in exposing white people's obliviousness to their own racism. "Unless my books are read I shall not be able to accomplish even the ethical purpose which I have in view," Chesnutt wrote to his publisher in 1901 (qtd. in Finseth 3). Yet popularity was not enough. His white readers loved the tales but missed the critique. In the two published novels that followed them, Chesnutt sought to make his critique more difficult to miss for his white readers, a desire that ended up hurting his popularity under the regime of realism.

A PARTIAL SOLUTION: REDUNDANCY IN *THE HOUSE BEHIND THE CEDARS*

The House Behind the Cedars shows how realist authors kept sentimental techniques in their locked trunk of narrative resources, for them to raid at will. Minoritized authors, however, could use them only sparingly or ingeniously before critics would question their realist bona fides. In her introduction to the Modern Library edition of *The House Behind the Cedars*, Judith Jackson Fossett asks: "Is it a tragic romance? Local-color fiction? Naturalist or Realist narrative?—the novel does not conform to just one genre" (xvii–xviii). The Purity Principle of realism mandates just such generic choosing, as if a single narrative cannot remain realist if it partakes of certain admixtures (and it's interesting in this regard that the first two alternatives, a romance or local color fiction, are genres associated with women writers).

The novel tells the story of Rena Walden, who attempts, along with her brother, to pass as white. Her attempt is temporarily successful. She becomes engaged to a white man, George Tryon, who eventually finds out her secret and rejects her, soon after which Rena falls ill and dies. The novel uses a technique that Susan Suleiman has deftly argued to be a characteristic feature of didactic novels, of which antebellum sentimental novels are exemplars: "a very high *degree* of redundancy" and the favoring of "certain *types* of redundancy" (171). Suleiman notes that one of the forms this redundancy takes in didactic novels is interpretive commentary on the characters. It's not enough that characters act and talk in certain ways according to which the reader can evaluate them. Didactic novels characteristically add commentary from the narrator or the other characters, and sometimes from paratextual sources too.

Redundancy sounds like a bad thing to those of us weaned on Strunk & White, but it can be a neutral description. As Suleiman points out, linguists use it nonjudgmentally when, for instance, they point out the redundancy of plural subjects necessitating plural verb forms. When it comes to didactic fiction, redundancy guards against the possibility of misinterpretation, something the didactic author, as opposed to, say, the surrealist one, is interested in preventing. Here's an example of redundancy from *Uncle Tom's Cabin*, in which you can see Stowe's strenuous efforts to avoid misinterpretation on the part of her readers. In chapter 20, the novel reveals that the enslaved girl Topsy has stolen a ribbon from her owner, Miss Ophelia: "The ribbon was pulled out of Topsy's own sleeve, yet was she not in the least disconcerted; she only looked at it with an air of the most surprised and unconscious innocence" (223). From this description, we can glean that Topsy is both a thief and a liar. In the first instance of redundancy, Miss Ophelia says to her, "Topsy, you naughty girl, don't you tell me a lie,—you stole that ribbon!" (223). But the novel doesn't stop there; a little later on Topsy herself admits: "I's mighty wicked, any how. I can't help it" (224). A little later than that, the narrator steps in and compares Eva to Topsy: Eva with "her spiritual, noble brow" and Topsy, "her black, keen, subtle, cringing, yet acute neighbor" (224), a description that references both Topsy's underhandedness ("subtle," "cringing" and possibly, for Stowe's white readers, "black") and the characteristics that equip her to succeed in her deceptions ("keen," "acute"). So there are at least three layers of redundancy offered in this representative passage, and if you happen to be reading the 1853 edition of *Uncle Tom's Cabin* published by Stannard and Dixon, a fourth: an illustration by Louisa Corbaux that features Topsy in borrowed (or stolen) finery, with a ribbon at her feet. It is captioned, redundantly, "Topsy At Her Tricks."

Redundancy is also a crucial feature of *The House Behind the Cedars*. Keeping with realist norms, the novel's narrator keeps his opinions much more to himself than the narrator in *Uncle Tom's Cabin* does. But there are some exceptions. Here is how *The House Behind the Cedar*'s narrator justifies a character's decision not to tell Rena's Black mother that he knows Rena is passing as white:

> If there be a dainty reader of this tale who scorns a lie, and who writes the story of his life upon his sleeve for all the world to read, let him uncurl his scornful lip and come down from the pedestal of superior morality, to which assured position and wide opportunity have lifted him, and put himself in the place of Rena and her brother, upon whom God had lavished his best gifts, and from whom society would have withheld all that made these gifts valuable. (86)

In this passage, the narrator alludes to the intrigue that propels the novel's plot: the racial passing attempted by Rena and her brother. Although not a direct address of the kind the narrator in *Uncle Tom's Cabin* is defamed for making, the narrator's interjection into the flow of the unfolding plot is addressed to a reader who is, with his "assured position and wide opportunity," coded as white. As happens in *Uncle Tom's Cabin*, Chesnutt invites this reader to put himself in the place of people he might assume to be vastly different from himself. But just as Stowe will do, the narrator highlights the similarities between the reader and the oppressed. Presumably the white reader also feels himself to have enjoyed God's "best gifts." This exculpatory narrative commentary makes redundant in part[11] the many incidents in the novel that also function to excuse Rena for the crime of passing: to name just two, the prejudice she faces in her hometown, where her identity as a Black woman is known, and her unjust rejection by her fiancé. These incidents, which excuse her decision to racially pass, also highlight Rena's white appearance. In this way, they make redundant in part the repeated descriptions of Rena that foreground her whiteness and suggest the inevitability and blamelessness of her choice to pass. For example, a white woman, Miss Leary, whom we'll soon meet again, asks a Black schoolchild, "Is your teacher white?" "No, Ma'm," he replies and goes on to say, redundantly: "She ain't w'ite; she's black. She looks lack she's w'ite, but she's black" (161). Thus we can see how the passage I began with, where the narrator tries to justify a character's decision, sets in motion a chain of redundancy.

In using a narrator who tells white readers just what to think and then tells them again and again, Chesnutt mirrors Stowe. Yet there is still a crucial difference between the narration in these two novels: what we might call the realist difference. This realist difference is, ironically, what requires Chesnutt to supply an interpretive narrator in the first place.[12] Stowe's narration does not focalize through any of the characters; Chesnutt's does.[13] Here is how Chesnutt describes a Black character, Frank, who is in love with Rena: "Frank, with an equal unconsciousness, clothed [Rena] with the attributes of the superior race. Only her drop of black blood, he conceived, gave him the right to feel toward her as he would never have felt without it; and if Rena guessed her faithful devotee's secret, the same reason saved his worship from presumption" (87). At first this can seem like an example of non-focalized third-person narration, but there are subtle clues it is not. In this passage, where does "superior race" come from? It's complicated, because the narrator highlights Frank's unconsciousness of how he perceives Rena. But this does not mean Frank is not thinking in terms of a "superior race" to which his own race is juxtaposed, only that he's unaware that he is doing so. I would contend that "superior race" grows out of Frank's perspective; certainly it's not something that the narrator would believe himself, according to the value system we extrapolate on the basis of the zero-focalized commentary (that is, not told from any particular character's perspective) in the dainty reader passage. Another clue that "superior race" is focalized through Frank comes in the next sentence with "he conceived," suggesting a continuation of the focalization. This is not objective narration but focalized narration even as many readers are invited to mistake it as the former. What's more, it's unreliable focalized narration: Frank thinks white people are superior, but they're not, a mistake on the part of Frank that the masterful reader is meant to clock.

Here's another example of focalization, this time involving a white character, Miss Leary, who makes a bid for Tryon's hand in marriage after he has rejected Rena. In examining this example of focalization, we can start to see why Chesnutt needs to offset it with redundancy in the form of an interpretive narrator. Tryon is about to propose to Miss Leary when a group of Black schoolchildren distract him: "How deeply the shadow of the Ethiopian had fallen upon her own happiness, Miss Leary of course could not guess" (161). We confront the same problem as with the passage about Frank: its subtlety. Is this focalized? As with Frank's passage, it's a single word or phrase that gives it away: "Ethiopian." It's a word the narrator would never use, in its connotation of a single source of African "blood."[14] Instead, it reveals Miss Leary's racist worldview, which includes the belief that Black people are homogenous. What's more, for Miss Leary, they're not Americans; they are "African." This last is a particularly absurd conclusion because the narrator has moments before described one of the boys in this group of schoolchildren as "a tall *yellow* boy" (160; emphasis added), suggesting with that one adjective a history of racial mixture, which gives the lie to the correctness of any African American being categorized in the postbellum period as "Ethiopian." The narrator's role in *The House Behind the Cedars* is to make clear what the novel's characters—especially the white characters—cannot acknowledge themselves. Miss Leary and other white characters in the novel see nothing incorrect in believing theirs to be the superior race, and their thoughts on this matter are such an unquestioned part of their racist worldview that they have no critical distance from them.[15] In articulating these unconscious thoughts via focalization, the narrator (and Chesnutt) opens these thoughts up to critique. Through this technique, Chesnutt suggests that it's possible for white readers *not* to see white people as superior if they can recognize this as unreliable focalization rather than objective narration.

Unreliable focalization becomes an important pedagogical technique of Chesnutt's. Once attuned to it, one can see that it's not just individual characters who unreliably focalize in *The House Behind the Cedars* but the entire white community. We can see it in a scene featuring a medieval tournament that takes place in Clarence, South Carolina, where Rena has settled with her brother, who had previously established himself there as a white attorney. The scene reveals the way that people in southern white society want to see themselves. Melissa Asher Rauterkus offers a wonderful close reading of this scene, revealing how the performances of the white knights (and we might think of another kind of white knight that was becoming popular in this period) "are symbolic demonstrations of Anglo-Saxon perfection that allow the people of Clarence to return to the feudal past" (133). Similarly, Aaron Ritzenberg talks about the tournament as "a communal wish-fulfillment for a culture of nobility and honor" (57).

I'd like to add a technical dimension to these points to help us understand why this scene leads critics to think in terms of white fantasies and white wish fulfillment. In this scene, instead of "we-narration," an unusual form of narration in the first-person plural that we find in novels like Jeffrey Eugenides's *The Virgin Suicides*, we have what we might call "we-focalization." For example, in this scene of the tournament, we are told that the "best people gradually filled the grand stand, while the poorer white and colored folks found seats outside" (30). The "best" is not an objective fact about these white people; it is how they see themselves. The self-congratulatory narration continues in the descriptions of the "skillful horsemanship" of the white men playing at being knights (33). The chapter demonstrates with great specificity how postbellum southern whites relied on an idea of their connection to Arthurian England, the idealized portrait of which they take from Walter Scott. (As the narrator informs us, "The local bookseller had closed out his entire stock of 'Ivanhoe'" before the tournament [30].) One indication that the novel invites masterful readers to be skeptical of this way of seeing the scene is that, as with Miss Leary's perception of American Blacks as Ethiopians, the novel will later give the lie to this focalization. It does so through subsequent details that contradict the white people's way of seeing themselves in this chapter, one of which Rauterkus mentions: Tryon's treatment of Rena once he discovers she is Black "peel[s] away [his] chivalrous veneer" (J. Lee Greene qtd. in Rauterkus 137).

Yet because the focalization in this novel is so subtle, it is easily mistaken for an omniscient narrator's zero-focalized, objective view. Because the novel has given us no reason to believe that the narration is anything other than reliable, there's a good chance that white readers will take these instances of unreliable focalization to be an accurate way to see the world. Frank's opinion of white people as a superior race becomes for gullible white readers an objective fact rather than a poignant, self-undermining belief. These are instances of rhetorical passing, but they reveal the problems with such a strategy: that gullible white readers will fail to transform into masterful readers who can recognize different characters' unreliability.

Because it's so easy to miss, the unreliable focalization in this novel raises a problem that Chesnutt hopes an interpretive narrator and other forms of redundancy can fix. By having the narrator tell white readers about the necessity and tragedy of racial passing, he hopes to subject his readers' perceptions of the world to "dramatic alteration" (4), to use Ryan Simmons's term. Yet although Chesnutt's redundancy reinforces his message, it's still not equivalent to Stowe's kind of redundancy in the sense that in one crucial way it's not actually all that redundant. Stowe's narrator articulates what other characters and the intended reader already know about racial difference. Topsy, we are told over and over, is a thief and a liar, and this information slots with ease into the mental schemata of Stowe's intended, white readers, who were already predisposed to doubt the truthfulness of Black people. The more progressive view of Topsy that Stowe advances—that Topsy's deceit is a direct result of her cruel upbringing—is enabled by Stowe's softening up her readers by first playing to their mental schemata. Before schooling them, Stowe meets her white-superiority-believing white readers where they are. But Chesnutt's redundancy doesn't do that. Although in the passage that excuses Rena's and John's attempts at racial passing there's a tiny nod to the white reader's many accomplishments, Chesnutt undertakes his lesson of cross-racial understanding without hooking that lesson onto any cherished racist beliefs the white reader holds. In other words, the narrative experiment Chesnutt launches with *The House Behind the Cedars* has to overcome obstacles that Stowe, with her plan to school her white readers in sympathizing with enslaved men, women, and children, did not.

As I mentioned, Suleiman shows how "redundancy" is regarded neutrally by linguists. But if we think instead about how it's used in common parlance, it allows us to distinguish between Stowe's and Chesnutt's use of it. In common parlance, redundancy connotes not just repetition but needless repetition; we don't perceive something as redundant unless it's something we already know and don't find any especial pleasure in hearing again. Stowe's portrait of Topsy's stealing is oft repeated, but the repetition did not seem unpleasant to her contemporaneous white readers (this is different from the reaction of many contemporary readers), as evidenced in the fact that Topsy was almost always included in the theatrical productions of *Uncle Tom's Cabin* that became so popular and that otherwise eliminated great swaths of the novel.

Chesnutt's use of redundancy does not fit this pattern: it doesn't flatter his white readers' racist worldview. The narrator's interpretive commentary and the elements in the narrative that later repeat it are thus less examples of redundancy, in its negative sense, than what I would call good pedagogy. (Chesnutt was a teacher and then the principal of a teaching college before becoming an author.) When I became a teacher, a mentor told me to say at least three times anything that I wanted students to remember. Chesnutt is guiding white readers to understand what they don't already know. He's giving them critical distance on themselves, and that takes time, a topic I'll return to in my discussion of *The Marrow of Tradition*.

It's hard to teach people a new thing if they're not able to hook it onto an old thing.[16] This was not a problem Stowe struggled with. Stowe manages to hook her new things onto old things: if not old prejudices then the self-perceptions of white antebellum readers that were both familiar and cherished, for example, that middle-class white women are self-sacrificing and gentle. The Quaker Rachel Halliday's commitment to helping escaped fugitive slaves goes down easy because she's exactly the sort of matriarch that Stowe's white women readers aspired to be. Chesnutt, unlike Stowe, does not share the prejudiced views of his white readers, although his unreliable focalization does cater to the prejudices and aspirations that he knew his white readers held dear. This is why white readers are always in danger of not realizing Chesnutt's moments of unreliability. They fail to understand that they should not, like Miss Leary, believe that the descriptor "Ethiopian" applied to a mixed-race schoolboy in Clarence, South Carolina, is accurate or that a restaging of a medieval tournament reveals anything but a southern white community's commitment to chivalry and honor. How do you dislodge your white readers from their obliviousness to their racism?

Chesnutt's rhetorical experiment in *The House Behind the Cedars* tests whether he can transform white readers by relying on unreliable focalization supplemented by an interpretive narrator who will tell white people how their perceptions of what's really going on are false. (You can see why people would want to label such a narrator "intrusive" rather than the more neutral "interpretive.") In this novel, Chesnutt needs to supplement realism's unreliable focalization, done with his habitually subtle touch, with one of sentimentality's favorite conventions, redundancy. But here is where duration becomes a problem: there's not much time in *The House Behind the Cedars* between the intervals of unreliable focalization and the commentary of the interpretive narrator that sets readers straight. That is, white readers do not have much time to identify with the unreliable white focalizers before they are told to desist, alerted that these white characters have gotten it wrong. Furthermore, the narrator's interpretive commentary makes recognition a cognitive matter for the reader. Readers are told that these white characters are wrong; they're not brought to feel it. Stowe brought in sympathy to help the medicine go down, a lesson Chesnutt will take on board himself with his next novel.

Another problem with Chesnutt's use of an intrusive—here it seems right to go back to the more common term "intrusive"—narrator in *The House Behind the Cedars* is its violation of realist norms and the consequences of that for an author who sought prestige from the literary establishment. In *Writing Realism*, Daniel H. Borus discusses how Howells's ideas about realist writing required authors to emphasize the "simple, natural, and honest," to quote the title of Borus's second chapter. Achieving this required authors to jettison narrative techniques that shattered the illusion of the novel as a true, closely observed history, one that transparently records the unfolding of events. As Henry James wrote, "It is impossible to imagine what a novelist takes himself to be unless he regards himself as an historian and his narrative as history" (qtd. in Borus 92). Intrusive narrators are often called upon, as Suleiman points out, to underline the moral of the novel. Howells and James disliked narrative techniques that threatened the mimetic illusion, and they hated sentimental didacticism even more. In *The House Behind the Cedars*, the presence of an intrusive narrator does not just prevent the reader from forging a bond with the white characters; it threatens Chesnutt's identity as a realist author.[17]

Both the conjure tales and *The House Behind the Cedars* experiment with balancing popularity and what was seen as artistry-robbing partisanship. Chesnutt moves, in the conjure tales, from an unreliable narrator without any but the most subtle clues readers are meant to distrust him to, in *The House Behind the Cedars*, a similarly subtle unreliable focalization coupled with an interpretive narrator. Chesnutt makes this move, I hazard, to prevent white readers from going off the interpretive rails. But neither experiment quite works. Either the unreliability fails because it is not recognized as unreliable, or readers aren't given time to settle in with their identification with characters whose worldviews they are immediately brought to question. Chesnutt will develop a new strategy with *The Marrow of Tradition*, which relies much less on an intrusive narrator than *The House Behind the Cedars*. Instead, it is built almost completely out of the unreliable focalization with which he lards the *The House Behind the Cedars*. Yet he also includes some additional methods to allow white readers to recognize their own racist schemata. Chesnutt works out a way to extend the duration of his readers' sympathetic identification with white characters but still force them to ultimately recognize these characters' unreliability. In other words, *The Marrow of Tradition* doubles down on both its realist and its sentimental techniques,[18] and in contrast to any of the other realist authors I've examined, Chesnutt, rather than oscillate between them, sometimes manages to wield both at once.

ANOTHER LINEAGE FOR CHESNUTT

Tess Chakkalalal has observed that critics have tended to place Chesnutt in an African American literary tradition, and early twentieth-century critics, as Stephen Knadler notes, did so to Chesnutt's detriment, highlighting what they saw as Chesnutt's accommodationist tendencies. Chakkalalal and

Knadler point out that, unlike Harlem Renaissance authors, who advocated Black solidarity, Chesnutt was appalled by the category of "Negro" being applied indiscriminately to a heterogenous Black population.[19] This earlier understanding of Chesnutt has long been put to rest, although contemporary critics still highlight his place in a tradition of African American writing. They have done this with regard to *The Marrow of Tradition* especially.[20] For example, Barbara McCaskill connects it to protest novels like *Iola Leroy* and *Contending Forces* in their shared desire to bring attention to "an abiding sense of white supremacy" in the post-Reconstruction period (489).

What other traditions might Chesnutt belong to? When critics like Knadler, Matthew Martin, and Matthew Wilson bring in white-authored works with which to compare *The Marrow of Tradition*, they choose works by white supremacists like Thomas Nelson Page and Thomas Dixon to register its clean contrast with them.[21] Putting Chesnutt in an African American literary tradition affords us an answer to the question I began the chapter with: the link between the conjure tales and *The Marrow of Tradition*. It nudges critics to focus on Chesnutt's subversive dismantling of the logic of white supremacy. Yet it doesn't explain what still seems to me to be the vastly different *feel* of these works, the slyness and indirection of the tales versus the brutal exposé of racial violence in *The Marrow of Tradition*. We cannot account for this difference if we simply look at the thematic continuities between them. We can account for it, however, by placing *The Marrow of Tradition* in another literary lineage, one that reveals the connection between Chesnutt's different works via his evolving adaptation of sentimental forms of persuasion.

If you were an author in the postbellum era and you wanted your oblivious white readers to aid in the work of ending racial injustice, what narrative resources were available? In 1911 the Black activist and educator Mary Church Terrell wrote an appreciation of *Uncle Tom's Cabin* that conveys the vividness and power the novel still retained for a portion of readers, even sixty years after it was published.[22] She wrote: "But, stand with Mrs. Stowe at the auction block, witness the agony of the mother torn from her child. . . . Hear the cries that are wrung from the broken hearts crushed by the master hand without one pang of remorse, if you would feel this woman's power and learn what slavery was." As I argued in chapter 2, even Twain and Howells, who defined the excellence of their own writing against what they saw as the sentimental dreck that came before them, relied on sentimental scenes at moments when they sought to enlist their readers' sympathy and deepen the ethical stakes of their work. An author who didn't want to choose between his principles and his success, Chesnutt found Stowe's narrative techniques promising. *Uncle Tom's Cabin* had, after all, achieved both commercial success and global influence. "Consider," Terrell asks, "how far-reaching were the impressions made by Uncle Tom's Cabin, of which 300,000 copies were sold in the first year in this country alone, more than a million and a half in England and the colonies." Chesnutt wrote to publishers that he wanted *The Marrow of Tradition* "to become lodged in the popular mind as the legitimate successor of *Uncle Tom's Cabin* . . . as depicting an era in our national history" (qtd. in Wilson, *Whiteness* 100). Chesnutt's eventual publisher, Houghton Mifflin, echoed his wish, advertising *The Marrow of Tradition* as "a novel that will recall at many points its great precursor 'Uncle Tom's Cabin'" (qtd. in Bufkin 234).[23]

In light of Chesnutt's explicit embrace of this lineage, the question arises about why it has been difficult for critics to acknowledge it. I would suggest that Howells's and Twain's impulse to distinguish their own works against sentimental ones has carried into modern criticism of Chesnutt. In fact, the critics who want to claim Chesnutt's importance and artistry link him to the realist tradition; those who want to disparage them link him to a didactic or sentimental one (although they only rarely use the term "sentimental"). For example, in *Chesnutt and Realism*, Simmons tries to counter Joseph McElrath's objection that Chesnutt's writing can be manipulative by pointing out, "If Chesnutt's writing can seem manipulative (and it can), it is more a function of his insistence that readers *do* something—react emotionally and, it is hoped, politically to the circumstances he portrays—than it is evidence that he abandoned realism in favor of political writing" (15). This seems to me a specious distinction. Simmons has described exactly what Stowe, a political writer par excellence, was trying to do with *Uncle Tom's Cabin*: make her readers respond emotionally to the characters and thus be compelled to act. Yet the taint of political/didactic (or sentimental) writing still causes enough concern that Simmons has to claim that a work does not belong to a "political" tradition even as he seems to demonstrate that the book belongs to it exactly. Here we have a problem that besets literary criticism of sentimental writing, a problem that I discussed in chapter 3: as soon as critics see a work (or character or scene) as sentimental, they disparage it; only if they don't identify a work as such can they recognize that work's power. A corollary to the rule is this: as soon as critics spot any sign of sentimentality in a realist work, they see it as wholly sentimental or didactic. In the previous chapter I associated this tendency with the logic of abjection, but in this chapter I have named it the "Purity Principle" of realism. To claim Chesnutt as a realist, Simmons must disavow Chesnutt's relationship to antebellum sentimental authors, who were engaged in "political writing." For both Simmons and McElrath, as for so many other critics, realism is a pure genre, not a mixed one.[24]

MARROW'S MIXTURE

Another continuity that unites Chesnutt's works is his challenge to readers to see not only allegedly distinct racial categories as mixed but realism that way as well. What does his version of a legitimate successor to *Uncle Tom's Cabin* look like? His legitimate successor means not just a departure from plantation fiction responses to *Uncle Tom's Cabin* like *Aunt Phillis's Cabin* (1852), Mary Henderson Eastman's southern apologist rebuttal. It looks like a novel that functions in the literary sphere the way a multiracial person functioned in the social one: as a challenge to binaries that uphold dominant hierarchies of value.[25] I will not claim, as McElrath does, that what many critics have taken to be realist works are in fact sentimental ones. I want to undermine the Purity Principle of realism.[26] I want to highlight the mix of realist and sentimental narrative elements contained in Chesnutt's novels and the narrative affordances such a mix provides.[27]

Like *Uncle Tom's Cabin*, *The Marrow of Tradition* aims to present a complete picture of a population, what John Wideman has called the novel's "panoramic view of Southern society" (128)—Black and white characters from all walks of life. Yet the perspectives from which these two novels are written at first seem very different. *Uncle Tom's Cabin* is written from a white perspective. As Hortense Spillers has argued, Stowe lays bare the "central nervous system of the African" (177). Spillers's tone suggests how egregious she finds Stowe's confidence. *The Marrow of Tradition* appears at first very different: it seems to center a Black perspective, both in terms of the events that *The Marrow of Tradition* depicts and in its upending of white supremacist norms. Knadler writes that "Chesnutt attempts to overturn the specificity of whiteness through . . . a surreptitious introduction of the liberal white reader to the point of view of the novel's black speakers" (429). He continues, noting that Chesnutt, in "borrowing modern experimental techniques in multiple perspectives and indirect discourse, . . . would release the repressed black gaze" (431). According to Knadler, Black people do the scrutinizing in *The Marrow of Tradition*.

Although Knadler's article is persuasive overall, I want to look more closely at the particular claim that *The Marrow of Tradition* is told from a Black perspective. It seems reflexively correct because the novel's critical view of the Wilmington coup/pogrom was in short supply at the time Chesnutt was writing. Thus, any "counter-history," as Ian Finseth terms the novel (16), which in this case focuses on the brutality of white people against the Black inhabitants of the fictional town of Wellington, would seem to come from a Black perspective. Yet if we look closely at how the narration works in *The Marrow of Tradition*, we realize that what is most often offered in the novel is the white perspective. Although the story spends some time focalized through Dr. Miller, a Black Wellington physician, and smaller amounts of time focalized through other Black characters like the militant Josh Green and the Uncle Tom–ish Jerry, the narration is overwhelmingly focalized through the white characters. In a literal sense, then, *The Marrow of Tradition* is told not from a Black perspective but from a white one, the better, as we shall see, to foment sympathetic identification between Chesnutt's white readers and his white characters.

Like Stowe, then, Chesnutt tells a story of Black oppression from a white perspective, but he does so with a big difference. Stowe focuses on, though does not focalize through, her white characters to model their own experiences of sympathetic identification, which require white characters to recognize similarities between themselves and the enslaved. Readers see white characters witnessing Black people's pain and the dissolution of Black people's nuclear families. Her white readers experience what she takes to be elemental aspects of shared humanity. The reader's sympathetic identification with white characters enables them to ultimately sympathize with the Black ones. In *The Marrow of Tradition*, white readers are also meant to sympathize with white characters—although the novel will eventually reveal that even the best of them are far from admirable. Yet here's Chesnutt's trick: he delays the revelation of his white characters' considerable ethical lapses, which derive from their racial misapprehensions, until white readers have had time to lock into sympathetic identification with them. The aim of this durable sympathetic identification is to enable white readers not so much to sympathetically identify with Black characters—what Stowe is aiming for—as to enable them to recognize in themselves the same ethical lapses that beset the white characters.

To invite his white readers to sympathetically identify with his white characters, Chesnutt learned from *The House Behind the Cedars* that he had to meet his readers where they lived. Rabinowitz has observed in *Before Reading* that readers bring to books expectations around genre, expectations that provide a set of rules for both authors and readers. For writers, these generic expectations take the form of "patterns or models that [they] follow in constructing texts"; for readers, they are "packages of rules that readers apply in construing them" (177). What would Chesnutt's post-Reconstruction realist white readers expect from a Black author who had just published the pointed, tragic *House Behind the Cedars*? They would likely expect a work that had a cause to plead. The "protest novel" tradition, strongly associated with both African American writers and sentimental ones, primes the reader to adopt certain reading protocols. They include the following: the assumption that the narrative commentary is zero-focalized; the assumption that the narrator is reliable; and the attribution of the beliefs of the narrator to the beliefs of the author. Let me reconstruct how a reader who believes *The Marrow of Tradition* to be an entry in the protest tradition would likely read its initial scene.

The first few lines lead readers to believe that this scene is a direct descendant of *Uncle Tom's Cabin*. The novel opens on a scene of distress: Olivia Carteret, the wife of the town's newspaper editor, Major Carteret, is unsuccessfully laboring with their long-awaited child. She is attended by Wellington's white doctor, Dr. Price. The descriptions in this initial scene seem highly symbolic. "The heavy scent of magnolias, overpowering even the strong smell of drugs in the sickroom, suggested death and funeral wreaths, sorrow and tears, the long home, the last sleep" (44). Readers are led to expect suffering, although what form that suffering will take they might mistakenly think will involve the death of Olivia and her newborn (who both end up surviving). Interspersed with these portents are other descriptions of the scene and its inhabitants that evoke strong feelings in the contemporaneous white reader: the "fine old house," Major Carteret's family as one of the "oldest and proudest in the state" (44), and his older brother as someone who "had sacrificed his life on the bloody altar of the lost cause" (44). These sentiments activate in white readers what would be, in the post-Reconstruction period, a familiar set of nostalgic feelings about the South, ones that Matthew Martin notes northern white readers shared with southern ones. In this initial scene, readers also meet a character called "Mammy Jane," with her "unctuous whisper" (45) and heavy dialect, who compliments the baby after he has finally been born: "Bless its 'ittle hea't! It's de ve'y spit an' image er its pappy!" (49), words that are undercut by some gentle humor from the narrator: "The tiny mite . . . bore as much resemblance to mature humanity as might be expected of an infant which had for only a few minutes drawn the breath of life" (49).

With the exception of its evocation of Lost Cause sentiments, this scene seems like it could come straight out of *Uncle Tom's Cabin* in its description of physical spaces that seem, as Jane Tompkins has noted about the spaces in *Uncle Tom's Cabin*, both actual and spiritual as well as in the hierarchy established between proper whites and the slightly ridiculous enslaved. "Mammy" Jane especially fits a familiar pattern.[28] Stowe garbs her mammy figure, Chloe, in a "well-starched checked turban" (18); Mammy Jane is bedecked with a "red bandana handkerchief coiled around her head by way of turban" (45). They also resemble each other in the intimacy between them and the white families they work for and in their love of their white charges. While Mammy Jane can't stop complimenting the baby, Aunt Chloe can't stop teasing and feeding (before she feeds her own children) her master's son George: "Aunt Chloe sat back in her chair, and indulged in a hearty guffaw of laughter, at this witticism [which wasn't that funny] of young Mas'r's, laughing till the tears rolled down her black, shining cheeks, and varying the exercise with playfully slapping and poking Mas'r Georgey" (21). As Katrina Dyonne Thompson notes about the figure of the mammy, "For almost two centuries, she continues to love white families even more than her own family" (59). The description of Chloe and Jane reassures contemporaneous white readers that, despite these Black women's place in the bosom of a white family, they constitute absolutely no threat at all. I'd like to assume that some version of the understanding of the first scene I have articulated is the one that most of Chesnutt's white readers would experience: objective description, a reliable narrator, and, for white readers, a familiar, comforting view of the racial order.

The Marrow of Tradition engages in another trick to encourage white readers to feel comfortable and identify with its white characters. It's not just the narrator who seems trustworthy; readers will also feel kindly toward Major Carteret and Dr. Price. As the novel progresses, however, Carteret and Price, as well as other important white characters in the novel, will, one by one, fall from grace. Chesnutt precipitates their fall by making it clear, at different, carefully calibrated points, that they are unreliable focalizers. Readers gradually become aware that there is a distance between their view of the world and that of the implied author, and they recognize that the implied author's view is more trustworthy. In analyzing this staggered series of falls and the different ways readers come to their new assessments of these characters, I will show how Chesnutt relies not just on sentimental narrative conventions but on realist ones—and invites readers to mistake one for the other. Chesnutt might have begun the novel banking on his readers' tendency to read his novel the way they would *Uncle Tom's Cabin*, but he comes to rely on their ability to read realistically, in particular their ability to recognize unreliable focalization and expect morally complex characters.

There is one set of white characters whom the novel reveals to be unreliable focalizers early on: the most evil ones. Here is how the most vulgar character in the novel, Captain McBane, thinks of what will result from the race riot he is involved in fomenting: "He would help these fellows carry the state for white supremacy, and then he would have his innings,—he would have more to say than they dreamed, as to who should fill the offices under the new deal" (95). Contemporaneous white readers might sympathize with McBane's desire to muffle the political voice Black men gained from Reconstruction, but they will have a hard time sympathizing with his vision of who will take the reins once "white supremacy" once again reigns supreme: slang-slinging class bounders like him, who put a bad face on the noble cause of white supremacy. This is focalized discourse that will be easily recognized by white readers who want to distance themselves from McBane and his preference for what shape the glorious new day will take. They are invited to conclude that this is a man whose view of the world is ethically suspect, although what they find ethically suspect about it (that vulgar men like McBane will hold political power) goes only so far. It doesn't necessarily extend to the idea of white supremacy in general.

Tom Delamere is the one other unalloyedly evil character in the novel, a "degenerate aristocrat" (104), as another character who is "an excellent judge of character" (104) pegs him, rather than an arriviste. He also sometimes acts as a focalizer, as readers can see in an interaction between him and McBane: "[Delamere's] aristocratic gorge rose at the presumption of this son of an overseer and ex-driver of convicts. McBane was good enough to win money from, or even to lose money to, but not good enough to be recognized as a social equal" (141). It's possible that in this passage the implied author is up to a trick we saw in *The House Behind the Cedars*: revealing aspects of a character's thinking that the character is himself unaware of. In this case, Delamere might be unaware of the cause of his visceral reaction to McBane. Regardless, readers likely grasp that they are seeing the world through Tom's snobbish eyes, and that Tom's view of the world is one they would do well to disavow, although again, the readers' flexing of their ethical muscles might not extend to recognizing that Delamere's reaction to McBane is one that they themselves likely share, a self-protective oversight cleverly invited by Chesnutt.

With regard to these utterly unsympathetic characters, their immediately exposed villainy makes it clear we should distrust their views of the world as revealed in their focalized narration. But in case we don't, Chesnutt employs another technique that Suleiman describes in her discussion of authoritarian fiction: what she calls "amalgamation," the alignment of the author's view of a character's ideological commitments with other traits the author depicts the character as having. For example, in an anticommunist novel, the character who loves Lenin will be ugly, treat his wife badly, and have terrible breath. Amalgamation is one of Stowe's favored narrative techniques, and Chesnutt takes it up too. McBane is introduced to us with this description: "His broad shoulders, burly form, square jaw, and heavy chin betokened strength, energy, and unscrupulousness" (63). He also has dandruff. Tom, although more pleasing physically, is also revealed, from very early on, as a gambler and a drinker. That the purely evil characters unreliably focalize in *The Marrow of Tradition* is easy for even gullible white readers to spot because, from the start, Chesnutt set up these readers to want to put distance between these characters' ways of thinking and their own. These characters thwart sympathetic identification: as in *The House Behind the Cedars*, there's just no time to identify with them before readers realize they are villains.

Chesnutt will figure out a way to delay the unmasking of other white characters, and he'll do so by relying on a convention not of sentimental writing but of realist writing: its rejection of amalgamated characters in favor of ones who contain a mix of good and bad traits. The villains of the novel fall in the readers' estimation early, but the two other members of what the novel calls the "Big Three," the men who orchestrate the race riot, take a little longer to fall. To understand their fall, one has to understand where in readers' estimation they started. We have seen, in the initial scene, where Major Carteret begins: as coming from a fine old family and upholding a noble southern way of life. We see a more mixed yet still mostly sympathetic initial portrait of the third member of the "Big Three," General Belmont: "General Belmont was not without a gentleman's distaste for meanness, but he permitted no fine scruples to stand in the way of success. He had once been minister, under a Democratic administration, to a small Central American state. Political rivals had characterized him as a tricky demagogue, which may of course have been a libel. He had an amiable disposition, possessed the gift of eloquence, and was a prime social favorite" (64). This is neither an unambivalent endorsement of Belmont (the passage's coy "may of course have been a libel" rather than "was a libel") nor an unambivalent condemnation (his amiability stands in the way of condemnation, as does, more complexly, his social standing). Unlike the pure villains, these two men are not revealed to be unreliable focalizers until the final section of the novel, which documents the events that lead immediately up to the coup/pogrom and the coup/pogrom itself.

I think even an astute early reader of *The Marrow of Tradition*, Wideman, is led astray by this final section, which the whole novel has been building toward. In his wonderful 1972 article, which made the case for Chesnutt's recovery, Wideman describes how he sees the novel changing starting with chapter 27 to something much more dramatic and fast-moving. He contrasts the tempo of this final section to the "leisurely pace of the early chapters . . . set by the voice of a narrator who does not hesitate to intrude himself into the action to make authorial judgements and asides" (132). Yet it's not in fact correct to consider the narrator's voice as dropping out in the final section. Starting with the last few pages of chapter 27, the action is wholly taken over by the voice of the narrator. Presumably the reason why this doesn't register to Wideman is that the narrator appears in realist camouflage. Rather than apostrophizing, the narrator recounts events and deploys facts; he uses, in other words, vaunted "objective" realist techniques of narration. The narrator also refers to events that readers know have occurred in the real world—the well-known realist habit of writing about topical issues. Here is a representative statement by the narrator from this section: "At the North, a new Pharaoh had risen, who knew not Israel,—a new generation, who knew little of the fierce passions which had played around the negro in a past epoch, and derived their opinions of him from the 'coon song' and the police reports" (190). Chesnutt's narrator has pulled back from his focus on Wellington to offer a wider assessment of the post-Reconstruction nation: we see that the actions of the southern whites will receive no check from northern qualms. Despite this not being written in the "feminine" voice of a chidingly intrusive narrator—the voice here is learned and calm (and male) in its impersonal authority—this line reveals the anti–white supremacist, "partisan" views of the narrator (and author).

Amidst this seeming avalanche of facts, both Belmont's and Carteret's nefariousness is exposed.[29] First, the narrator reveals, factually and impersonally, that General Belmont has been entrusted with helping the grandfather of the degenerate aristocrat Tom Delamere to write his last will and testament. Old Delamere has been the character most sympathetic to the Black inhabitants of Wellington; he dies shortly after the will is written. (His death, the removal of the last bastion of white decency, symbolically enables the riot.) Instead of leaving his money to the villainous Tom, old Delamere leaves it to Dr. Miller's hospital, which has been built to serve the Black citizens of the town. Yet the will, which had been witnessed by and entrusted to General Belmont, does not appear. The explanation for this disappearance begins with the statement "This suppression was justified by the usual race argument: Miller's hospital was already well established. . . . Mr. Delamere's property belonged of right to the white race" (188). We learn in the next couple of sentences that it was General Belmont who "reached this conclusion" and that in fact he has "locked [the will] carefully away in his safe" (188). It's not that readers have not received hints about General Belmont's untrustworthiness—certainly his alcoholism is a problem—but not until this late stage of the novel does the reader have incontrovertible proof. But we should note that his nefarious actions regarding the will are "justified" by his allegiance to white entitlement. The hope in deeming Belmont's actions unethical, of course, is that readers will question the justification that sponsored them.

The narrator also reveals Carteret's less than robust moral character in this final section, which is both realistic and didactic at once. Carteret, more than Belmont, is linked to the real-world historical currents recounted in chapter 28: "The state was at the mercy of venal and self-seeking politicians, bent upon regaining their ascendency at any cost. . . . Carteret, as spokesman of the campaign [for white supremacy] . . . performed prodigies of labor. . . . [T]he major made a tour of the state, rousing the white people of the better class to an appreciation of the terrible danger which confronted them in the possibility that a few negroes might hold a few offices" (191). These facts reveal that Carteret is a scoundrel. It does so in the realist manner: it uses what seems like realist objectivity and realist topicality instead of the denunciations of an intrusive narrator. Yet even as the intrusive narrator goes missing, his outrage and moral guidance remain. The novel's final section offers the same kind of ethical guidance that is provided by an intrusive narrator, even as it looks like realist writing. This is extraordinary narration: the seamless melding of sentimental outrage in the guise of realist objectivity.

The novel functions like a slowly collapsing house of cards, with the cards being white readers' identification with Chesnutt's white characters, who are unmasked, in stages, as not just vulgar or snobbish or untrustworthy but ethically deficient. Furthermore, the novel links these deficiencies to their commitment to white supremacy. No reader will likely sympathetically identify with McBane or Delamere, but some might have identified with Belmont or Carteret, who is from a "fine, old family" after all. And many white readers will presumably identify with Dr. Price, whom we met in the first scene. They will likely also identify with another very sympathetic character, the young journalist Lee Ellis, who works for Carteret. These characters would have invited identification particularly from northern liberal white readers, the type who would have known Chesnutt from his earliest days as an author publishing stories in *Harper's* and the *Atlantic*. Dr. Price and Ellis evince liberal northern attitudes about race, appearing even to endorse racial equality—within limits.

But they don't stay sympathetic either: they fall at the very end of the novel, having provided the greatest amount of time for readers to develop strong sympathetic ties with them. At the beginning of the novel, Ellis seems purely admirable: his "honest gray eyes" (51) are our first indication of his good character, which is affirmed by further descriptions ("there was no element of the sneak in Lee Ellis's make-up" [55]) and by his function in the novel to act as a foil to Tom Delamere. Like Dr. Price, he is coded as politically progressive,[30] a man "whose Quaker father had never owned any slaves" (61). Presumably the apple does not fall far from the racially progressive tree.

In realist novels, even the protagonist will be fallible, for instance, tenderhearted but dim as in the case of Huck Finn or loyal but pigheaded as in the case of Silas Lapham. Fans of realism tout this quality; in their estimation, it makes realism more realistic, and it also differentiates realist characters from what they deem to be the boring, morally black-and-white sentimental or "romanticistic" characters that preceded them. Geordie Hamilton, for example, has pointed out how realism relies on morally complex characters. According to Hamilton, "Howells deliberately—and artfully—guides the reader to listen carefully and sympathetically to the morality of many characters, . . . but Howells also subtly introduces doubts and qualifications that lead the authorial audience to reject unquestioning reliance on any single character or class viewpoint as an unambiguous moral standard" (20). For readers who see *The Marrow of Tradition* as replete with characters who are not easily summed up, whose evaluation needs to be pondered, they are left with a sense of *The Marrow of Tradition* as a deeply realist novel. But what makes *The Marrow of Tradition* most realistic—the moral complexity of many of Chesnutt's white characters—also makes it, ironically, most didactic: a message about how much racism resides even in white characters who see themselves and are seen by others as progressive, honest, and intelligent. But before that message has been made clear, the novel has invited white readers to sympathetically identify with these characters. *Telling* readers how to feel about racist characters did not work in *The House Behind the Cedars*, but inviting sympathetic identification with them might finally get the message across about white readers' own commitment to white supremacy.

When it comes to Ellis, the foundation of a more complex assessment is laid fairly early, but only for masterful readers. Chapter 16 depicts an incident involving Delamere and Ellis, who has been told by a Black bellboy that Delamere is in an upstairs room in the hotel that they're both visiting. Ellis focalizes the ensuing action in the following manner: "[Ellis] could imagine circumstances under which he would not care to speak to Delamere; he would merely pass through the hall and glance into the room casually, as any one else might do, and see what the darky downstairs might have meant by his impudence" (134). Ellis's disregard for Black people, suggested in his casual use of "darky" and his reference to the bellboy's "impudence," are reinforced at other points in the novel. For masterful readers, this passage reveals Ellis's inhumanity. Yet the passage works differently for Chesnutt's contemporaneous, gullible white readers. Readers of the time would not find anything objectionable in this passage: they believe that "darky" is an acceptable term and Black bellboys who suggest they are aware of white foibles are deserving of censure. For these readers, the passage would seem zero-focalized, just the narrator's neutral description of what happened. So even as, for some readers, the game is up, for others, their relationship to Ellis remains unchanged.

It's plausible that readers find Ellis wholly sympathetic even after reading this troubling passage; it's harder, though, to maintain this relationship with him through the final five chapters, which detail the coup/pogrom. Both he and Dr. Price are portrayed in this final section as fatally passive. Mrs. Carteret, in desperate need of finding a doctor who can minister to her sickly son, hears that "[Dr. Price] had gone up the river this morning to attend a patient, and would not be back until to-morrow. Mrs. Price thought that he had anticipated some kind of trouble in the town to-day, and had preferred to be where he could not be called upon to assume any responsibility" (235–36). Dr. Price's efforts to remain above the fray match those of Ellis, whose love interest has inquired if anything can be done "to stop this terrible affair" (235). "'I wish I could do something,' he murmured fervently, taking both her trembling hands in his own broad palms, where they rested with a surrendering trustfulness which he has never since had occasion to doubt. 'It has gone too far, already, and the end, I fear, is not yet; but it cannot grow much worse'" (235). Ellis is wrong that it cannot get worse, and Dr. Price is wrong that it's possible not to take responsibility. In demonstrating this, Chesnutt complicates what was for gullible readers the purely admiring relationship established with these characters. These characters, indeed, are stand-ins for his northern readers, whose liberal bona fides did not motivate them to intervene in white southerners' inhumane treatment of Black people. Chesnutt obeys the diktat that realist authors create morally complex characters, but in making them so, he sends a didactic message worthy of Stowe: that there's no ethical place to stand outside the fray of racial injustice.

So the most sympathetic characters are the last to fall, and the time the novel spends cultivating white readers' sympathetic identification with them is Chesnutt's Hail Mary pass after two failed attempts, in the form of his earlier works, to teach white readers what they need to learn. The problem with both the conjure tales and *The House Behind the Cedars* was that contemporaneous white readers never understood them as the supple rhetorical performances they are: with the conjure tales, gullible readers never understood John to be unreliable, and with *The House Behind the Cedars*, readers never had time to identify with Chesnutt's white characters before the veil was ripped from their eyes. *The Marrow of Tradition* combines these features, offering evidence that Chesnutt understood the problem as I have laid it out. In *The Marrow of Tradition*, he reveals, through a seamless mix of realist and sentimental narrative conventions, the unreliability of these white characters, in perfectly staggered stages keyed to just how sympathetic they first seem to be.

THE MARROW OF TRADITION'S SENTIMENTAL EDUCATION

The final section of *The Marrow of Tradition* manifests what Simmons calls realism's "objectivity of narration," in this case an objective, neutrally narrated series of events modeled closely on a set of actual events. That, at least, is how Wideman reads it. I want, however, to add something to this account. This final section is also didactic. In the previous section, I observed how it reveals the views that the implied author has about both white supremacy and the ethical lapses of what had seemed to be sympathetic white characters, though not through an intrusive narrator. There are other sentimental elements in the final section of the novel: the trope of the nuclear family under threat of dissolution, a critique of realist distance, and a climax in the form of the inclusion of a sentimental scene of distress.

I'll begin by observing that the final events the novel recounts are framed by a doubled sentimental plot: two efforts to keep two families intact during the riot, undertaken by two sets of characters, Black and white, who are themselves twinned. The threat of family dissolution is the sentimental motor that drives *Uncle Tom's Cabin*, part of what produces, as Winfried Flück has argued, the heightened emotional reaction that drove many of Stowe's readers to commit themselves to ending slavery. The families under threat of dissolution in *The Marrow of Tradition* are the Carterets and the Millers. Dr. Miller is the gifted Black doctor of Wellington, whom Carteret had previously turned away from his house after Dr. Miller was invited there by Dr. Price. (Carteret will not have a Black doctor in his house.) Janet Miller, Dr. Miller's wife, is the mixed-race sister of Olivia Carteret, who has, right before the riot began, destroyed her father's will and marriage certificate to his second wife, his Black former housekeeper and the mother of Janet. (There's a lot of will-destroying in *The Marrow of Tradition*.) The novel twins Olivia and Janet, as we can see in the statement, repeated at intervals throughout the novel, that they could be mistaken for each other.

But the novel twins Carteret and Dr. Miller as well. They're twinned in their refinement, their wealth, and in another important way—their preference for critical distance. Dr. Miller prefers to view events from on high: "Miller was something of a philosopher. He had long ago had the conclusion forced upon him that an educated man of his race, in order to live comfortably in the United States, must be either a philosopher or a fool; and since he wished to be happy, and was not exactly a fool, he had cultivated philosophy" (81). Carteret also prefers to view events from on high, as demonstrated in the narrator's description of a morning's work writing an editorial: "He had argued, with entire conviction, that the white and black races could never attain social and political harmony by commingling their blood; he had proved by several historical parallels that no two unassimilable races could ever live together except in the relation of superior and inferior; and he was just dipping his gold pen into the ink to indite his conclusions from the premises thus established, when Jerry, the porter, announced two visitors" (62). We can see from the passage's verbs—"argued," "proved," "indite[d] his conclusions"—that while Dr. Miller dons the mantle of philosophy, Carteret uses its tools. Philosophy, in this construction, is synonymous with critical distance, a preference to see the problem of the color line from on high, avoiding the committed partisanship that comes with viewing life only from one's particular vantage point. Whom do Carteret and Dr. Miller resemble in this regard? No one so much as the realist author. Yet even as we read the description of Carteret's editorial, masterful readers catch Chesnutt's critique of it; for example, the "gold pen" is a clue that Carteret's view of the races is just that much easier to hold if one counts his membership in the "superior" (and richer) one. Yet even Dr. Miller's much more benign embrace of philosophy will come under pressure. The final section of the novel reveals the impossibility of holding oneself above the fray of racial violence.

Chesnutt reveals a problem with the realist author's touted critical distance. This distance is created, in part, by the realist's reliance on morally complex characters, who offer different perspectives from each other, with the resulting sense that truth resides in the play of perspectives rather than the authority of any single one. The problem that Chesnutt identifies is the realist text's inability to make final ethical judgments even as it so clearly poses ethical questions. Because realist texts engage readers in the process of ethical evaluation, critics tend to overlook their antipathy to final judgments: many critics still insist their preferred realist text comes down on the right side of history. For example, Simmons explores the realist narrative techniques that *The Marrow of Tradition* uses. In the process, he focuses on the different perspectives Chesnutt depicts in it. According to Simmons, "The novel's social purpose can largely be explained in terms of Chesnutt's conviction that truthful knowledge, although always tenuous and partial, must ultimately reveal that racism is in almost no one's self-interest; however, because of its tenuous, partial nature, such knowledge can only be achieved discursively, though one's immersion in many different voices" (102–103). Simmons seems to be claiming that this ultimate revelation will be reached by considering different perspectives, yet the final step remains mysterious. How does one go from polyphony to social purpose? How does a chorus of conflicting views become a monovocal rallying cry against racial oppression? Simmons claims both that Chesnutt should be considered a realist author and that "for Chesnutt . . . a realist aesthetic and an implied stance of political advocacy are not mutually exclusive positions" (15). Certainly an author can combine a realist aesthetic with political advocacy, but that advocacy will be registered much more easily if the critic is willing to dispense with the Purity Principle of realism. More often, though, they hew to it and ignore when a realist author writes sentimentally. Simmons, for example, seems to resist the idea that Chesnutt strays from the "realist aesthetic."[31] I don't resist the idea; instead I believe that Chesnutt believed that his advocacy needed more narrative resourcing than the proliferation of different perspectives. In *The Marrow of Tradition*, he needed to draw on the sentimental scene to supplement the realist aesthetic's narrative limitations.

To demonstrate how he integrates these sentimental elements, I return to an analysis of the novel's depiction of Ellis, that son of a Quaker father, to explain why Chesnutt has to venture beyond realist narrative techniques. Some readers miss the focalization of the bellboy passage, in which case Ellis becomes much less morally complex throughout the novel because he remains purely sympathetic. In this gullible reading, Ellis simply exhibits the admirable traits that the narrator and other characters have described him as having. In this case, because his actions and the descriptions of his character line up, he's an amalgamation. Yet masterful readers register the unreliable focalization of the bellboy passage, which makes the novel more realist in its characterization, but it also involves these readers in the typical evaluative process inspired by realist novels: How do we balance Ellis's honesty with his racism? Does it matter that the kind of racism he exhibits is more benign than that exhibited by someone like McBane? The process of weighing these factors involves us in ethical evaluation. But we're distanced from Ellis while making these calculations; we have adopted the same philosophical stance that Dr. Miller and Major Carteret prefer. Either way, the novel points out the problem with critical distance—its incompatibility with political advocacy—even as it inculcates it in its masterful readers. Both masterful and gullible white readers of Ellis face problems, but they are different ones. Masterful readers are distanced from Ellis, whereas gullible readers think he's admirable. In neither case does the white reader both recognize the problem with Ellis and feel complicit in his racism via their previous sympathetic identification with him. Both of these things—sympathy and recognition—need to occur in order for the white reader to recognize their own racist schemata.

The final section of the novel tries to solve this problem. We can see this if we recognize Chesnutt's debt to Stowe and the innovations Chesnutt rings upon her scenes of sympathy. Instead, critics have taken this final section as proof positive that this is a realist novel, with "realist novel" understood according to the Purity Principle. Here is where the intrusive narrator finally absents himself, as Wideman claims, and here is where the novel seems to depict the actual events of the Wilmington riot most closely, as Joyce Pettis has shown. But here is also where the novel wants to teach its white readers some of its most important lessons. For gullible readers who have persisted in thinking Ellis is sympathetic and reliable, the final section reveals him to be compromised. For masterful readers, who never developed an emotional connection to Ellis or any of the other white characters and thus never felt the self-critique embedded in their ultimate unmasking, the final section offers one more chance for them to be moved, culminating as it does in a scene that could have been taken out of *Uncle Tom's Cabin*. If the novel's depiction of the coup/pogrom smuggled outrage into seemingly objective and polyphonic realist narration, the final scene of the final section of the novel makes that outrage much harder to miss.

In this final scene, Chesnutt both takes up Stowe's sentimental technique of evoking sympathy and utterly transforms it. Olivia Carteret, the proud white wife of Major Carteret and mother of that sickly son, is reduced to "poor humanity" (243) at the prospect of losing said son. Let me recount once again that ur-scene of sympathetic identification from *Uncle Tom's Cabin* to detail how these scenes of potential maternal loss work. The enslaved woman Eliza has run away to prevent her young son from being sold away. To protect Harry, Eliza will do anything, including risk a life-endangering crossing of the Ohio River by jumping from one patch of ice to another. Once she crosses the river, she seeks help at the house of a senator and his wife, Mrs. Bird. Upon first seeing this "young and slender woman, with garments torn and frozen, with one shoe gone" (74), Mrs. Bird exclaims, "'Poor creature!'" (74). Mrs. Bird is primed to feel for her as an example of suffering humanity, but the sympathetic identification between them is fully accomplished when Eliza, recovered from her swoon, notes that Mrs. Bird is "dressed in deep mourning" (76) and asks, "Have you ever lost a child?" (76). Indeed, Mrs. Bird has: "It was only a month since a darling child of the family had been laid in the grave" (76). Out of this conversation is born a deep connection because Mrs. Bird realizes how alike she is to Eliza in their shared vulnerability and experience of maternal suffering even though Eliza has "the impress of the despised race on her face" (74). The scene shows that sympathy is contagious: taking their cues from Mrs. Bird and Eliza, Mrs. Bird's sons weep, as does their "colored domestic" (74), Dinah; even the senator vents his sorrow. A little later, the senator sympathizes not just with Eliza but with her son, to whom Mrs. Bird has given some of the clothes of their own dead child. "[The senator] had never thought that a fugitive might be a hapless mother, a defenceless child,—like that one which was now wearing his lost boy's little well-known cap" (81). Sentimental identification is based on imagined similarity, often cued by a visual marker: this person looks just like me or just like someone I love.

Stowe's sentimental scene sets up multiple entry points for the reader, and it also proposes a plan of action. Even if you yourself are not a bereft mother, you are witness to a scene of bereft mothers and can model yourself on one of the weeping witnesses to this scene. Weeping, although often looked on with distaste by critics as a mark of sentimentality's manipulation or dishonesty, can instead be seen as a guarantor of sincerity. As the eighteenth-century actor and elocutionist Thomas Sheridan theorized, "Whenever the force of these passions is extreme, words give place to inarticulate sounds: sighs, murmurings, in love; sobs, groans, and cries in grief; half choked sounds in rage; and shrieks in terrour, are then the only language heard" (102). Because strong passions lead to weeping, weeping assures us that strong passions are being experienced. Weeping also galvanizes readers to act: after witnessing this sentimental scene between Eliza and his wife, Senator Bird decides to help Eliza escape, and the other members of the household also pledge themselves to help. The scene both models how readers are meant to feel and channels that feeling into an array of actions from which the reader can choose. Nonetheless, despite the options it makes available for the reader, there's one thing that's not an option: failing to feel sympathy. In the world of *Uncle Tom's Cabin*, everyone who is not a slave catcher (and even some of them who are) is susceptible to sympathy, and everyone is galvanized to act once they fall under the "magic of the real presence of distress."

As do other realist authors, Chesnutt uses this sentimental scene to remove the critical distance that realist narrative techniques foster and signal how important it is for readers to do something. In this, *The Marrow of Tradition*'s final scene, Olivia Carteret comes to the door of Dr. Miller and Janet, her previously unacknowledged half-sister, to beg Dr. Miller to come attend her son, who yet again is gravely ill. All of Wellington's white doctors either have stayed out of town or are occupied with the violence her husband, Major Carteret, was instrumental in unleashing. Dr. Miller initially refuses her request on the grounds that her husband was responsible for the riot that has killed his only child. Mrs. Carteret does not take this rejection well: "'Ah, Dr. Miller!' she cried, with his wife's voice,—she never knew how much in that dark hour, she owed to that resemblance—'it is *my* child . . . my only child. . . . Oh, Dr. Miller, dear Dr. Miller, if you have a heart, come and save my child!'" (243). Dr. Miller decides to leave it up to his wife, who listens to her sister's appeals: "It is my only one—my sweet child—my ewe lamb" (244); and "You will not let my baby die! You are my sister" (245); and "You *are* my lawful sister" (245). Janet rebuts all of Olivia's appeals: it was Janet's only child, too, who died; Olivia never acknowledged their kinship until now; what use is the recognition of the legitimacy of her maiden name now that she has a married one? Yet Janet decides to show mercy on her sister anyway: "But that you may know that a woman may be foully wronged, and yet may have a heart to feel, even for one who has injured her, you may have you child's life, if my husband can save it!" (246).

You can see how similar this scene is to Stowe's: the references to the dissolution of the nuclear family, the experience of overwhelming emotion, the appeal to maternal feeling, sympathy as offering the possibility of interracial connection in its ability to dissolve what otherwise seem like insuperable differences. They even share similar wording: Stowe's "poor creature" is reflected in Chesnutt's "poor humanity" (243). Suffering does not get more elemental than this; these characters are vivid in their pain. In other words, this is a *sentimental* scene, not a realist one (although, to be fair, most critics do not see this very final scene in the novel the same way they see the rest of the final section). It serves many purposes in Chesnutt's novel, not least of which is to solve the problem of proliferating perspectives brought up by the realist methods he uses elsewhere.

In what James Phelan would call its "thematic" aspect, the final scene and its lead-up reveal to readers the interdependence of the Black and white townspeople in Wellington. Dr. Carteret has previously failed to acknowledge this interdependence; in fact, he thinks that he and his fellow white people are only disadvantaged by Black people, not potentially saved by them. If Mammy Jane's collateral death during the riot doesn't convince him (and white readers) of this interdependence, then the closing off of options to help his child via the steel trap of the white supremacist machine he has so diligently constructed does: he literally cannot find a white doctor to save his child so must resort to seeking help from a Black doctor, whom he previously denied entry to his home.

This final scene attempts to solve, via its sentimental evocation of sympathy, the problem of critical distance, specifically the problem of white readers either feeling only critical distance from the white characters they so much resemble or feeling sympathy for them but failing to recognize these characters' deficiencies. To explain how that works, I return to the Eliza scene in *Uncle Tom's Cabin*. I've pointed out the similarities between these two scenes, similarities that strike me as so profound that I suspect that Chesnutt might have had this specific scene in mind when he wrote his own. But I am also struck by their differences, and these can be brought out by alluding to another passage from *Uncle Tom's Cabin*. This one might have been another explicit intertext for Chesnutt, one that pungently registers Stowe's belief in racial essentialism. Stowe's tableau involves two girls, the angelic little Eva and the enslaved Topsy: "There stood the two children, representatives of the two extremes of society. The fair, high-bred child, with her golden head, her deep eyes, her spiritual, noble brow, and prince-like movements; and her black, keen, subtle, cringing, yet acute neighbor. They stood the representatives of their races. The Saxon, born of ages of cultivation, command, education, physical and moral eminence; the Afric, born of ages of oppression, submission, ignorance, toil, and vice!" (224–25). In *The Marrow of Tradition*, it's as if Chesnutt crafts a tableau of Eva and Topsy grown up: "The two women [Janet Miller and Olivia Carteret] stood confronting each other across the body of the dead child.... Standing thus face to face, each under the stress of the deepest emotions, the resemblance between them was even more striking than it had seemed to Miller" (244). On the one hand, in her tableau, Stowe emphasizes what seem like insuperable differences, all the better to highlight the power of sympathy in bringing "representatives of the two extremes of society" together; Chesnutt, on the other hand, emphasizes insuperable similarities in an effort to highlight how white supremacist thinking distorts reality.

There are more differences. In Stowe's sentimental scenes, Black people do the imploring; in Chesnutt's climactic scene, it is a white woman who implores a Black one. In *Uncle Tom's Cabin*, a white character learns to stop seeing the enslaved as an abstraction. But in *The Marrow of Tradition*, it is only in abstracting from the individuality of Olivia Carteret that Janet can bring herself to sympathize with her. I can show this by quoting more fully the response Janet makes to her sister upon hearing how Olivia will now acknowledge their familial connection: "I throw you back your father's name, your father's wealth, your sisterly recognition. I want none of them,—they are bought too dear! . . . But that you may know that a woman may be foully wronged, and yet may have a heart to feel, even for one who has injured her, you may have your child's life, if my husband can save it!" (246). Janet needs to reject the particularities of this woman, this situation, and this lineage in order to sympathize with her because they are what, in turn, particularized Janet into a victim: made her into a bastard and left her destitute and kinless. These wrongs were all caused by white people's perception of her race, what white people see as her insuperable difference from them, which, unlike Eliza's, is visually absent: as the novel points out again and again, Janet and Olivia look almost identical to each other. Janet Miller will sympathize with Olivia but only as suffering human to suffering human rather than Black woman to white woman.

Chesnutt reverses the usual direction of the flow of sympathy. Instead of flowing from white woman to Black woman, it flows from Black woman to white woman, and Janet can sympathize with her sister only if she strips her of her individuality, including her racial particularity. In the process, Chesnutt reveals something about literary sympathy's general mechanics: literary sympathy strips characters of racial particularity regardless of the direction it flows in. In the case of cross-racial experiences of sympathy, racial particularity is a species of difference, and sympathy works on the basis of perceived (or projected) similarities. Stowe's belief in racial essentialism is actually at odds with sympathy's workings in her novel. For Chesnutt, by contrast, sympathy's mechanics align with his belief in how much the white supremacist belief in a racial binary distorts the actual similarities between white people and Black people in the postbellum United States, in terms of both the reality of racial admixture and Black and white people's connected interests. With this final scene, Chesnutt invites us to recognize the absurdity of cross-racial sentimental sympathy's being achievable—barely—only in a time of emergency.

Why end *The Marrow of Tradition* with what is, even with all of Chesnutt's innovations, a sentimental scene? Such scenes model within the storyworld what authors want to happen in the real world. Characters recognize themselves in other characters once they sympathize with them; readers are also meant to identify with them and recognize themselves in them. Mrs. Bird sympathizes with Eliza, and white readers are meant to recognize themselves in the senator's wife and thus also feel what she does: sympathy for Eliza. Sentimental sympathy often involves triangulated relationships. This formation reveals how sentimental sympathy flows from readers in two ways: one, a reflexive, unconscious way, such as in the experience of sympathy that readers feel toward characters they feel are like themselves, and the other a more effortful way, mediated by a proxy, where in a burst of recognition readers realize how very similar they are to people they had previously assumed to be very different from themselves. White readers sympathize with Mrs. Bird (unconsciously), and through Mrs. Bird they also sympathize with Eliza (more effortfully).

How does this triangulation work in the final scene of *The Marrow of Tradition*? We might think the scene asks white readers to unconsciously identify with Janet as they see her effortfully sympathizing with her white sister, Olivia. But in fact I would argue that Chesnutt doesn't think that Janet could be, for white readers, an object of the unconscious kind of sympathy I've described. Instead, the unconscious object of identification would seem to be the white, well-off Olivia, with her obvious similarities to Chesnutt's white readers. But Chesnutt has made Olivia somewhat unsympathetic to contemporaneous readers in her cruel treatment of her sister (she's completely nefarious to most contemporary readers), summed up in Janet's justified reaction to her sister's belated recognition of their blood tie. As Janet notes, voicing what seems like a very reasonable position, "Now, when this tardy recognition comes, for which I have waited so long, it is tainted with fraud and crime and blood" (246). In sum, it hardly seems as if this scene is aiming to establish sympathy for Janet via the proxy of Olivia (this is not the direction in which sympathy flows in this final scene) or for Olivia via the proxy of Janet (whose sympathy for her, though it exists, is not particularly robust).

Instead, there's a different triangulation of sympathy going on. It requires us to recognize that another Olivia has come into existence in this final scene, one who is humble where the old Olivia had been proud, one who is desperate for her Black sister's recognition when before she had always scorned it. Olivia even looks different from how she usually looks: "Her long dark hair . . . had fallen down, and hung disheveled about her shoulders" (243). New-Olivia has been undone. New-Olivia, however, finally recognizes similarities between this new self and her old self. She understands, finally, that she has always been legitimately related to her Black sister; she realizes she has never actually possessed the racial invulnerability she thought she did. The connection between these two selves was hidden by her own white supremacist views. Olivia's old way of seeing the world, shared by the other white characters as well as Chesnutt's white readers, has given way to a new and newly self-aware version of herself.

It is this new version of Olivia that the scene asks the white reader to (effortfully) sympathize with by recognizing their own similarities to her via the conduit of the old-Olivia, with whom the white reader has already unconsciously bonded, at least to some extent, at least at first. Thus, the thematic aspect—the "lesson"—of this last scene dovetails with its emotional impact. In recognizing what her white supremacist views have wrought, Olivia "tottered under the stress of her emotions" (246), and so, it is hoped, will the white reader. I'd like to call what goes on in the final scene "sentimental self-identification."[32] Olivia recognizes how distorted her view of the racial order has been up to this point. As is the way with sentimental scenes, what happens within the text models what should happen outside it. Sentimental sympathy makes vivid and compelling to white readers the possibility of a new, ethically redeemed version of themselves.

Sentimental self-identification aims to correct the two inversely related problems that beset Chesnutt's earlier published work: first, the problem of white readers either unconsciously identifying with a character they failed to realize is racist and, second, the problem of recognizing that a character is racist but failing to sympathetically identify with them. Only upon a second reading of *The Marrow of Tradition* should white readers recognize, from the beginning, that the unreliable focalization characterizes not just Chesnutt's villainous white characters but also the most admirable ones. Chesnutt needs white readers to unconsciously identify with the covertly villainous, racist white characters long enough so that, when these readers, like Olivia, are tottering under the stress of their blooming sympathetic self-identification, they can finally identify their own racist schemata. Ironically, sympathy is what finally allows white readers to realize that *all* the white characters have been unreliable focalizers and that they themselves share much in common with them. In other words, in *The Marrow of Tradition*, it is sympathy that enables the one kind of critical distance Chesnutt seems to condone: white readers' critical distance from themselves, which allows them to recognize their own racist schemata, coupled, he hopes, with the enticements of sympathy for a new, more vulnerable version of themselves and a newfound commitment to act against the existing racial order.

My claim that Chesnutt asks his white readers to sympathize with Olivia (however "new" she is) might seem difficult to swallow for my own contemporary readers. They can rightly point out how much the text has signaled Olivia's ethical deficiencies throughout the novel and contrasted them to Janet's admirable character traits. I'd ask these readers to consider two things.

First, there is the distinction between intended reader and actual reader. Intended readers—the postbellum white reader, whether progressive or conservative, whether northern or southern—likely sympathized with Olivia's reluctance to acknowledge her Black sister. This is very difficult for the contemporary (white) reader to accept because they know if they were in Olivia's place, they would not act that way. And even if many postbellum white readers, in fact, wouldn't have sympathized with Olivia in this way, all we need to establish is that Chesnutt thought they would. As a person who had, for his whole life, been systematically excluded from the cultural and social opportunities offered to white people, as Richard H. Brodhead delineates in his introduction to Chesnutt's journals, I don't find it very hard to believe that Chesnutt believed that his intended white readers would sympathize with Olivia. Second, Chesnutt could not more strongly signal in this final scene that he believes an improvement in race relations cannot be delayed another second. The novel ends with a character calling out to Dr. Miller, "There's time enough, but none to spare" (195). The character is referring to the possibility of saving Olivia's son, but of course, this is also Chesnutt sending the white reader the same message about the larger emergency of race relations and the probability of the coup/pogroms to come. This kind of emergency calls for a solution, not further questions or the further proliferation of perspectives. In times of emergency, authors call on sympathy, and hard as it will be for white readers to change their minds about the insuperable differences between themselves and the Black people with whom they share a country, Chesnutt calls on Olivia—and sentimental sympathy—to show them how.

ASPIRATIONAL SYMPATHY

The Marrow of Tradition is a brilliant novel, but it did not inspire white readers the way *Uncle Tom's Cabin* did. Why *didn't* the novel engage contemporaneous readers in a process of sentimental self-identification of their own racist schemata?[33] In her invaluable article "Beyond 'Bitter': Chesnutt's *The Marrow of Tradition*," Sydney Bufkin describes how white readers of *The Marrow of Tradition* deflected its criticism.[34] She finds that contemporaneous reviewers of the novel typically pictured a public that was either geographically or ideologically distant from themselves to be the target of Chesnutt's critique. Northern reviewers felt *The Marrow of Tradition* to be a most salutary book for southerners to read since southerners needed to be exposed to points of view not included in books like Thomas Nelson Page's popular plantation fiction novel *Red Rock*; southern reviewers believed *The Marrow of Tradition* to be directed at northerners and used their reviews to rebut the novel's portrait of the Wilmington massacre. As Bufkin writes, "The record indicates ... that many reviewers were perfectly willing to read the novel in ways that moderated or displaced [Chesnutt's] very critique [of race hatred]" (248).

Bufkin is more interested in revealing the reception of the novel than exploring why this displacement happens. I'd like to build on her work by suggesting an explanation. Howells and Twain constructed an argument for the literary value of realism by unfavorably comparing sentimental novels to their own, but in doing so, they did more than establish the merit of their work. Their metric of literary value frames realism as antithetical to sentimental writing, as if they could never exist together in a single work, an assumption all the more powerful for its being simply an implicit corollary to what they explicitly argue. In this way, readers have been persuaded to see a novel as either realist *or* sentimental.

Howells is anomalous not just in taking *The Marrow of Tradition*'s critique to heart; he's also one of the few contemporaneous reviewers who claimed it to be a realist novel. In his review he notes, "I am not saying that [Chesnutt] is so inartistic as to play the advocate" ("A Psychological Counter-Current" 882), advocacy, in Howells's opinion, being the thing that would align Chesnutt's novel with sentimentality rather than realism. We can note the lukewarmness of Howells's defense in his double negative, and it is further vitiated by another judgment Howells makes that "[Chesnutt] is too clearly of a judgment that is made up" (882). Howells notices the way that Chesnutt offers different perspectives in the novel even as Chesnutt exposes their shortcomings (presumably the "judgment" that Howells refers to). Howells could not admit of a realist author playing the advocate yet remaining a realist.[35] He is following the Purity Principle of realism.

Other contemporaneous reviewers, however, far from downplaying the novel's advocacy, linked its advocacy to its power over readers. Furthermore, they did not hesitate to suggest its similarity to *Uncle Tom's Cabin*. The *New York Press* reviewer thought that in its "dramatic qualities, as well as in theme, it bears a decided likeness to 'Uncle Tom's Cabin,'" and the novel's connection to *Uncle Tom's Cabin* is mentioned in many contemporaneous reviews, with accompanying descriptors suggestive of sentimental writing: "dramatic," "passionate," "feeling." For example, the *Brooklyn Daily Eagle* echoes the *New*

York Press's citation of the novel's "dramatic qualities" by describing the final section as depicting a "dramatic incident, which is handled with unusual power and intensity," and the review sums up the novel by saying it "has come at white heat from the author's heart." Even though many reviewers recognized the novel's dramatic intensity, they failed to take its cause to heart. Why did they assume that its lessons were intended for other readers?

This was not the effect of *Uncle Tom's Cabin*, as we might recall from the first chapter. Readers felt inspired to take up the antislavery cause themselves. Yet if we compare how each book structures its scenes of sympathy, we can start to glimpse what I'd like to call the aspirational nature of literary sympathy—what, I hypothesize, caused contemporaneous readers to deflect the novel's invitation to identify one's own ethical deficiencies. In the Eliza scene, we recall how Mrs. Bird's sympathy for Eliza is evoked by a sense of their shared suffering. (Both have lost or are in danger of losing a young child.) That's how the scene works within the storyworld, but in the real world, Mrs. Bird functions as a stand-in for the reader, a character with whom readers are meant to sympathetically identify, an identification made stronger if the reader, as was likely, had herself suffered the loss of a close family member. Through Mrs. Bird, we feel the rush of sympathy for Eliza that she does. Thus, the scene allows opportunities for the two kinds of sympathetic readerly reactions I discussed earlier: the unconscious kinds of identification we feel with characters we assume to be the same as we are and the more effortful experiences of sympathy with characters we imagine to be different from ourselves.

Contemporary scholars who write about sympathy have emphasized two aspects of it: its reliance on scenes of suffering and its reliance on imagined similarities between the sympathizer and the object of sympathy. For now, let me focus on the latter. As I noted in the introduction, Suzanne Keen claims that "we humans, like other primates, tend to experience empathy most readily and accurately for those who seem like us" (x). The sympathizer imagines that the sufferer is like them, and this feature of sympathy has given critics great pause. As I have observed throughout this book, for many critics, sympathy results in a variety of ethical problems. For them, the problem with sympathy lies in the sympathizer's failure to recognize difference: the way that the experiences of the object of sympathy might not align with her own, for instance, how being an enslaved fugitive might be different from being a senator's wife. I'd like to think about how the sympathizer herself might be different from how she perceives herself to be in the moment of sympathizing. Mrs. Bird imagines herself to be as fierce and brave as Eliza in her efforts to protect her son, and the reader imagines herself to be the same in her mediated sympathy with Eliza. Similarly, in her unconscious identification with Mrs. Bird, the reader imagines herself to possess the good qualities of this petite exemplar of true womanhood: a perfect housekeeper, a wife who knows her husband better than he does, a fierce defender of the defenseless, and so on. Probably only a tiny sliver of Stowe's white women readers were these things. Yet *all* of Stowe's white women readers aspired to these qualities. This is the aspirational feature of literary sympathy: we sympathize with characters who present us a picture of how we would like to be and, in that moment of sympathetic identification, imagine we really are.

That sympathy works aspirationally is the aspect of sympathy that, I hypothesize, helped to short-circuit *The Marrow of Tradition*'s ability to induce readers to take to heart the lesson of the novel. There's something gnarled and knotty about the flow of sympathy in the novel, not unlike the grapevines that populate Chesnutt's famous short story. My description of the novel as a text that can rhetorically pass until its last section depends on a wholly gullible reader, one who won't apprehend the unreliable focalization of the white characters until their actions overtly contradict their self-justifications. But actual readers exist on a continuum of gullible to masterful. Different readers will recognize a given white character's unreliability at different stages of the novel. For example, one might start doubting Major Carteret's good character much earlier than the final few chapters.[36] As soon as a reader does, not only will that reader withdraw her unconscious identification from that point forward, but also it's possible she might forget that she had ever extended it. Although there are circumstances when readers sympathize with unreliable narrators (and unreliably focalizing characters),[37] they do not when that unreliable character holds beliefs or values that the reader would like to think conflict with her own. It's not that Chesnutt is wrong in delineating how white readers' judgments and perceptions are distorted by their sense of race privilege; the problem is that his white characters capture the phenomenon precisely. Readers sympathize not with characters that reflect how they are but with those that reflect *how they would like to be*, and this aspect of sympathy, which has gone unnoted as far as I can tell by critics both unsympathetic and sympathetic to sympathy, is what causes the deflection on the part of readers that Bufkin documents.

The aspirational nature of sympathy can give us added insight into *The Marrow of Tradition*'s final, sentimental scene. An obstacle that Olivia Carteret encounters in her efforts to make Janet Miller sympathize with her is this: Olivia appeals to an image of Janet that Janet has rejected. By promising her wealth and a family name, Olivia paints a picture of Janet as someone who seeks charity and is ashamed of her own Blackness. Janet firmly rejects that image: "Now, when I have married a man who can supply my needs, you offer me back the money which you and your friends have robbed me of! . . . Now, when an honest man has given me a name of which I can be proud, you offer me the one of which you robbed me, and of which I can make no use" (246). It's not just that Olivia's appeal reveals her ignorance of her sister (she should take lessons from the discerning Eliza and her accurate assessment of Mrs. Bird); it's that Olivia doesn't know that if you want to induce someone to sympathize with you, you must offer to the hoped for sympathizer an image of themselves they would happily accept.

Olivia also reverses the power hierarchy of sympathy: normally the sympathizer is the one offering largesse. In *Uncle Tom's Cabin*, Mrs. Bird, the wealthy white potential sympathizer, can offer Eliza the resources to continue her flight from slavery, and it is typical for the sympathizer to be in the more powerful social position. But Olivia asks Janet to take on a subservient role even though Janet is the sympathizer. Not surprisingly, Janet rejects the dependent position Olivia offers her and decides to offer Olivia her sympathy only on her own terms. As I mentioned earlier, Janet says, "But that you may know that a woman may be foully wronged, and yet may have a heart to feel, even for one who has injured her, you may have your child's life" (246). Janet offers a picture of herself that runs counter to the one Olivia has offered her: Janet wants to be self-sacrificing yet dominant in her role as Olivia's teacher. Olivia will thus learn not just something about sympathy but something about race: Janet deserves to be addressed as "a woman," not as a "n—" or "Negro," as Olivia has earlier been wont to address her. Far from taking on the subservient position that Olivia's proffers of money and name would force her to occupy, she finds a way to take the high ground, and she attains it by trying to teach this white person a lesson.

The interaction between Olivia and Janet highlights the very difficult dynamics of transracial sympathy for Black authors in both the antebellum and postbellum periods, if not today. White characters are happy to make Black characters into objects of sympathy with the concomitant picture of themselves as powerful benefactors. Robyn Warhol has written of how Harriet Jacobs refuses the role of subservient and transparent object of sympathy in Jacobs's autobiography *Incidents in the Life of a Slave Girl* ("Reader, Can You Imagine"). In many of Jacobs's apostrophes to her white women readers, she refuses to take on a beseeching role, insisting instead, as Warhol sums it up, "because you have not seen/done/lived what I have, you *cannot* feel the same way I feel" ("Reader" 65). One of the many things that makes Warhol's article important is Warhol's acumen in discerning Jacobs's resistance to taking on a subservient role. It's not that I doubt the existence of Jacobs's resistance—far from it—but it seems crucial that Jacobs's contemporaneous white readers not detect it. Jacobs meant for her text to rhetorically pass. If her contemporaneous readers had detected her resistance to their positioning themselves as her benefactors, they would not have felt sympathy for her. Instead, Jacobs would have been offering a picture of them to themselves (as subservient to a Black woman) that they would likely have refused. It is a tragedy of *The Marrow of Tradition* that the moment when Chesnutt needed the veil to finally fall from his readers' eyes is the moment when he called on them to recognize their prior sympathy with a spate of characters they now had critical distance from. This state of affairs accounts for how a representative contemporaneous reviewer could get it both so right and so wrong. Writing in 1901, a reviewer for the *Chatauquan* writes that if *The Marrow of Tradition* shall "avail to give the advocates of 'white supremacy' ... a glimpse of themselves as others see them, it will have rendered honorable and welcome service in a time of desperate need" (qtd. in Bufkin 240). Both the sentiment and the scare quotes put the reviewer at a distance from the "advocates of white supremacy" that he identifies as the book's target. Like Chesnutt's other white readers, the reviewer recognizes the political purpose of *The Marrow of Tradition* but fails to consider whether he himself might be a candidate for the self-critique Chesnutt prescribes.

Afterword

A Case against the (Solely) Discerning Reader

Have contemporary literary scholars done better at understanding Charles Chesnutt's intent than his contemporaneous readers? I ended the previous chapter with the observation that Chesnutt's contemporaneous white readers failed to recognize themselves as the target of Chesnutt's racial critique in *The Marrow of Tradition*. Chesnutt's criticism of the postbellum racial order depended on his readers' sympathizing with the white characters in this novel, but they likely ceased to sympathize (and maybe even ceased to remember they had previously sympathized) with the characters as soon as they perceived them to be ethically wanting. It seems obvious that Chesnutt would desire future white literary critics to recognize their own racist schemata via sympathetic identification, and it seems equally obvious that this has not happened even as they and other literary critics have excavated, persuasively and thoroughly, the racial critique that *The Marrow of Tradition* offers.

One reason for this failure is likely the novel's temporal distance. For one thing, the novel features white characters whose speech patterns and gender relations seem antiquated, and the modern white reader's recognition of these differences allows them to feel distanced from the novel's white characters. There's also the aspirational aspect of sympathetic identification, which I discuss in the previous chapter. But I believe there's another reason why contemporary literary critics are unlikely to sympathetically identify with *The Marrow of Tradition*'s characters. In the process of critiquing racist schemata, Chesnutt reveals the limits of the reading practices that realist authors encouraged, practices that foster the cultivation of critical distance to the exclusion of other stances. These reading practices have been widely adopted by literary critics. Another reason, then, why contemporary literary critics avoid identifying with the (white) characters in *The Marrow of Tradition* is the reason we avoid sympathetically identifying with any characters (or at least writing about that experience of identification): to do so strikes critics as entailing that we abandon our hard-won reading practices and the value they hold for us.

My own process in writing the previous chapter attests to the relevance of Chesnutt's critique of modern literary critical practice. I have a confession to make: the interpretation of the first scene of *Marrow* I offered in the previous chapter didn't reflect how I read it even the first time. I analyzed this scene as if I were a more gullible reader than the reader I actually am. You'll recall that this first scene focuses on Mrs. Carteret and her infant son. When I analyzed the scene in the previous chapter, I took on the guise of a reader who does not register its critique of Lost Cause ideology until a second reading of the novel. Instead, by the third paragraph I had decided that Chesnutt was up to similar tricks to the ones he had played in the conjure tales. Here is the sentence that did it, the description of Major Carteret I alluded to in the last chapter: "Long ago, while yet a mere boy in years, he had come back from Appomattox to find his family, one of the oldest and proudest in the state, hopelessly impoverished by the war,—even their ancestral home swallowed up in the common ruin" (44). Two phrases triggered my alarm system: "oldest and proudest in the state" and "ancestral home," both of which seemed to me to reveal the importance Carteret places on what he sees as his aristocratic white lineage. These phrases are ones Carteret himself would use, not an objective narrator, and certainly not Chesnutt himself. These ideologically loaded phrases conjure up the Arthurian-inflected account of the antebellum South that so many postbellum southern whites favored. The refinement of Carteret's pedigree is meant to contrast starkly with the never-to-be-acknowledged lineage of the Black people they live beside. This passage, I concluded, must be focalized through Major Carteret. What's more, this description seemed to me to be not just focalized but unreliably focalized: readers are intended to register a distance between Major Carteret's judgments about his family and the Old South and a more truthful account of them. In registering this distance, we are brought closer to the judgments of Chesnutt. The rest of the scene continues to create a distance between the other oblivious white characters and Chesnutt, who is skeptical of these characters' self-regarding, racist beliefs.

Unlike the gullible interpretation I offered in the previous chapter, this interpretation of the initial scene does not find Chesnutt to be imitating *Uncle Tom's Cabin*; instead, he is eviscerating it. For example, later in the first scene, the masterful reader sees Chesnutt critiquing—not adopting, as I suggested in the previous chapter—Stowe's characterization of the mammy figure in *Uncle Tom's Cabin*. In *The Marrow of Tradition*, this figure is even called "Mammy." Mammy Jane seems to be a descendant of Aunt Chloe, Uncle Tom's wife, yet in contrast to Aunt Chloe's guilelessness and devotion to her white "family," Mammy Jane slyly and knowingly reveals the lie white people adopt that they are not dependent on—even related to—their Black neighbors. Mammy Jane tells the origin story of Mrs. Carteret's half-sister, Janet Miller (45–49). This story of racial intermixing is prophetic; it foreshadows the future dependence of Mrs. Carteret on Janet Miller in the final scene, and it also foreshadows the broader interdependence and intermixing of the white and Black residents of Wellington. Yet its prophecy goes unheeded. Dr. Price, the white doctor in attendance on Mrs. Carteret, who is liberal in his own eyes and the eyes of the town, meets Mammy Jane's story with a yawn (46). The novel thus also foreshadows white people's unfailing unresponsiveness to revelations made by Black people. By allowing some white readers to believe that they might be more discerning than Dr. Price, the novel seems to compliment them (i.e., me) on their precocious understanding of its thematic lessons.

There are many pleasures to be had from never being a gullible reader of Chesnutt, but there's also a price to pay. It matters that this initial scene be able to pass for two reasons. For one thing, it allows Chesnutt to maintain his integrity. Stowe shares her white readers' prejudices, as we can see in our first introduction to Uncle Tom's literal cabin, a scene that caters to antebellum white readers' presumed sophistication: "In one corner of it stood a bed, covered neatly with a snowy spread; and by the side of it was a piece of carpeting, of some considerable size. On this piece of carpeting Aunt Chloe took her stand, as being decidedly in the upper walks of life" (*Uncle Tom's Cabin* 18). The narrator shares the readers' prejudices about Tom's "rude" dwelling, and because this is a didactic novel, we can assume Stowe does too. But Chesnutt does not share the prejudices of his contemporaneous white readers. Richard H. Brodhead's bleak assessment of what Chesnutt sacrificed in producing the conjure tales—"[Chesnutt] has served one group's life up as the stuff of another group's entertainment" (*Cultures* 205)—strikes me as off the mark because it does not consider how the stories rhetorically pass. The first scene of *The Marrow of Tradition* works similarly: it caters to Chesnutt's white readers' prejudices while offering proof that Chesnutt does not share in them.

If this first reason depends on there being masterful readers who can recognize Chesnutt's rhetorical passing, the second reason has to do with the readers who don't recognize it. The gullible reading of this scene makes Chesnutt's criticism of the racial order particularly powerful. If white readers fail to sympathize with any of his characters, they won't feel a pang at their unmasking or, even better, recognize the extent to which they share in their mental schemata. Chesnutt stated that his goal as an author was "to lead [the reading public] on imperceptibly, unconsciously, step by step to the desired state of feeling (*Journals* 140). Like Stowe with her much-maligned admonition at the end of *Uncle Tom's Cabin* that readers *"feel right,"* Chesnutt highlights the role of feeling in changing readers' minds.

HOW TO RECONCILE SYMPATHY AND CRITIQUE?

I want us to hold in the same hand two recent phenomena in my discipline: (1) the popularity of Rita Felski's study *The Limits of Critique* and (2) the discipline's consensus view of the inevitable ethical deficiencies of sentimental sympathy. On the one hand, members of the discipline seem open to new ways of reading that don't require critical distance or honor the preference to be "neither shaken nor stirred" (64), to use Felski's wonderful pun. On the other, they remain wary of allowing themselves to identify with characters or engage in the other uncritical reading practices invited by sentimental sympathy. Holding these two positions simultaneously puts people in a box. This book suggests one way we might lift one of its flaps.

I mentioned Mary Henderson Eastman's proslavery *Aunt Phillis's Cabin* (1852) in the previous chapter. That book stands as a potent reminder that sentimental sympathy can work in the service of nefarious aims. Yet it can also work to further admirable ones. In this book I have tried to argue for sentimental sympathy's ethical flexibility. There is no way to tell in advance the ethical effects of sentimental sympathy. But we can tell in advance that, for good or ill, it will work powerfully to further an author's thematic aims.

Apart from ethical qualms, could it be that there's another reason why it's been hard for professional readers to approach sentimental sympathy without prejudgment? Felski describes critique as a "charismatic mode of thought" (3), noting that it is "virtually synonymous with intellectual rigor, theoretical sophistication, and intransigent opposition to the status quo" (7).

Who in the academy doesn't like associating themselves with such things? If we consider the rhetorically passing text in particular, we can add to the list of critique's pleasures. Masterful readers feel pleasure in figuring out when rhetorical passing is taking place. It makes them feel bonded with the author, similar to the way that Wayne Booth envisions the reader's recognition of irony as fostering friendships between authors and readers.[1]

We might imagine that authors like Nella Larsen and Chesnutt would have felt particularly friendly toward their masterful readers—including the future literary critics who so perceptively ferret out the double-voiced meaning of their rhetorically passing texts. And when it comes to the rhetorically passing text that depends on a reader's racist schemata to pass successfully, there's an added incentive not to fall for it. A masterful reading assures them that they don't possess such schemata. The discerning white literary critic immediately feels both above and distant from Chesnutt's reprehensible white characters: these characters are not like what such a reader imagines herself to be, so there's no impulse to identify with them. The masterful reading of Chesnutt also allies contemporary white critics with historical Black readers, who presumably quickly saw through the self-serving focalizations of characters like Major Carteret. As an anonymous reviewer for *The Appeal*, a Black weekly, writes of *The Marrow of Tradition*, "[Chesnutt] punctures not only the demagogue, but white respectability which endures and tolerates with such charming composure the Southern mob and its bloody work" (Review of *Marrow*, *The Appeal*). This masterful reading corresponds with my own, and I derive great pleasure from knowing that I'm allied with this reviewer in our shared sense of Chesnutt's clever, eviscerating treatment of respectable white people.

But there's a grave problem with being, from the start, a masterful white reader of *Marrow*. It was important for Chesnutt that white readers remain gullible throughout at least some of the novel, so that he can show them they see the world similarly to how his white characters do. He wants to demonstrate to these white readers the murderous results of this kind of thinking. (This is a different situation from that of Woolson. In her case, she seems to prize the discerning reader because such a reader will not see her as simply a local colorist striving to be just as good as the male realists; instead, they will register her criticism of the realist old boy club.) Masterful reading allows us to ally with literary authors whom we see as equally masterful. Masterful reading, however, makes it hard to sympathize with—to feel for and with—literary characters. This uncritical, emotional reading practice has not been comfortable for literary critics to engage in for a long time. Many critics date its beginning to the "Affective Fallacy,"[2] but I've sought to push back its date of origin to the reading protocols explicitly advocated by Howells and Twain.

As I suggested earlier, Chesnutt's and Woolson's critique extends beyond race and gender privilege; it's also a criticism of the critical distance cultivated by realist narrative conventions and touted by realism's celebrators. It's a criticism of the stance required by "critique." It's possible that many white literary scholars do not hold the particular racist beliefs that Chesnutt's white characters do, but I think most of us do hold the idea that we are very good readers. I want my analysis of *Marrow* to challenge contemporary literary critics to consider the idea that discerning reading habits can obscure the power and ethical weight of a text. Sometimes, as in the case of Woolson, literary critics who recognize an author's unreliable narration can plausibly think that they are that author's ideal readers. But not in the case of Chesnutt. Chesnutt invites literary critics to question our interpretive practices and what they miss.

The case of Chesnutt also invites us to keep in mind the distinction between intended and actual readers. Let's acknowledge that it's not just time, place, or status that determines an author's intended readers but also the reading practices that a group of readers have adopted, which the text they are reading might itself try to uproot, as *Uncle Tom's Cabin* does. We should also keep in mind that the reading practices of the intended reader might not resemble the contemporary critic's own. Chesnutt can help us see that masterful reading is not the only, let alone the only valid, reading practice possible. His own method of protest—and here he is just like Stowe—depended on his white readers' lack of suspicion. When critical distance erases the possibility of experiencing sentimental sympathy, we're affirmed in our cleverness without realizing that this cleverness obscures from our view important aspects of what we're reading.

CRITIQUE AND SYMPATHY

I've been suggesting that sympathy and critique oppose each other in the distinctive reading practices they each cultivate. To the extent that the word "critique" names a critical act that depends on the critic's stance of critical distance, I can't use the term to describe what Chesnutt is trying to achieve by inviting his readers to feel sentimental sympathy toward his characters. But to the extent that "critique" means "criticism," Chesnutt shows they are not opposed.

In fact, his criticism of the racial order depends on sentimental sympathy: in the absence of experiencing it, readers can certainly recognize and admire how he criticizes the existing racial order, but they won't feel the power of how he's done it or take up his invitation to engage in admittedly painful self-critique.

If Chesnutt manages the feat of writing realistically and sentimentally at the same time, Twain and Howells alternate between them. They also chose not to abandon sentimentality, despite the headlines, because realist narrative conventions have limitations that sentimental ones supplement. The same is true in the other direction—realist narrative conventions supplement the limitations of sentimental ones—although so much ink has already been expended in pointing out the limitations of sentimentality that it has seemed more urgent to spend time on the limitations of realist writing. But a pluralist strategy can be applied to literary scholars' own critical and pedagogical practices: we need neither replace critique with sympathetic identification nor, as is the case now, let critique crowd out sympathy.

My advocacy of this kind of critical pluralism is not meant to tarnish realism nor to suggest it's not really realism after all. Even as realist authors relied on sentimental sympathy to supplement critical distance, they either denied or masked the fact they were doing so. We need not follow them in this. Acknowledging realist authors' reliance on or generous thinking about sentimentality does not, I think, threaten the identity of realism, in the same way that engaging in (or at least appreciating) sentimental sympathy need not threaten the identity of literary critics. It does mean, however, abandoning what I've called the Purity Principle of realism.

Abandoning this principle doesn't, as I've said, mean we stop thinking of works as realist, but it does change what the label means.[3] Sentimental narrative techniques allowed realist authors to accomplish things that realist narrative conventions could not achieve on their own, even as realist narrative conventions produce their own valuable effects. On the one hand, acknowledging this complementarity means that realism loses the cachet it garners from positioning sentimentality as its debased other. On the other hand, acknowledging it allows us to glimpse more of the richness and contradictoriness of realist works. This complementarity also allows those of us in the discipline to see ourselves more clearly: What values do we hold as literary critics that predispose us to overlook or deny sentimental sympathy's affordances?

Here's one possibility. As John Guillory argues, we literary critics value our difference from lay readers. We've been able to think of ourselves as special because we've renounced the consolations of lesser readers—their susceptibility to immersion and one of its most powerful motors, sympathetic identification.[4] We are indeed special in this way, but I'm recommending that we allow ourselves to engage in, or at least appreciate, a sympathetic reading practice that many of us had no trouble engaging in before we became English majors. My suspicion is that perhaps many of us still do read that way; it's just that we don't generally write about it in our research. But sometimes we do. Janice Radway acknowledges her own continuing capacity to read (and watch) uncritically in her description of her experience viewing *It's a Wonderful Life* with her family after a year spent reading Marx: "For me, on that particular occasion, there were two experiences of *It's a Wonderful Life*—the familiar family experience of it and another, more critical experience traceable to a set of interpretive procedures I had learned as a professional critic of popular culture" (276). Robyn Warhol ends one of her articles with this thought: "I propose we envision a community of readers empowered by their relationship to sentimental texts, fully conscious of how strategies 'get to them,' and free to enjoy having a good cry. Once that community's sense of embarrassment and isolation has been dispelled, its potential for participating in the transformation of culture and society will be considerable" ("As You Stand" 121–22). Radway suggests that the critical–uncritical divide leads many of us to feel we have split reading lives. (Radway points out she keeps her Marxist interpretations from her family.) You'll notice, too, that Warhol only implies—as I have only ever implied in this book—that she has cried at certain sentimental scenes and characters. Yet such acknowledgments of uncritical reading have led Radway to investigate how reading practices can be formed collectively and Warhol to investigate the ethical power of tears.

Engaging in uncritical reading habits like sympathetic identification, even if not written about directly (how do you write about them directly and still sound professional?), can, ironically, nonetheless be enormously generative for literary critics. Uncritical versus critical reading is not an either/or. Acknowledging that critical reading might itself be augmented by uncritical reading practices enables critics to generate new insights (as I hope I have generated new insights) by paying better attention to both a text's *intended* readers, who are often very different from the literary critic, and its reception by *actual* readers.

There's also a pedagogical benefit to allowing ourselves to rely on our capacities to be uncritical when engaged in the act of interpretation. In "Uncritical

Reading," Michael Warner observes that "our common enterprise [as English professors] is to discipline students out of their uncritical habits into critical reading" (13–14). Teaching others to be critical readers helps generate an identity we are proud of: we are professionals when it comes to literary interpretation, and our students' reading practices set our own into relief. In *Clueless in Academe*, Gerald Graff aims to lay bare the otherwise opaque interpretive practices used by those well ensconced in the discipline. Although I respect Graff's project enormously, it is premised on the fact that the way we write about literary texts is (and should be) so different from what our students would otherwise do that it will remain opaque to them unless we teach it transparently. Joanna Wolfe and Laura Wilder's *Digging into Literature*, which I've enthusiastically assigned for many years, does similar demystifying work. In its first chapter it introduces the idea of "Discourse Communities as Parlors" (5) and establishes how the particular parlor that literary critics inhabit has different conversational rules from the ones students are already acquainted with. The book's considerable value grows out of the way it "clarif[ies] the strategies of argumentation that literary critics and literature instructors use—and expect others to use—in their discourse community" (6). Its second chapter etches the borders of literary analysis even more deeply by distinguishing literary analysis from statements of evaluation (as seen in book reviews), statements that assert causality (as seen in author biographies), and proposals (as seen in editorials about whether a book should be banned). In demystifying literary interpretation, Wolfe and Wilder suggest its distance from what lay readers do. This establishment of firm boundaries is a problem because it can demotivate students by making them think they have to abandon what they already know how to do as readers, as if there's nothing they can build on.

Submerged in both Graff's and Wolfe and Wilder's ideas are hints of a different stance we could adopt. Graff discusses "the academic potential of [students'] argumentative talents" (226), and Wolfe and Wilder, addressing students, note that "your ability to listen closely to what has already been said and to politely agree or disagree with others will help you participate in the academic discourse community that college exposes you to" (5–6). Graff and Wolfe and Wilder suggest there are continuities between what our students already do and what they will do in the English classroom, although the list of interpretive strategies Wolfe and Wilder are so wonderful at articulating for students does not include their ability to feel for and with different characters. This small supplement to the repertoire of interpretive strategies we can use would entail a large and helpful change in how professional readers approach the reading habits our students come equipped with. We could say to students, you don't have to leave behind this aspect of how you read; you already possess not just valuable experience listening and arguing but valuable experience in feeling sympathy when you read.

When I began to teach as a graduate student, I remember there was one question students would ask that I hated more than any other: Wouldn't university English classes destroy the pleasure they took in reading? For the first many years I taught, I simply dismissed the question as evidence of my students' ignorance and my own expertise, proved by the fact that although I didn't know how to answer it, I knew not to ask it myself. This was followed by a revelation: that I did have an answer to this question. The pleasure that students lost in giving up their old ways of reading would be replaced by the pleasure they would find in dissecting a literary text, a different kind of pleasure to be sure but one that I felt more and more strongly as I grew into my professional identity. But I've begun to think that there might be an even better answer. I can now say to students, you don't have to put aside your accustomed pleasures. Realist authors couldn't achieve a full spectrum of effects on their readers without relying on sentimental sympathy, and literary critics offer only partial interpretations if they don't account for the narrative power and possible ethical benefits of this sympathy. Let's appreciate the full range of effects that literary texts produce and the full range of resources that authors can avail themselves of.

Notes

INTRODUCTION

1. Even otherwise sympathetic accounts of sentimentality suggest this withering away: Mary Louise Kete, for example, describes how the postbellum period saw a rejection of "what might be called the ideological . . . functions of sentimentality (148). Nina Baym argues that "in the late 1860s and 1870s . . . the [sentimental] genre had run its course" (13).
2. This is the account offered by David Shi in *Facing Facts*. He mentions how many realist authors began as journalists, adding that "newspaper work honed their skills at precise observation" (95). Later critics have challenged the idea of realism's objectivity, perhaps most famously Amy Kaplan, who reveals realism's saturation by ideology.
3. Alfred Habegger was an early critic to uncover the close relationship between the realists and the antebellum sentimental writers who came before them. In *Gender, Fantasy, and Realism in the American Novel*, Habegger characterizes Howells and James as "middle men" (65), intermediaries between the popular women novelists and (in his account) the more masculine naturalists. In *Henry James and the "Woman Business,"* Habegger sees James as closely connected to the antebellum sentimentalists via the intervening link of the "Civil War women agonists" (23), authors like Louisa May Alcott and Elizabeth Stoddard who wrote about loveless marriages.
4. Although my focus will remain on the affordances that realist writers found in sentimental writing, there's evidence that the conventional story of the withering away of sentimental novels in the postbellum period is wrong from an empirical perspective as well. The authors of *What Middletown Read*, an account of the Muncie, Indiana, public library and its borrowers between 1891 and 1902, report that middle-class women made up the largest group of adult borrowers, and the books they borrowed most by far were "the romantic, sentimental, and domestic fiction that circulated widely in late Victorian America" (Felsenstein et al. 118).
5. Phillip Barrish also notes the close relationship between realism and sentimentality, but whereas for him the connection comes from noting the realism in sentimentality, for instance, the way *Little Women* accumulates a mass of quotidian details (20–21), for me the connection comes from seeing the sentimentality in realism.
6. Hoeller's work is an exception to this rule. She attends to the aesthetic dimension of sentimentality, by which she means its characteristics as a distinctive literary tradition. I share her assumption that sentimentality is describable in more than political or philosophical terms even as we come to different conclusions about some of its aesthetic characteristics. For example, I see sentimental writers as trying to downplay the synthetic aspects of their texts, whereas she sees the typical sentimental work as "almost rejoic[ing] in its constructedness" (31).

7. Even Camfield, who so effectively demonstrates the intellectual complexities of sentimental moral philosophy, hints at his own distaste for sentimentality when he writes that "although we may dislike the sentimental overtones of much of Clemens's later work, it diminishes that work to explain it exclusively in psychological terms" (241).
8. For an argument about the difficulty of maintaining a distinction between sympathy and empathy, see my article "Closeness through Unreliability."
9. See Katherine Lundeen for a critique of sympathy on the grounds that it involves cultural appropriation; see Noble (*Rethinking*), Susan Bernstein, and Amy Shuman for a critique of sympathy on the grounds that it disregards the otherness of the other; see Lauren Berlant (*Female Complaint*, "Poor Eliza") and Lynn Festa for a critique on the grounds that it prevents structural critique.
10. One reason it might fail to elicit a strong emotional reaction is that "difference-insisting sympathy" might not actually be sympathy at all, in a hardwired or evolutionary sense. Keen, who understands empathy in evolutionary terms, does not see difference recognition as playing a part in empathy. As she notes, "We humans, like other primates, tend to experience empathy most readily and accurately for those who seem like us" (x).
11. Robert Scholes describes the problem that besets novice English majors when confronting literary texts "as one of difference, or otherness—a difficulty in moving from the words of the text to some set of intentions that are different from one's own and possibly opposed to them" ("The Transition to College Reading" 166). Critical reading, with its emphasis on recognizing differences, has functioned in the university English classroom as the cure for this problem.
12. Here and elsewhere I quote scholars who use "sympathy" and "identification" synonymously. I also use them synonymously myself, even though, as McGlothlin points out, "the intimate relationship between 'narrative empathy' and 'reader identification' is a complicated one" (256). It's sufficient for my purposes to understand identification as very closely related to sameness-asserting sympathy.
13. Nancy Bentley notes how "the analytic instinct," a phrase coined by Henry James, characterizes the American realists: James "was only the most overt of the writers devoted to creating art that could offer, in James's words, 'a more analytic consideration of appearances'" (11). I hope to make plausible a through line between this analytic instinct and the value English professors place on critical reading.
14. One reason I find Phelan's approach so useful is that he also values readers' emotional responses. Phelan defines narrative as "somebody telling somebody else on some occasion and for some purpose(s) that something happened" (*Somebody* 5). Out of this rhetorical concern grows a concern with how "authors of narratives offer their audiences . . . communications that invite or even require their audiences to engage with them cognitively, psychically, emotionally, and ethically" (*Living* 5). Far from proscribing literary critics from acknowledging readers' emotional reactions, a rhetorical narrative approach suggests that we cannot offer a comprehensive picture of how a given narrative works without attending to them.
15. Nancy Glazener attributes the association of emotional excess with romances and sentimental literature to a whole range of reviewers and authors associated with what she calls "the *Atlantic* group," the magazines associated with the *Atlantic Monthly*. See especially chapter 3 of *Reading for Realism*, "Addictive Reading and Professional Authorship." She also points out how the *Atlantic* group defined realism "relationally," that is, against other, and what it considered lesser, genres (13).
16. Borus and William Roscoe Thayer do diverge, however, in the judgment they make of this seeming objectivity. Borus remains neutral; Thayer is critical of it.

17. Guillory makes a similar point in *Professing Criticism* when he notes that "lay reading is a *condition* of professional reading, more specifically, an *antithetical origin*. . . . [T]his condition results in lay reading's construction as the other of professional reading, even its antagonist" (323).
18. Berlant notes that both "social progressives" and "the racist/patriarchal/capitalist world" have represented the world "in tactically sentimental ways," the former to reveal "the ordinary of structural suffering" and the latter "to describe the psychic effects of feminism/multiculturalism on those who once felt truly free" (*Female Complaint* 22).
19. According to this model, authors use different narrative resources to influence their readers. Phelan and Sarah Copland have also suggested that authors consider readers' probable reactions to what they're reading as they construct their narratives ("The Ideal Narratee"). Phelan does not provide an exhaustive list of resources; he leaves it to other critics to supplement the list he provides, as I do by framing "sentimentality" as just such a narrative resource. For more details of this model, see Phelan's "Authors, Resources, Audiences: Toward a Rhetorical Poetics of Narrative" and chapter 1 of *Somebody Telling Somebody Else: A Rhetorical Poetics of Narrative*.
20. In her foundational *Woman's Fiction*, Nina Baym sees sentimental novels as following this plot: "the story of a young girl who is deprived of the supports that she had rightly or wrongly depended on to sustain her throughout life and is faced with the necessity of winning her own way in the world" (11). Note how much this could apply to Crane's *Maggie*, which is not a sentimental novel. For a detailed analysis of how *Maggie* challenges a plot-centered definition of sentimentality, see *Sentimental Readers*, xii–xv.
21. I discuss Rabinowitz's model of audience in chapter 1. In Rabinowitzian terms, sentimental authors expect the intended audience to stop believing at some point that their fiction is an artifice. Stowe reinforces such a belief with her *Key to Uncle Tom's Cabin*, which asserts that the characters and events in *Uncle Tom's Cabin* are based on real ones.
22. Phelan's model of narrative as rhetoric makes central the analysis of relations between "tellers" and audiences, so the explication of this relationship is featured in many of his works. Phelan's "Authors, Resources, Audiences," however, provides an excellent explanation for "the prominence" in rhetorical narrative theory "of tellers, audiences, and purposes" (1).
23. Narration appears objective and omniscient when it is in the third person, when the narration is not tethered to any one character, and when the narrator knows things about the storyworld that the characters do not know themselves. In "Omniscience," Jonathan Culler offers an incisive critique of the concept of omniscience, demonstrating that it often confuses helpful distinctions in how a text's narration is functioning.
24. Unreliable narrators are almost always first-person narrators. As Monika Fludernik has written, "Only first-person narrators can be properly unreliable" (213). In chapter 8 of *The Distinction of Fiction*, however, Dorrit Cohn provides an example of an unreliable heterodiegetic (or third-person) narrator.
25. For a pointed critique of the idea of realist writing as democratic, see Glazener.
26. I choose to use "literary critic" rather than "literary scholar" throughout this book to signal the ubiquity of critical, distanced reading in the discipline, a ubiquity that Felski has documented in *The Limits of Critique*.
27. The claim that previous classics were marred by unrealistic characters is a leitmotif of Howells's *Criticism and Fiction*. You can see it in what has become his famous passage about cardboard grasshoppers, discussed in chapter 2, and you can see it in how he laments the benightedness of some literary critics: "Some of these poor fellows [critics], however, still contend . . . that human feelings and motives, as God made them and as

men know them, are not good enough for novel-readers" (27). Edith Wharton levels a similar charge in the first section of *The Writing of Fiction*: "The next advance [in fiction writing] was made when the protagonists of this new inner drama were transformed from conventionalized puppets—the hero, the heroine, the villain, the heavy father, and so on—into breathing and recognizable human beings" (4).
28. See chapter 1 for examples of this reaction from William Lloyd Garrison, Henry Ward Beecher, and Georgiana May.
29. These stories fit into another sentimental pattern that Warhol identifies, the way that sentimental characters often violate type: "Contrary to popular belief, sentimental texts do not present two-dimensionally 'stereotyped' characters, but rather rely on characterization that mixes traits to work against the types that have been established in the text [or in the culture]. This strategy works together with the unexpected reversals of plots to produce a reader's emotion" ("As You Stand" 119). In other words, typical characters often change in order to support cherished cultural narratives; or we might say that cherished cultural narratives often center on a character whose type of deficiency is seen as a problem and requires them to change into something better.
30. In fact, the very paucity of explicit character traits might be not an obstacle to a sense of a character's vividness but a catalyst for it. The psychologists Max Louwerse and Don Kuiken note that "empathy may involve the projection of possibilities for comprehending character development" (170). Glossing this point, Keen suggests that "empathy may work as a gap-filling mechanism, by which a reader supplements given character traits with a fuller psychologically resonant portrait" (217). In other words, an author does not have to provide multiple and varied characteristics for that character to seem round to the reader; the reader feels a character to be round even if that character is described simply or scantily as long as the reader's empathy has been triggered.
31. Flück writes: "I think it is fair to say that for the modern reader the novel becomes increasingly difficult to handle the more it typologizes itself. For while the analogy of the family is still familiar and can be revived and reimbued with meaning . . . the typological affirmation of a moral order, as Jane Tompkins in turn has shown, is no longer a code on which the modern reader can or wants to draw" (331).
32. As evidence, I offer a scene from Dennis Lehane's 2023 bestseller *Small Mercies* (stop reading now if you don't want spoilers). The main character, Mary Pat, a white woman from South Boston, has developed a friendship with Calliope, a Black woman she works with. When Mary Pat realizes her daughter, who has recently been murdered, had a hand in killing Calliope's son, she approaches Calliope and her husband to offer her sympathy. After all, they both have children who have been murdered. In an extremely moving scene (at least to this reader), Calliope could not reject Mary Pat's sympathy more firmly. Calliope responds to Mary Pat's "I'm sorry for your loss" with this: "You raised a child who thought hating people because God made them a different shade of skin was okay. You allowed that hate. You probably fostered it. And your little child and her racist friends, who were all raised by racist parents just like you, were sent out into the world like little fucking hand grenades of hate and stupidity and, and, and *you can go fuck yourself*, Mary Pat, if you think for one second I'm okay with that" (ch. 27). To use Raymond Williams's heuristic, the once dominant cherished cultural narrative of people from across the racial divide becoming friends because of common tragic experiences is here being replaced by an emerging cherished cultural narrative of a sinned-against minoritized person refusing to be part of a sympathetic exchange.

CHAPTER 1: Word Become Flesh

1. Gillian Brown also identifies the centrality of reading to Stowe's political project. For Stowe, "the project of making people feel right, then, involves, [sic] making people read rightly" (78–79). Like me, Brown is interested in the different reading practices Stowe advocates, but she develops a different taxonomy from mine: "experiential" and "prophetic."
2. I owe a huge debt to Barbara Hochman's *Uncle Tom's Cabin and the Reading Revolution*, which details how antebellum readers read the novel. Hochman also recurs to a history of reading to contextualize their responses.
3. That the intended audience of *Uncle Tom's Cabin* is white did not prevent Black readers from taking up the novel with great interest. Marva Banks and Robert S. Levine both describe the responses by antebellum northern Black readers (although they differ in their interpretation of them).
4. Throughout the novel, we see Stowe's favored characters reading to others with ease but struggling to write. This distinction reflects the relative emphases placed on teaching students to read and write in the antebellum period. Historians of the book and of rhetoric trace the gradual movement, as the century progresses, away from oral reading and memorization toward silent reading and original composition. See, for example, Ronald Zboray; Jean Ferguson Carr, Stephen L. Carr, and Lucille M. Schultz; Elizabeth Larsen; and P. David Pearson and Susie M. Goodin, who all detail this shift.
5. George M. Fredrickson, the scholar who first explicated the doctrine of "romantic racialism," describes it thus: "Although romantic racialists acknowledged that blacks were different from whites and probably always would be, they projected an image of the Negro that could be construed as flattering or laudatory in the context of some currently accepted ideals of human behavior and sensibility" (101–2).
6. For a detailed analysis of how Stowe adapts traditions of blackface, see Christina Zwarg's "Fathering and Blackface in *Uncle Tom's Cabin*."
7. Brown describes the popular antebellum author Sarah Prentiss's novel *Stepping Heavenward* as "exemplify[ying] an evangelical hermeneutics of daily experience as intrinsicallly sacred in meaning" (104–5).
8. Even when Tom is reading alone, the words he reads bear the mark of orality: "His Bible was thus marked through, from one end to the other, with a variety of styles and designations; so he could in a moment seize upon his favorite passages" (132). These marks resemble the breathing marks that orators made on the text of their speeches.
9. In her "Farewell to Readers," which followed the last installment of *Uncle Tom's Cabin* in *The National Era* but does not appear in the Norton Critical Edition of the novel, Stowe writes, "The thought of the pleasant family circles that she has been meeting in spirit week after week has been a constant refreshment to her" (qtd. in Charles Edward Stowe 157). Stowe imagines *Uncle Tom's Cabin* being read aloud in a family-binding weekly ritual.
10. These "Concluding Remarks" enjoin readers to act on what they have just read. Contained within this final section of the novel is a passage that distills many contemporary critics' sense of just what is wrong with this novel: "But, what can any individual do? Of that, every individual can judge. There is one thing that every individual can do,—they can see to it that *they feel right*" (404). Critics point out that it does not matter how people feel; it matters how they act, but for Stowe, action was inspired by feeling. For a discussion of the inextricability of feeling and action for Stowe and others in her era, see Warhol's "As You Stand, So You Feel and Are."
11. Suleiman writes that, like the exemplum, the "tendency" of the *roman à thèse* "is always

designed to lead to a *prise de conscience* [realization], and eventually to an action on the part of the reader or listener" (146).

12. For an extensive list of criticism about the dangers of sentimental texts that assume an equivalence between two suffering people regardless of their class or racial difference, see footnote 2 of Noble's essay "The Courage to Speak and Hear the Truth," which argues that Stowe backs away from such an easy sense of identification in one of her later novels, *The Minister's Wooing*.
13. Robyn Warhol makes a similar point in "Poetics and Persuasion," as does Elizabeth Barnes.
14. It is easy to dismiss the slaveholders' self-interested unease with Stowe's method of depiction, but there are contemporary critics who are also made uneasy by it. Kenneth Dauber writes that "the passion of [Stowe's] commitment is assured by the dispassion of her knowledge" (29); that is, Stowe presents the "facts" of her novel as if they will compel the reactions to them that she desires. But whereas I think Dauber finds Stowe's method of depiction ethically troubling regardless of context, I see it as ethically flexible, an argument I develop throughout the book.
15. See chapter 1 of Hochman's *Uncle Tom's Cabin and the Reading Revolution*.
16. If we focus on the oral aspect of the kind of reading practice that Stowe advocates, we should acknowledge that, as Robert Darnton observes, "for most people throughout most of history, books had audiences rather than readers. They were better heard than seen" (14).
17. In a reappraisal of his earlier work, David D. Hall counsels against seeing what happens between the eighteenth and nineteenth centuries as a reading "revolution" ("Readers and Reading" 354–56). Many recent historians of reading and the book find different reading practices coexisting in the same period. For example, according to David Finkelstein and Alistair McCleery, by the Middle Ages there had arisen a population of silent readers "who . . . had belonged to segments of the society that had long been literate" (107). That said, new reading practices were gaining cultural cachet during the early nineteenth century with the expansion of the book trade. See Barbara Sicherman for a description of postbellum family reading practices.
18. Jerome Tharaud provides an excellent discussion of this early work and Stowe's involvement in evangelical print culture.
19. In *The Word in the World*, Brown discusses the ways that evangelicals extended what she calls the "evangelical canon" in the nineteenth century and the different genres that made up this canon.
20. I want to thank one of the external readers for suggesting that St. Clare has Marxist sympathies.
21. That Stowe associates Tom with Eva in terms of their ideal literacy becomes a source of pain for the modern reader just as her mentions of enslaved adults' childlike nature are painful: they dovetail so neatly with the paternalistic beliefs of slaveholders as well as white supremacist thinking in general. When Stowe figures Tom as reversing his "g's" and "q's," she's suggesting Tom's difficulty in adopting conventional literate practice—which, according to the values of the novel, turns out to be a wonderful thing. It's hard to feel the same way, especially in light of the prohibition against teaching enslaved men and women to read and the insight that conventional literacy often helped freedom seekers on the path to freedom, a point made by Frederick Douglass in his *Narrative* and twentieth-century scholars of African American literature.
22. Newkirk recommends that modern students read passages aloud and memorize them. He calls these practices "as old as the hills" (9), and frames them, as Stowe did, as opposed

to the practices valued in their own day. That Newkirk's piece was considered publishable suggests both the distance we have journeyed from these methods and, ironically, their connection to other nostalgic forms of consumption currently in vogue like "slow food."

23. There's a certain irony in using the term "lay reader" to describe the kind of reader Stowe is trying to create because this reader, in Stowe's imagination, is a religious, Christian one. Nonetheless, this reader shares things in common with the contemporary "lay reader" in terms of the habit of reading empathetically and without critical distance. See Hannah Pardey for a discussion of such a reader's approach to global literature.

24. Rabinowitz calls this the "authorial audience," but I'll refer to it as the "intended audience" because it's a more common term.

25. The distinction between actual readers and intended readers provides the implicit impetus for the articles by Banks and Levine that I refer to in an earlier endnote. The fact that Stowe's intended audience was white did not prevent antebellum Black readers from reading her novel, although it did, for a long time, prevent white critics from searching out their reactions.

26. In case you're having trouble imagining what it means to be part of the "narrative audience," James Phelan explains how becoming part of the narrative audience means assuming "an observer position within the storyworld" (*Living* 7). Instead of being a person who inhabits the real world and knows they are reading a fictional account of a Mr. and Mrs. Bird who help a character named Eliza escape from slavery, as a member of the narrative audience you are in the kitchen with them, witnessing the unfolding scene.

27. Rabinowitz's model contains a fourth audience, which I mention for the sake of comprehensiveness (it's not one that comes up in the arguments I make in this book), the "ideal narrative audience," which occurs in the case of narratives that have unreliable narrators. This is the audience who believe the unreliable narrator's account. When Phelan uses this model, he replaces "ideal narrative audience" with "narratee."

28. Ironically, this makes our students better readers of *Uncle Tom's Cabin* than the professors who insist on critical distance, which makes it extremely hard for readers to become part of the novel's narrative audience.

29. I am grateful for Hildegard Hoeller's heuristic of distinguishing realist writing from sentimental writing. The former, she observes, is characterized by "economy," the latter by "excess."

30. In claiming to have created fiction based on real people and incidents, Stowe was cannily participating in a debate in the evangelical community, described by Brown (*The Word* 95–105), over the value of fiction, assuaging those evangelicals who rejected fiction reading as dangerous self-indulgence. But she could also garner support from those evangelicals who had begun to embrace "useful" fiction and the imaginative force it exercised over its readers.

31. Stowe's method mandates that we reject the surface meaning of proslavery accounts, even when they seem to be based on facts. As Weinstein states, Stowe "uses the language of literary analysis in order to illustrate the point that the facts of slavery as presented in pro-slavery sources must be interpreted because defenders of slavery know no 'scorn of dissimulation'" (90).

32. Stowe wrote the preface to the 1858 version of Henson's autobiography, and Henson titled the third version of his autobiography *"Uncle Tom's Story of His Life." An Autobiography of the Rev. Josiah Henson (Mrs. Harriet Beecher Stowe's "Uncle Tom"), from 1789 to 1876*.

33. Henrik Skov Nielsen, James Phelan, and Richard Walsh use the same analogy to explain a different narrative phenomenon in "Ten Theses about Fictionality" (a fact I was unaware of at the time I originally wrote this chapter).

34. This challenge might explain the otherwise strange fact that Hawthorne himself uses apostrophes and certain sentimental tropes like the innocent child, although he uses these things in a different way. He embraced a literacy based on solitary readers and clashing interpretations. See my discussion of Hawthorne in chapter 3 of *Sentimental Readers*.
35. See the opening of Douglass's novella *The Heroic Slave*, where Listwell, the white stand-in for the reader, overhears rather than sees Madison Washington, the heroic slave of the title, and only thus can acknowledge the man's superior qualities.
36. With this locution of "fictionalizing themselves," I am invoking Walter Ong's powerful model concerning the way that readers must imagine themselves into becoming part of a writer's audience.

CHAPTER 2: William Dean Howells, Mark Twain, and the Sentimental Red Herring

1. For example, here is how the novella renders Maggie's first impressions of Pete, her cur of a boyfriend: "Maggie thought he must be a very elegant and graceful bartender" (20).
2. Claudia Stokes describes how Howells touted "the power of the literary professional to adjudicate and supervise public literary taste" (*Writers* 105).
3. This and all subsequent quotations from *Adventures of Huckleberry Finn* are from the Bedford edition.
4. R. Kent Rasmussen, editor of the Penguin edition of *Huck Finn*, makes this association.
5. See Scharnhorst's *In Defense of Literary Biography* for more details on this stage of Twain's career.
6. As John T. Frederick notes, Hawthorne penned this phrase to his publisher William D. Ticknor in 1855 (231; emphasis added). What is not frequently quoted from is the letter he wrote two weeks later in which he partially recants his view (or at least its stridency) and praises Fanny Fern: "I bestowed some vituperation on female authors. I have since been reading 'Ruth Hall'; and I must say I enjoyed it a good deal.... If you meet [Fanny Fern], I wish you would let her know how much I admire her" (Hawthorne qtd. in Wallace 204–5). I must mention, however, that what I left out of the quotation praising Fern is the statement that "generally women write like emasculated men, and are only to be distinguished from male authors by greater feebleness and folly; but when they throw off the restraints of decency, and come before the public stark naked, as it were—then their books are sure to possess character and value" (Hawthorne qtd. in Wallace 204–5). I'm not sure but that Hawthorne didn't dig himself a deeper hole with his recantation. For an article that makes the case that Hawthorne's ideas about women writers were not as simple as the scribbling women comment makes them appear, see Wallace.
7. One example of how aesthetic complaints against sentimentality have persisted into the present day is demonstrated in Hoeller's discussion of "The Agonies of Rediscovering Sentimental Fiction" (2–10). Hoeller points out that one problem that contributes to these agonies is that even many recovery critics, the feminist critics who recovered nineteenth-century women writers from obscurity, recoil from the quality of sentimental writing. As Hoeller notes, even as these critics questioned their "aesthetic standards," they were not able "to transcend [their] taste" (8).
8. Although my focus is on the discussion of *Tears, Idle Tears* during this dinner party, this is also the dinner party at which a drunken Silas Lapham embarrasses himself in front of his future in-laws, an incident Howells is said to have modeled on a similar embarrassing performance by Twain at a birthday dinner at the home of John Greenleaf Whittier (Daugherty, "William Dean Howells" 12).

9. For example, Stokes sees Howells using Sewell as a tool "who offers Penelope Lapham the final word in pragmatist literary criticism" (*Writers* 162). Hoeller also sees Howells using Sewell as a mouthpiece (see her analysis of *The Rise of Silas Lapham* 13–17).
10. See Amanda Claybaugh's extended analysis of how Twain critiques the efficacy of sentimental reform in *Adventures of Huckleberry Finn* and *A Connecticut Yankee in King Arthur's Court*. Claybaugh observes how *Connecticut Yankee* reveals sympathy to be both fleeting and built on a faulty foundation, a belief in "a shared humanness that does not in fact exist" (178). I return to Claybaugh and *A Connecticut Yankee* later in the chapter.
11. Twain evinces similar values in his discussion of how James Fenimore Cooper violates the rule that "when the personages of a tale deal in conversation, the talk shall sound like human talk, and be talk such as human beings would be likely to talk in the given circumstances . . . and be interesting to the reader, and help out the tale, and stop when the people cannot think of anything more to say" ("Fenimore Cooper's Literary Offenses" 181).
12. In a less dismissive context, Stowe is in fact often seen as a foremother to later regionalists. According to David Minter, "The writers who contributed most to the [regionalist] movement were, significantly, women. It is not too much to call them the literary daughters of Harriet Beecher Stowe" (767).
13. By picking an adolescent poetess to represent the sentimental author, Twain suggests that the main producers and consumers of sentimentality are genteel girls. Although Huck Finn himself is awed by Emmeline's productions, when left to his own devices he prefers adventure stories. As Barbara Hochman notes, "Advocates of 'realism,' launching a concerted attack on sentiment and romance, took the young girl not only as the prototypical novel-reader, but also as 'the iron Madonna' whose taste was destroying American literature" (*Uncle* 142). Until the 1990s, most critics assumed that only women produced sentimental works. For scholarship that finally debunked this idea, see Mary Chapman and Glenn Hendler's *Sentimental Men*, which builds on the claims made by a special issue of *American Literature* called *No More Separate Spheres!* (Davidson), one of the first works to question the association of women and sentimentality.
14. In *The Writing of Fiction*, first serialized in Scribner's (1924–25) and later collected into a book (1925), Wharton has ideas about how to construct a modern character similar to Howells's. She praises Balzac as "the first not only to see his people, physically and morally, in their habit as they lived . . . but to draw his dramatic action as much from the relation of his characters to their houses, streets, towns, professions, inherited habits and opinions, as from their fortuitous contacts with each other" (5). Characters have distinctive characteristics and backstories; they're not types. This characterization of characterization suggests Wharton's view of the impoverished state of sentimental characterization. See Hoeller for an extended discussion of Wharton's ideas about how to create modern characters that she laid out in *The Writing of Fiction*.
15. "Reading" in the sense literary critics use it often means "interpreting," so it can apply to both what real people do in the world and what they do with books. Realist authors often model what their readers should do (how they should read) by depicting what a character does within the storyworld (how she interprets the people and events around her).
16. Boudreau also offers a thematic analysis of *Annie Kilburn*, arguing that Howells uses the novel to illuminate how charity reinforces class differences rather than ameliorates them.
17. Claybaugh has shown that not just this novel but realist novels in general draw and meditate on not just an American culture of benevolence but a transatlantic tradition of reform.
18. Howells does not often use the word "sentimentality" in the novel (he does use "sentimental" and "sentimentalist" once each), but he describes certain dispositions of his characters

and certain artistic productions in ways that parallel the attacks on sentimentality that would become a staple of twentieth-century criticism.

19. "Mortally Wounded," anonymously published in 1863 and widely recirculated, was one of the most popular poems during the Civil War. It was commonly understood to have been written by a dying Civil War soldier but was actually written by Mary Woolsey Howland, a resident of Astoria, New York, as Ellen Gruber Garvey has revealed.

20. For example, in one representative conversation early in the novel, Dr. Morrill responds to the very sincere things Annie says about sympathy and reform "with a laugh lurking under his gravity" (733), by "laugh[ing] outright" (733), and by "laugh[ing] again" (736). Finally, the conversation "end[s] with another laugh, in which after a moment of indignant self-question, she joined him" (736). Sentimental reform—how amusing!

21. John Beckman discusses Twain's and Howells's dedication to the idea of "pure facts" as a realist ideal even as realist authors, according to Beckman, resorted to adding hybrid elements to their realist novels to defend that ideal. Beckman's idea of realism as a mixed genre is similar to Fredric Jameson's, although the elements he sees it mixed with—mainly satire and burlesque—do not include sentimentality.

22. I've discussed "unreliable focalization" in earlier chapters, but here's a refresher. Unreliable focalization works similarly to the unreliable narration found in first-person narratives: the author has designed the text so that the reader finds that she must reject the facts, perceptions, or judgments of the focalizing character, from whose perspective the reader is seeing the world.

23. For more details about disingenuous eloquence and the sentimental response, see my *Sentimental Readers*.

24. For Stowe, one cannot feel right without doing right. Feeling right is not separable from doing right in two senses: one cannot feel at peace unless one has acted morally, and sympathetic identification cannot but function as a spur to action, as *Uncle Tom's Cabin* shows over and over, pace Suzanne Keen, one of whose interesting points in *Empathy and the Novel* is that sympathy does not necessarily result in pro-social action. In my opinion, the passage about feeling right is one of the most misunderstood in Stowe's novel.

25. By "breakthrough New York novel," Bremer means that *Hazard* ushers in a new paradigm for writing about cities, breaking with an older tradition of writing about cities as if they were "overgrown towns" (296).

26. I am indebted to Nancy Bentley's *Frantic Panoramas* and its claim that realist literature is preoccupied with clashing elements, both in terms of its themes and its structure (99). In terms of the latter, Bentley notes "realism's reliance on the mass forms it opposes" (99). Along these lines, she observes that *A Hazard of New Fortunes* examines "the costs and violent conflicts of an economics of culture" (99).

27. For example, Phillip Barrish writes that one of the major themes of his *Cambridge Introduction to American Literary Realism* will be "the claim by William Dean Howells . . . that literary realism would help America more fully to achieve its democratic principles of equality, unity, and the toleration of difference" (6). Barrish goes on: "For Howells, American literary realism had the potential to represent 'democracy in literature.' 'Men are more like than unlike one another,' Howells proclaimed" (6).

28. But not always. At times the commentary about a character could not be clearer. For example, the narrator begins his description of how Dryfoos made his fortune with this statement: "[Dryfoos's] moral decay began with his perception of the opportunity of making money quickly and abundantly" (263). From such condemnations, we are encouraged to condemn the blunt, proud, stubborn Dryfoos's attitude toward his son Conrad.

29. One example of this ambiguity happens in a passage that discusses a stroll that Basil takes

down Mott Street in the second part's chapter 11. Howells intersperses in this description what seem to be a stream of indications that this tour is being focalized through March: "March had a sense . . . It was a fancy, of course . . . March understood . . . He said . . ." (186). But this is in fact not a steady stream but more of a trickle. There are sentences of description seemingly untethered to Basil ("Their numbers . . . there") and there are also instances that lie in between.

30. Claybaugh's insight that realist writers wrote "novels of purpose" can explain Howells's rejection of Basil's purely aesthetic response to poverty. Where my interpretation of these novels differs from Claybaugh's is in her sense that the realists rejected sentimental modes of writing and sentimental understandings of reform even as they kept many other features of antebellum reform novels.
31. Howells once remarked that "[James] felt obliged to prove his familiarity with continental literature by insulting ours" (qtd. in Daugherty, "William Dean Howells" 14).
32. We can contrast Howells's method to Martha Nussbaum's. In *Love's Knowledge*, Nussbaum is, like Howells, interested in pursuing the question of "how [best] should a human being live" (25). Nussbaum chooses to follow what she calls "the Aristotelian procedure," which "tells us to be respectful of difference; but it also instructs us to look for a consistent and shareable answer to the 'how to live' question, one that will capture what is deepest and most basic, even though it will, of necessity, to achieve that aim, have to give up certain other things" (28). As does *Hazard*, Nussbaum requires that we consider different perspectives, but she also requires that we eventually stop the considerations and settle on an answer, even knowing that it will result in losing certain possibilities. How different an agenda this seems to be from *Hazard*'s own, for most of the novel.
33. For a detailed account of Howells's reaction to the riots and his subsequent defense of the anarchists involved, four of whom were eventually hanged, see Boudreau's *Sympathy in American Literature* 150–53.
34. See Claudia Stokes's discussion in "The Religious Novel" of the tensions between "Muscular Christianity" and its antithesis, the Social Gospel movement.
35. "Mask narration" is a term taken from James Phelan (*Somebody* 99).
36. Claybaugh analyzes this moment differently: she sees it as part of Twain's attack on sentimentality.
37. This is not the only sentimental scene in the novel. There is also a sentimental scene, in chapter 21, involving a slave coffle and the separation of an enslaved husband and wife, and another scene, in chapter 40, involving Hank's nursing of his daughter, Hello-Central, in which scene her existence transcends the joke of her name and she flares briefly into life.
38. See Steven Wandler, "Hogs, Not Maidens," for an investigation of this question. Wandler's article is especially interesting for the way it apprehends what seems like a clear case of "sympathy" as "objectivity," which enables him to position realism as trafficking in objectivity rather than sympathy.
39. William Manierre alludes to how *The Rise of Silas Lapham* is "generally granted" to be Howells's "masterpiece" (357), and Brook Thomas calls *Adventures of Huckleberry Finn* "mythical" ("*Adventures*" 1).
40. By contrast, many instructors have disqualified it as a classroom text because of its innumerable repetitions (211 times according to David E. E. Sloane) of the "N-word."
41. Yet they have also come in for critique from scholars of disability. In "Disabling Assumptions," Dynnelle Fields et al. describe a deaf student's appalled reaction to hearing how Jim received the news of his daughter's deafness as a tragedy (95).

CHAPTER 3: The Unmastering of Henry James, or, Searching for Sentimentality in *The Bostonians*

1. There are too many examples of this sense of mastery to cite, but I'll point out that even two critical works that take James's debt to the sentimentalists seriously still find occasion to disparage their fiction. In her excellent article that traces a genealogy from nineteenth-century domestic novels to modernist works, using *The Spoils of Poynton* as her example, Bonita Rhoads calls sentimental fiction "saccharine and overblown" (147). Habegger, who aims to defend this literature against what he sees as James's dismissal of it, nevertheless reveals he finds it immature when he talks at one point about how women's fiction "was beginning to grow up" in the 1860s (*Henry James* 22).
2. One can see this contempt in a passage from James's review of Stowe's *We and Our Neighbors*: "The reader remains in an atmosphere of dense backstairs detail which makes him feel as if he were reading an interminable file of tradesmen's bills" (qtd. in Habegger, *Henry James* 14).
3. An early work of this kind is Jane Tompkins's *Sensational Designs*, the work in which her chapter on *Uncle Tom's Cabin*, "Sentimental Power," appears; a more recent work is Barbara Hochman's *Uncle Tom's Cabin and the Reading Revolution*, which charts how dramatically the estimation of Stowe's novel changed in the postbellum period, becoming a defanged and nostalgic artifact rather than the immersive and revolutionary document it had originally been.
4. The most obvious example of a person using Verena for profit is her father, who allows Verena to live with Olive in return for a check. Through this transaction, however, Olive is complicit in the "thingifying" of Verena as well: as Hochman puts it, Olive "literally leases Verena from her father for a year at a time" ("Reading Historically" 275).
5. Aaron Shaheen attributes this propensity to Basil rather than James: Basil "refuses to credit her with the subjectivity she tries time and again to claim for herself" (186). I'm unsure whether Verena is trying to claim her own subjectivity throughout the novel, but it is not just Basil who refuses to credit her subjectivity but also James (via his narrator). Further, I believe that this is not a reactionary move on James's part but a potentially liberatory one.
6. One final reason I classify Verena as an "object" is to connect my argument to Jane Thrailkill's discussion of James in *Affecting Fictions*. I cannot here do justice to Thrailkill's brilliant and complex analysis, but I can note a couple of points of convergence: our shared sense of James's investigation of the wonder that people can imbue objects with and our shared sense of his commitment to constructing women characters whose most salient aspect is their receptiveness. (Thrailkill sees Milly Theale this way.) I attempt to add to her discussion by discussing the effect of the distinction I explore later in this chapter between how characters in the storyworld react to Verena (with wonder) and how James's intended readers do (less with wonder than with curiosity about a mystery that James refuses to solve).
7. In "Reclaiming Sentimental Literature," Dobson demonstrates that she is the intended reader of *Uncle Tom's Cabin*, as we can see when she discusses the scene in which Eva gives away locks of her hair: "Eva's generosity is constructed within a cultural and historical context where all too often children *did* die, were snatched incomprehensibly from the arms of helpless families—as Harriet Beecher Stowe knew only too painfully" (273). Here Dobson recurs to the reality of what Stowe was writing about, taking on a tone of anguish herself (as well as taking on Stowe's love of dashes). I greatly admire Dobson's approach to *Uncle Tom's Cabin*, so rare among literary critics, at the same time that I think

this approach makes it difficult to explore Stowe's sentimental techniques since it tends to deny they are techniques at all.
8. For example, Weinstein's paradigm-enlarging third chapter, "Thinking through Sympathy: Kemble, Hentz, Stowe" (66–94), shows how the discourse of sympathy is deployed across the ideological spectrum in both anti- and proslavery texts. Through intricate close readings, Weinstein identifies how the three authors named in the title enjoin their readers to feel sympathetic to very different populations and by means of different formal techniques.
9. Bayley himself attributes this lack of sentimentality to James's healthy respect for money. According to Bayley, discussing *The Golden Bowl*, James would not understand a reader's lack of sympathy for Maggie and her father on the basis of their vast wealth, "the economic scales . . . weighted so overwhelmingly in their favor." For Bayley, "James, the least sentimental of writers, would not feel himself bound to defer to the tendency to side with penniless passion" (235).
10. The impulse to measure James's artistry according to how far he has departed from earlier genres does not die out after Bayley. See Lee Ann Johnson for more details.
11. For an insightful account of the way that women's rights activists in the latter part of the nineteenth century used the metaphor of "enslavement" to describe white women's plight, see Karen Sanchez-Eppler.
12. For an alternative account of the conventionality of sentimental poetry, see Claudia Stokes, who in "The Poetics of Unoriginality" highlights how the conventionality of Lucretia Davidson's poetry allowed her to transform herself into a figure of moral authority for her readers.
13. Evaluation in sentimental novels works differently. For example, on the very first page of *Uncle Tom's Cabin*, we meet a slave trader named Haley: "He was a short, thick-set man, with coarse, commonplace features, and that swaggering air of pretension which marks a low man who is trying to elbow his way upward in the world" (1). The reader knows exactly how to judge Haley, and all of his later actions confirm this judgment.
14. In *Uncle Tom's Cabin*, characters sometimes render judgments of other characters, but these judgments are themselves easy to assess: if the character is sympathetic, the judgment is trustworthy; if he is unsympathetic, it is not. James's species of judgment—judgment as something that might be only partially trustworthy and as something that is as revealing of the judger as the judged—is absent in *Uncle Tom's Cabin*.
15. For a different view, see Lynn Wardley, who argues for James's support for a qualified form of women's public voice.
16. Victoria Coulson makes a similar point in her characterization of James's "profound imaginative kinship with women, an affiliative communion with feminine structures of subjectivity that is unparalleled elsewhere in the work of nineteenth-century male writers" (*Henry James* 5).
17. Here is how Herbert Ross Brown characterizes the scribbling women: "Imbued with a lyric faith in the perfectibility of man, they regarded the America of their own day as a mere vestibule to Utopia. They preferred to dwell in a cozy cloudland of sentiment, secure in a haven of dreams" (359). This characterization of the sentimentalists as incapable of deep or rebellious thinking is picked up by Douglas.
18. I use this term advisedly in light of the critique Jonathan D. Culler has made of the concept of "omniscient narrator." I justify its use in this context because so many readers still use the term and will identify the narrator of *The Bostonians* as such. If we were to use Shlomith Rimmon-Kenan's terminology, we would call it external focalization, narration that "is felt to be close to the narrating agent" (76), in this case close to the heterodiegetic narrator.

19. Against this assessment is an interpretation of *The Bostonians* developed in Glenn Hendler's excellent article "The Limits of Sympathy," which sees the "paradox of sympathetic politics . . . viciously satirized" (700) in this novel, which, according to Hendler, finds James "unambiguously assert[ing] the impossibility of reconciling sentimental femininity with liberal individualism" (701). Hendler perceives similarities between Miss Birdseye and Verena which propel him to see James as dismissing them both, whereas I see the novel as handling them differently in its narrative technique, a distinction that leads to my own conclusion about the undecidability of James's attitude toward the sentimental object and, by extension, reform efforts that use sentimental appeals.
20. Nancy Glazener discusses the high realist contempt for what she calls "addictive" reading practices in chapter 3 of *Reading for Realism*.

CHAPTER 4: Constance Fenimore Woolson's Rhetorical Passing

1. Anne Boyd Rioux's biography *Constance Fenimore Woolson: Portrait of a Lady Novelist*, came out in 2016, the same year as her edited collection of Woolson's stories, *Miss Grief and Other Stories*. Another collection of Woolson's stories had come out in 2004: *Constance Fenimore Woolson: Selected Stories and Travel Narratives*, edited by Victoria Brehm and Sharon L. Dean.
2. Such binary judgments also ignore how even *Uncle Tom's Cabin* works narratively. *Uncle Tom's Cabin* isn't sentimental all the time; it's studded with sarcasm, description, and political invective. Nonetheless, it is sentimental a lot of the time, leading to a ratio that makes it fair, I think, to call it a "sentimental novel."
3. Howells, Twain, and of course James share an interest in home decor. In *Adventures of Huckleberry Finn*, Twain mocks, through Huck's ingenuous perspective, the Grangerfords' parlor, and Howells spends time in both *The Rise of Silas Lapham* and *A Hazard of New Fortunes* describing the interiors of his characters' houses and apartments; like Twain, he uses these interior spaces not just to illuminate the characters from whose perspectives we see these rooms but to hone his readers' taste in domestic appointments.
4. According to Rioux, Woolson did sometimes receive unmixed praise from discriminating male critics ("A New Era"). Among her admirers was Charles Dudley Warner, Twain's coauthor on *The Gilded Age* and member of the editorial staff of *Harper's Monthly Magazine* from 1884 to 1892. As well as plagiarizing from Woolson in an early draft of *The Gilded Age* (Rioux, *Portrait* 81), he also wrote, according to Rioux, "one of the most admiring obituaries she received" (*Portrait* 82). Yet even in Warner's glowing obituary, we can discern an element that less admiring male critics latched onto. Warner wrote that Woolson "was an observer, a sympathetic observer and a refined observer, entering sufficiently into the analytic mode of the time, but she had *courage to deal with the passions*, and life as it is" (967; emphasis added). What Warner calls "dealing with the passions" seems another way of naming the sentimentality that other less admiring male readers highlight and that, a century later, feminist critics would disavow.
5. According to Edel, Woolson "had come to Europe half in love with James from her close reading of his works. . . . She was a somewhat deaf spinster, trim, compulsive, and meticulous, who wrote popular fiction for the women's magazines" (xvi–xvii).
6. Here's the full quotation from Harvey, who was editor of *Harper's* from 1901 through 1913: "At that time our women were writing fiction, not eminent in constructive art or for wit, humor, or philosophy, as compared with their brother writers, but nearer to nature and more intimately human" (961). Among these postbellum women writers Harvey includes Woolson, who along with a few others of "initiated a more native . . . fiction" (961).

Hovering over this characterization of Woolson and other of "our women" is the suggestion that they are subject to biological imperatives, which prevent them from representing life so much as transcribing what they see around them, a familiar way of characterizing the antebellum sentimentalists, who were artless, according to later critics, not in the sense that they were honest but in the sense that they lacked the ability to produce art.

7. This claim about their artistry was established after some initial rescue assessments that downplayed it, for example, when Nina Baym, in *Woman's Fiction*, conceded that "a reexamination of this fiction may well show it to lack the esthetic, intellectual, and moral complexity and artistry that we demand of great literature" (14), a claim she qualified in subsequent editions. In the case of Woolson herself, as Rioux has observed, her embrace by feminist critics was complicated somewhat by the fact that her stories didn't always take a female point of view ("A New Era"). As I try to demonstrate, however, the feminist critics who rescued Woolson followed broader feminist rescue trends in highlighting her artistry.

8. In previous chapters I've focused on the bond that sentimental writing instantiates between characters and readers, but sentimental authors can also bring readers to feel close to their narrators and to themselves. This happens in *Uncle Tom's Cabin*. It happens intertextually because Stowe's narrator functions as Stowe's mouthpiece, so readers are invited to see Stowe as their guide and friend. It also happens epitextually, when a reader finds out that Stowe was inspired to write *Uncle Tom's Cabin* by the death of her son Charley and thus is invited to see Stowe as someone who, like Eliza, Mrs. Bird, and possibly the reader, has also lost a child. Although concerned with first-person narrators, Susan Lanser, in "The 'I' of the Beholder," discusses the conditions that lead readers to associate narrators with authors.

9. Let me review these terms briefly. Unreliable narration occurs when a narrative is in the first person and we are meant to perceive a distance between the narrator's perceptions, judgments, or evaluations and our own. Unreliable focalization functions similarly but occurs when a third-person narrative is told from the perspective of an unreliable character. Focalized narration is sometimes called "free indirect discourse," although that is a subset of unreliable focalization. (Focalization can also be signaled by direct discourse.)

10. This is not to say that critics never call the occasional Woolson narrator unreliable. For example, Rioux calls the narrator of "'Miss Grief'" unreliable in "Anticipating James, Anticipating Grief." She does not use the term, however, in her more recent biography of Woolson. "Unreliability" for most literary scholars does not have the significance that it does for narratologists. Within narrative studies, "narrative unreliability" has both a precise definition and a host of accompanying debates. For an excellent overview of how it works and the debates around it, see James Phelan's *Living to Tell about It*.

11. In what follows, I'll reserve the term "masterful" for readings and readers that recognize the subtext in texts that rhetorically pass; I'll continue to use "discerning" reading for the kind of critically distanced reading that Twain, Howells, Wharton, and James advocate and teach their readers to perform.

12. Although Deborah E. McDowell does not use the term "rhetorical passing," she has also identified the lesbian subtext in *Passing* in her introduction to the Rutgers University Press edition of *Passing*.

13. It's not named as such in this story, but it is named in another story by Woolson, "St. Clair Flats." Zoar was also an actual village in Ohio, founded by German separatists.

14. What to make of the fact that Sol can produce his masterpiece only after being schooled by Erminia, the eastern sophisticate? Sol might need the technical lesson in perspective Erminia teaches him, but Woolson emphasizes that what Erminia teaches him is mere empty form: "the merely mechanical hand [of Erminia] explaining its art to [Sol's] ignorant

fingers of genius" (64). In comparing their hands, Woolson once again highlights, for the masterful reader, the emptiness of the lives of Erminia and the narrator versus the emotionally rich lives of Sol and Dorcas.

15. For example, Joan Myers Weimer focuses on Catherine, the failed artist figure in Woolson's 1876 short story "Felipa." Weimer writes that "Woolson's identification with her women artist characters is more complex in this story . . . because here both the repressed woman painter and her wild alter ego Felipa represent parts of Woolson herself" (xxxiv–v).

16. Phelan distinguishes six different kinds of unreliability, along the axes of reporting, interpreting, and judging. Narrators can get facts wrong or not convey salient ones; they can err in their interpretation of characters or events, either interpreting them incorrectly or not going far enough in their interpretation; or they can judge an event or character wrongly or judge them correctly but again not go far enough (*Living* 49–53).

17. Building on the idea of Miss Grief's odd and unfeminine appearance, Kristin M. Comment identifies Miss Grief as a queer figure and her writing as queer writing. While I agree that Miss Grief's unfashionableness supports a queer reading, I think it also evokes the postbellum dismissal of sentimental writing as unfashionable and unsophisticated.

18. Here I am referring to a heuristic developed by Sandra Gustafson in *Eloquence Is Power* to describe an influential way people in nineteenth-century America thought about the relationship between print and orality.

19. I realize this point can seem to contradict what I've said elsewhere about sentimentality: that it has less to do with content (what happens) than with establishing an intimate relationship between tellers, characters, and readers. An appeal to the primacy of pain and suffering can establish a sentimental relationship very quickly because it so directly evokes sympathy. It's not that one cannot depict pain in a realist manner but that this depiction will lead to different kinds of (more distanced) relationships between text and reader.

20. "The Birth-Mark" ends with the protagonist's successful removal of the birthmark from the cheek of his wife, Georgiana, but with one unfortunate side effect: her death: "As the last crimson tint of the birth-mark—that sole token of human imperfection—faded from her cheek, the parting breath of the now perfect woman passed into the atmosphere" (193). There's a remarkable parallel between that story and "'Miss Grief'" as we can see when the narrator comments, "The scattered rays of splendor in Miss Grief's drama had made me forget the dark spots, which were numerous and disfiguring; or, rather, the splendor had made me anxious to have the spots removed" (168–69).

21. Annie Fields, a friend of Stowe's and wife of her publisher, published in *Life and Letters* a reminiscence of a friend of Stowe's named Mrs. Howard. When Mrs. Howard inquired of Stowe how she could have written *Uncle Tom's Cabin* without ever having been to the South, Stowe responded that the novel "all came before me in visions, one after another, and I put them down in words." When Mrs. Howard pressed her that she must at least have arranged the events in her novel, Stowe disagreed: "'No,' said she, 'your Annie reproached me for letting Eva die. Why! I could not help it" (164).

22. In *Criticism and Fiction*, Howells writes that critics should be "gentle, dispassionate, [and] scientific" (55).

23. For an explanation of authorial versus narrative audience, see chapter 1, pp. 44–46.

24. Thinking along similar lines, Naomi Greyser describes the effect of the sentimental as "intimacy-at-a-distance" (9) Greyser writes that authors who use sentimentality "value intimacy as a social and individual good" (10).

25. For a critique of the view of characters that sees them simply as not real and readers who do see them as such as naïve, see Marie-Laure Ryan's "What Are Characters Made Of?"

26. I have discussed only two "failed artist" stories by Woolson, but we can apply this paradigm

of unreliable narration and rhetorical passing to other stories of hers. For example, the aunt who homodiegetically narrates "Jeannette" is fascinated by and yet denigrates Jeannette, a girl of both white and Indigenous descent, who also contains traces of the sentimental artist. Jeannette is a powerful reciter of artistic works, and she is defined against the artfulness and refinement of the white characters in the story. The overt love story contains not just a covert story of lesbian desire on the aunt's part but a covert story of sentimental desire on Woolson's.

27. For example, Jane Tompkins writes, in 1978, when "Sentimental Power" was first published, that "Stowe reconceives the role of men in human history" (146), and in 1981, Nina Baym demonstrated how canonical American literature had up to that point radically favored "melodramas of beset manhood" in a chapter in *Feminism and Literary History* of the same name.

28. For details about the intentional fallacy, see, of course, William K. Wimsatt and Monroe C. Beardsley's famous essay of the same name. Two other famous declarers of the death of the author are Roland Barthes ("The Death of the Author") and Michel Foucault ("What Is an Author?").

CHAPTER 5: Weaponizing Sympathy

1. Stephen Knadler and Matthew Wilson (*Whiteness*) have provided fascinating answers to the question of why *The Marrow of Tradition* sold badly.
2. For example, the *New York Times*, in an 1898 article, explained the killing of Black men during the riot by asserting how they either fired first or refused to follow directions: one Black man "hailed by a guard, but refus[ing] to halt, and, continuing to advance, was shot" ("Nineteen Negroes Shot to Death").
3. To name but a few of these readings: as far back as 1974, William L. Andrews noted how Chesnutt constructed the conjure tales to point out slavery as the cause of the Black characters' struggles; Matthew Martin discusses Chesnutt's subversion of plantation fiction such as that written by Thomas Nelson Page; Ben Slote warns professors not to teach "The Goophered Grapevine" in a way that mirrors its original reception as apolitical; Jennifer Fleissner analyzes the conjure tale "Lonesome Ben" and uses Ben's clay-eating to illuminate Chesnutt's "diasporic regionalism"; Mary Kuhn explores the "ecocritical critique" Chesnutt mounts in the conjure tales (as well as in later works) against not just the devastation the turpentine industry was wreaking on the pine forests in the South but the racism of the conservation movement.
4. Darryl Hattenhauer recognizes this formal property with regard to *The House Behind the Cedars*, calling it "unreliable narration in the third person" (34). It's not, however, the narrator who is unreliable in this novel as well as *Marrow*; it's the focalized characters.
5. Werner asserts the lack of connection between the tales and *The Marrow of Tradition* when he remarks that Chesnutt "wrote the 'conventional' novels (*The House Behind the Cedars, The Marrow of Tradition, The Colonel's Dream*) which have veiled the complexity of the works which frame them," namely, *The Conjure Woman* and the short story "Baxter's Procrustes" (19).
6. The portrait of Chesnutt driven by a desire for literary and financial success has been drawn most clearly by Michael Nowlin. Elizabeth Hewitt is the rare critic who puts these portraits together by considering Chesnutt's interest in capitalism and financial autonomy as the foundation for his critique of slavery.
7. For example, Matthew Wilson carefully documents Chesnutt's evolving belief that "the ideology of whiteness was the fundamental problem in trying to ameliorate American

racism" ("Who Has the Right" 29). Knadler has characterized Chesnutt's attitude about race "as less a stigma against blacks, or an advantage for whites, than a cultural practice by which all are marked" (426). Craig Werner offers an explicitly deconstructionist reading of Chesnutt (and sees Chesnutt as a fellow deconstructionist), claiming that John is a figure designed to "subvert the binary oppositions on which racial privilege depends" (12).

8. Many contemporaneous reviews of *The Conjure Woman* use "venerable" to describe Julius, including James MacArthur's review in *Outlook,* anonymous reviews from the *Nebraska State Journal* and the *Daily Inter Ocean,* and Florence A. H. Morgan's review in the *Bookman*.

9. Here is how Uncle Julius subtly lets readers know about the state of near starvation the enslaved were kept in: "I reckon it ain' so much so nowadays, but befo' de wah, in slab'ry times, a [N-word] didn' mine goin' fi' er ten mile in a night, w'en dey wuz sump'n good ter eat at de yuther een" (7). Here is how he describes the enslavers' methods in finding enslaved freedom seekers: "Now it happen dat one er de [N-words] on de nex' plantation, one er ole Mars Henry Brayboy's [N-words], had runned away de day befo', en tuk ter de swamp, en ole Mars Dugal' en some er de yuther nabor w'ite folks had gone out wid dere guns en dere dogs fer ter he'p 'em hunt fer de [N-word]" (9). Unless otherwise noted, citations of "The Goophered Grapevine" are from the 2012 Norton edition of *The Conjure Stories*.

10. One such discerning reader is Hamilton Wright Mabie, who in a 1900 review in *The Outlook* writes that "none of [the tales] lacks those quiet touches of humor which are so characteristic of the negro character; but they are also full of side-lights on the tragedy of slave life—a tragedy which is brought into more striking relief because it comes out, so to speak, incidentally and by the way."

11. I say "in part" because, as a rule, a given passage will have multiple functions in a narrative. For example, the descriptions of the prejudice that Rena faces in her hometown don't just help explain why passing would be a natural choice; they also underline the inflexible nature of the color line and move the plot forward.

12. In this chapter I use the more neutral term "interpretive narrator" rather than "intrusive narrator."

13. Stowe's narrator does report different characters' thoughts and feelings, but those thoughts and feelings do not take over the narration: "'To-night!' Eliza repeated, 'to-night!' The words lost all meaning to her; her head was dreamy and confused" (126). This is not a description of what Eliza is thinking about herself; it's a description, from an external perspective, of what's going on in Eliza's head, what Dorrit Cohn calls "psycho-narration" (*Transparent Minds*).

14. A small remark by the narrator will, I hope, illustrate the extent to which the narrator rejects the idea that Black people and white people belong to separate races in the postbellum period. The narrator is commenting on Rena's accent and how it shares something of the accent of an "old black woman," an attribute her brother does not perceive: "That it had a faint suggestiveness of the old woman's accent he hardly noticed, for the current Southern speech, including his own, was rarely without a touch of it. The corruption of the white people's speech was one element—only one—of the negro's unconscious revenge for his own debasement" (6). The ironies of this passage are many. Here is a white-passing Black man unaware of the way the two "races" have intermingled linguistically (and, from the evidence of Rena's brother's appearance, in other ways, too). Here is a narrator who breaches the defenses of his white readers with the idea of linguistic "corruption." Yet later in the same sentence, this corruption is attributed to revenge by southern Black people, with the unspoken point being that there's something that white people have done to them to warrant it.

15. Another passage that evinces white people's sense of racial superiority occurs at a luncheon Tryon attends that features one of the attendees offering up the toast "The Anglo-Saxon race: may it remain forever, as now, the head and front of creation" (92), a sentiment heartily endorsed by Tryon, "who felt in this company a thrill of that pleasure which accompanies conscious superiority" (92).
16. This is a tenet of good pedagogy found in the scholarship of teaching and learning; for example, the first chapter of *How Learning Works* explains how instructors need to take advantage of students' prior knowledge.
17. The presence of this interpretive narrator is likely one of the reasons why an anonymous reviewer in the *Detroit Free Press* introduces the novel as a "novel of purpose" ("An Issue" 11), and an anonymous reviewer in the *Denver Times* labels it a "sorrowful tragedy" ("The Mixture" 13).
18. Maria Windell also frames sentimentality as a strategy that can be used by authors, particularly marginalized ones. She asserts "the importance of conceiving of sentimentalism as a strategic tool, rather than a morally or emotionally freighted discourse" (2). I'd only add that its utility as a strategy depends on its being such a discourse.
19. Knadler justifies this move as Chesnutt's response to white supremacists who saw Blacks as a homogenous (and inferior) race.
20. Ian Finseth has also noted how critics want to "[advance] our understanding of Chesnutt's contribution to the African American literary tradition" (1).
21. Matthew Martin might seem to be an exception to this rule, but in his article comparing the conjure tales to Page's plantation stories, he stresses the similarities only at the beginning of the article. He devotes the latter part to enumerating Chesnutt's differences from them.
22. Barbara Hochman has shown, however, that the novel did not retain its power for many other readers. By the postbellum period, the book had only a historical significance for them. As she puts it, "An emphasis on the book's historical significance soon became the most popular strategy for promoting it" (*Uncle Tom's Cabin* 145).
23. This connection between Chesnutt and *Uncle Tom's Cabin* was one that contemporaneous reviewers also made. I quoted from the *New York Press* reviewer earlier. An anonymous reviewer for the *Illustrated Buffalo Express* writes that the novel is "'Uncle Tom's Cabin' under modern conditions—the conditions that have led to the cry of 'no negro domination,' to disfranchisement of the black man, to mob, murder and race riot" ("From the Negro Side").
24. For Glazener, unlike for McElrath and Simmons, the sentimental tradition had not been abandoned in the postbellum period. Glazener discusses a romantic tradition that existed alongside a postbellum realist one. My own emphasis, however, is on how narrative conventions from what are seen as different traditions can exist within a single work.
25. Chesnutt wrote to Jerome Howard while he was working on *Marrow*: "The notion that a man with such a drop of blood can have the same intelligence, culture, aspirations, ideas, foibles, and weakness as a 'real' white man can't be knocked into some people with a club.... [But] I believe it can be surreptitiously introduced by just such a story as you know so well how to write" (qtd. in Knadler 429).
26. Knadler's excellent article on Chesnutt's views of race nevertheless conforms to the Purity Principle of realism, asserting that *The Marrow of Tradition* "is a hard novel to classify." He goes on to say that "it at times seems realistic, at other times cloyingly melodramatic" (429). It's hard to classify only if we hold on to the idea that realist novels do not contain sentimental scenes and characters.

27. Eric Sundquist has spoken more generally of the mixing of Black (including both African American and African) and white cultural forms, especially in terms of the cakewalk, which he sees as the central trope of *The Marrow of Tradition*.
28. See Katrina Dyonne Thompson's historical tracing of this figure from *Uncle Tom's Cabin* to *The Help*.
29. Contemporary readers might disagree with my claim that it's only in the last part of the novel that they stand revealed; contemporary readers recognize early on that they're not just scoundrels but racists of the deepest hue. I discuss this possibility in detail in the Afterword.
30. The narrator describes Price as "a liberal man, from his point of view" (*Marrow* 86). Readers can easily pass by "from his point of view."
31. Simmons does not consider the final scene of *The Marrow of Tradition* to be sentimental. He writes, "I do not wish to discount the pyrotechnics of scenes such as the last chapter of *The Marrow of Tradition*, since such scenes are central to [Chesnutt's] vision and part of his realist approach, but I also hope to show that such dramatic moments are not cheap effects but the payoff of a carefully controlled depiction of reality" (7). The subtext of this sentence, as I read it, is the worry that such a scene will be taken to be sentimental because of its "pyrotechnics" and "dramatic moments." We can also read this worry in his assurances that this scene is in fact "carefully controlled": sentimental writing is often thought of as excessive or sloppy.
32. The groundwork is laid for sentimental self-identification in the penultimate scene: "Carteret possessed a narrow, but a logical mind, and except when confused or blinded by his prejudices, had always tried to be a just man. In the agony of his own predicament,—in the horror of the situation at Miller's house,—for a moment the veil of race prejudice was rent in twain, and he saw things as they were, in their correct proportions and relations,—saw clearly and convincingly that he had no standing here, in the presence of death, in the home of this stricken family" (241). Here's hoping, Reader, that the same may happen to you via this passage rather than via your son's imminent threat of death.
33. Christine Wooley also alludes to the failure of Chesnutt's body of work to much alter white readers' perceptions of their role in maintaining the racial order, but she sees Chesnutt as embedding that recognition of probable failure, what she calls "the limits of American literary realism" (198), in the works themselves. Discussing *The Colonel's Dream*, Wooley argues how it "shows us that interventions in falsities and assumptions do not necessarily result in justice" (198). Wooley sees this failure as tied to the realist project and what in retrospect seems like its naïve belief that pointing out facts in their proper relation will cause (white) readers to acknowledge them. I am building on her excellent work by noting that the failure might also arise from an inherent feature of sentimental sympathy.
34. Other literary critics have taken Howells to be a stand-in for the novel's typical reader, which is why his remark about its bitterness almost inevitably appears somewhere in contemporary articles about the novel. Bufkin shows that his assessment of the novel, specifically the way he seems to feel personally attacked by it, is, in fact, anomalous.
35. Yet this view did not preclude other reviewers from citing its realism. For example, a 1901 review says of the novel that "it is the highest type of realism, for it presents certain phases of contemporaneous life of which the public should have full knowledge if existing evils are ever to be eradicated" (Review of *Marrow, Daily Time*). Similarly, another review claims that "the riot he describes ought have been photographed in a dozen Southern towns ... and even minor details and atmospheric effects of the book carry with them the conviction of actuality" (Review of *Marrow, Times*). These reviewers, however, seem to be thinking about the novel's realism in the sense of its being realistic rather than as a genre of literary fiction the way that Howells does.

36. For example, in chapter 27, Major Carteret "suavely" (184) explains to Mr. Delamere why the proposed lynching of old Mr. Delamere's loyal Black servant Sandy is a noble endeavor: "The white men of this city, impelled by the highest and holiest sentiments, were about to take steps to defend their hearthstones and maintain the purity and ascendancy of their race" (184). This oratorical effusion is met with a yell of "'Rah, 'rah!" by a "tipsy sailor" (184). One can easily imagine a contemporaneous white reader who might have held on to his sympathy for Major Carteret up to this point withdrawing it upon reading this passage. Regardless of whether or not that reader in fact embraces Carteret's view, they might not want to align themselves with a "tipsy sailor."
37. See Phelan's "Estranging Unreliability, Bonding Unreliability, and the Ethics of *Lolita*" and my "Closeness through Unreliability: Sympathy, Empathy, and Ethics in Narrative Communication" for details on when this can happen.

AFTERWORD

1. Here is how Booth describes what happens when a reader reconstructs an ironic passage: "I see that it completes a more astonishing communal achievement than most accounts have recognized. . . . [E]ven the most simple-minded irony, when it succeeds, reveals in both participants [the author and reader] a kind of meeting with other minds that contradicts a great deal that gets said about who we are and whether we can know each other" (*A Rhetoric of Irony* 13).
2. For a thorough account of how the Affective Fallacy instantiated a discomfort with embodied, emotional reading and of the payoff for literary criticism of embracing it, see Jane Thrailkill's introduction to *Affecting Fictions*.
3. There are other hierarchies that changing the meaning of the label "realism" would overturn, and I list them in ascending order of how difficult I think they would be to realize: that our emotional reactions to literary works should not be ignored; that sentimentality is not a debased or inherently ethically problematic literary mode; and that literary sympathy is as capable of producing positive social change as it is of obfuscating structural forms of oppression.
4. Michael Warner includes "identification" in his list of uncritical reading practices but adds other practices, including "self-forgetfulness, reverie, sentimentality, enthusiasm, literalism, aversion, distraction" (15).

Works Cited

A Carolinian. "Slavery in the Southern States." *Littell's Living Age*, vol. 35, no. 446, 1852, pp. 433–42.
Abeln, Paul. *William Dean Howells and the Ends of Realism*. Routledge, 2016.
Ambrose, Susan A., et al. *How Learning Works: Seven Research-Based Principles for Smart Teaching*. Jossey-Bass, 2010.
Anderson, Benedict. *Imagined Communities: Reflections on the Origin and Spread of Nationalism*. Verso, 1991.
Andrews, William L. "The Significance of Charles W. Chesnutt's 'Conjure Stories.'" *Southern Literary Journal*, vol. 7, no. 1, 1974, pp. 78–99.
Artese, Brian. "Overhearing Testimony: James in the Shadow of Sentimentalism." *Henry James Review*, vol. 27, no. 2, 2006, pp. 103–25.
Ashton, Susanna, and Bill Hardwig. *Approaches to Teaching the Works of Charles W. Chesnutt*. MLA, 2017.
Avrich, Paul. *The Haymarket Tragedy*. Princeton UP, 1984.
Baldwin, James. "Everybody's Protest Novel." 1955. *Uncle Tom's Cabin* by Harriet Beecher Stowe. Edited by Elizabeth Ammons, 2nd edition, Norton, 2010, pp. 495–501.
Banks, Marva. "*Uncle Tom's Cabin* and Antebellum Black Response." *Readers in History: Nineteenth-Century American Literature and the Contexts of Response*, edited by James L. Machor, Johns Hopkins UP, 1993, pp. 209–25.
Barnes, Elizabeth. *States of Sympathy: Seduction and Democracy in the American Novel*. Cornell UP, 1997.
Barrish, Phillip J. *The Cambridge Introduction to American Literary Realism*. Cambridge UP, 2011.
Barthes, Roland. "The Death of the Author." *The Norton Anthology of Theory and Criticism*, edited by Vincent B. Leitch, Norton, 2010, pp. 1322–26.
Batson, C. Daniel. "These Things Called Empathy: Eight Related but Distinct Phenomena." *The Social Neuroscience of Empathy*, MIT Press, 2009, pp. 3–15.

Bayley, John. *The Characters of Love: A Study in the Literature of Personality.* Constable, 1960.

Baym, Nina. *Feminism and Literary History.* Rutgers UP, 1981.

———. *Woman's Fiction: A Guide to Novels by and about Women in America, 1820–1870.* 1978. U of Illinois P, 1993.

Beam, Dorri. "Henry James, Constance Fenimore Woolson, and the Figure in the Carpet." *American Literature's Aesthetic Dimensions*, edited by Cindy Weinstein and Christopher Looby, Columbia UP, 2012, pp. 137–55.

Bean, Judith Mattson, and Joel Myerson, editors. *Margaret Fuller, Critic: Writings from the New-York Tribune, 1844–1846.* Columbia UP, 2002.

Beckman, John. "The Church of Fact: Genre Hybridity in *Huckleberry Finn* and *Silas Lapham*." *Arizona Quarterly*, vol. 69, no. 3, 2013, pp. 23–48.

Bentley, Nancy. *Frantic Panoramas: American Literature and Mass Culture, 1870–1920.* U of Pennsylvania P, 2009.

Berlant, Lauren. *The Female Complaint: The Unfinished Business of Sentimentality in American Culture.* Duke UP, 2008.

———. "Poor Eliza." *American Literature*, vol. 70, no. 3, 1998, pp. 635–68.

Bernstein, Susan. "Promiscuous Reading: The Problem of Identification and Anne Frank's Diary." *Witnessing the Disaster: Essays on Representation and the Holocaust*, edited by Michael F. Bernard-Donals and Richard R. Glejzer, U of Wisconsin P, 2003, pp. 141–61.

Best, Stephen, and Sharon Marcus. "Surface Reading: An Introduction." *Representations*, vol. 108, no. 1, 2009, pp. 1–21.

The Bible. New King James Version, HarperCollins, 1982.

"Book Review of *The Conjure Woman*." *Outlook*, vol. 61, 1899, p. 884. *Charles Chesnutt Digital Archive*, https://chesnuttarchive.org/item/ccda.rev00031.

Booth, Wayne C. *The Rhetoric of Fiction.* 1961. U of Chicago P, 2008.

———. *A Rhetoric of Irony.* U of Chicago P, 1974.

Borus, Daniel H. *Writing Realism: Howells, James, and Norris in the Mass Market.* U of North Carolina P, 1989.

Boudreau, Kristin. *Sympathy in American Literature: American Sentiments from Jefferson to the Jameses.* UP of Florida, 2002.

Brehm, Victoria. "*Castle Somewhere*: Constance Fenimore Woolson's Reconstructed Great Lakes." *Constance Fenimore Woolson's Nineteenth Century: Essays*, edited by Victoria Brehm, Wayne State UP, 2001, pp. 99–110.

———. "Introduction." *Constance Fenimore Woolson's Nineteenth Century: Essays*, edited by Victoria Brehm, Wayne State UP, 2001, pp. 7–17.

Brehm, Victoria, and Sharon L. Dean. "Introduction." *Constance Fenimore Woolson: Selected Stories and Travel Narratives*, edited by Victoria Brehm and Sharon L. Dean, U of Tennessee P, 2004, pp. xv–xxvi.

Bremer, Sidney H. "Fiction's Many Cities." *A Companion to American Fiction, 1865–1914*, edited by Robert Paul Lamb and G. R. Thompson, Wiley-Blackwell, 2009, pp. 296–317.

Brodhead, Richard. *Cultures of Letters: Scenes of Reading and Writing in Nineteenth-Century America*. U of Chicago P, 1993.

———. Introduction. *The Journals of Charles W. Chesnutt*, edited by Richard Brodhead, Duke UP, 1993, pp. 1–36.

Brown, Candy Gunther. *The Word in the World: Evangelical Writing, Publishing, and Reading in America, 1789–1880*. U of North Carolina P, 2004.

Brown, Gillian. "Reading and Children: *Uncle Tom's Cabin* and *The Pearl of Orr's Island*." *The Cambridge Companion to Harriet Beecher Stowe*, edited by Cindy Weinstein, Cambridge UP, 2004, pp. 77–95.

Brown, Herbert Ross. *The Sentimental Novel in America, 1789–1860*. Duke UP, 1940.

Bufkin, Sydney. "'Beyond 'Bitter': Chesnutt's *The Marrow of Tradition*." *American Literary Realism*, vol. 46, no. 3, 2014, pp. 230–50.

Camfield, Gregg. *Sentimental Twain: Samuel Clemens in the Maze of Moral Philosophy*. U of Pennsylvania P, 1994.

Campbell, Donna. "Regionalism and Local Color Fiction, 1865–1895." *Washington State University*, https://public.wsu.edu/~campbelld/amlit/lcolor.html.

Carr, Jean Ferguson, Stephen L. Carr, and Lucille M. Schultz. *Archives of Instruction: Nineteenth-Century Rhetorics, Readers, and Composition Books in the United States*. Southern Illinois UP, 2005.

Carter, Everett. "William Dean Howells' Theory of Critical Realism." *ELH*, vol. 16, no. 2, 1949, pp. 151–66. *JSTOR*, doi:10.2307/2871516.

Castiglia, Christopher. "Pedagogical Discipline and the Creation of White Citizenship: John Witherspoon, Robert Finley, and the Colonization Society." *Early American Literature*, vol. 33, no. 2, 1998, pp. 192–214.

Chakkalakal, Tess. "Who Was Charles Chesnutt?" *C19 Podcast*, season 1, episode 5, *C19*, 2018, https://www.c19society.org/podcast-season1.

Chapman, Mary, and Glenn Hendler, editors. *Sentimental Men: Masculinity and the Politics of Affect in American Culture*. U of California P, 1999.

Chesnutt, Charles. *The Conjure Stories*. Edited by Robert B. Stepto and Jennifer Rae Greeson, Norton, 2012.

———. "The Goophered Grapevine." *Atlantic Monthly*, vol. 60, 1887, no. 358, pp. 254–60.

———. "The Goophered Grapevine." *The Conjure Stories*. Edited by Robert B. Stepto and Jennifer Rae Greeson, Norton, 2012, pp. 3–14. [Based on the version that was printed in *The Conjure Woman*.]

———. *The House Behind the Cedars*. 1900. Dover, 2007.

———. *The Journals of Charles W. Chesnutt*. Edited by Richard H. Brodhead, Duke UP, 2001.

———. *The Marrow of Tradition*. 1901. Edited by Nancy Bentley and Sandra Gunning, Bedford/St. Martin's, 2002.

———. "Po' Sandy." *The Conjure Stories*. Edited by Robert B. Stepto and Jennifer Rae Greeson, Norton, 2012, pp. 14–22.

Claybaugh, Amanda. *The Novel of Purpose: Literature and Social Reform in the Anglo-American World*. Cornell UP, 2007.

Cohn, Dorrit. *The Distinction of Fiction*. John Hopkins UP, 1999.

———. *Transparent Minds: Narrative Modes for Presenting Consciousness in Fiction*. Princeton UP, 1978.

Comment, Kristin M. "The Lesbian 'Impossibilities' of Miss Grief's 'Armor.'" *Constance Fenimore Woolson's Nineteenth Century: Essays*, edited by Victoria Brehm, Wayne State UP, 2001, pp. 207–23.

Coplan, Amy. "Understanding Empathy: Its Features and Effects." *Empathy: Philosophical and Psychological Perspectives*, edited by Coplan and Peter Goldie, Oxford UP, 2014, pp. 3–18.

Corbaux, Louisa. "Topsy at Her Tricks." *Uncle Tom's Cabin* by Harriet Beecher Stowe. Stannard & Dixon, 1853, https://www.britishmuseum.org/collection/object/P_1976-0515-21.

Coulson, Victoria. *Henry James, Women and Realism*. Cambridge UP, 2007.

———. "Teacups and Love Letters: Constance Fenimore Woolson and Henry James." *Henry James Review*, vol. 26, no. 1, 2005, pp. 82–98.

Cox, James M. "Attacks on the Ending and Twain's Attack on Conscience." *Adventures of Huckleberry Finn: A Case Study in Critical Controversy*, edited by Gerald Graff and James Phelan, Bedford, 1995, pp. 305–11.

Crane, Stephen. *Maggie, a Girl of the Streets*. 1893. Modern Library, 2001.

Culler, Jonathan D. "Apostrophe." *The Pursuit of Signs: Semiotics, Literature, Deconstruction*, Cornell UP, 1981, pp. 149–71.

———. "Omniscience." *Narrative*, vol. 12, 2004, pp. 22–34. *JSTOR*, https://www.jstor.org/stable/20107328.

Cummins, Maria Susanna. *The Lamplighter*. 1854. Edited by Joanne Dobson et al., Rutgers UP, 1988.

Darnton, Robert. "First Steps toward a History of Reading." *Australian Journal of French Studies*, vol. 23, no. 1, 1986, pp. 5–30.

Dauber, Kenneth. *The Logic of Sentiment: Stowe, Hawthorne, Melville*. Bloomsbury, 2020.

Daugherty, Sarah B. "Howells, Tolstoy, and the Limits of Realism: The Case of 'Annie Kilburn.'" *American Literary Realism*, vol. 19, no. 1, 1986, pp. 21–41.

———. "William Dean Howells and Mark Twain: The Realism War as a Campaign That Failed." *American Literary Realism*, vol. 29, no. 1, 1996, pp. 12–28.

Davidson, Cathy. "Preface: No More Separate Spheres!" *American Literature*, vol. 70, no. 3, 1998, pp. 443–63.

Dawson, Melanie. *Emotional Reinventions: Realist-Era Representations beyond Sympathy*. U of Michigan P, 2018.

DeLombard, Jeannine. "'Eye-Witness to the Cruelty': Southern Violence and Northern Testimony in Frederick Douglass's 1845 *Narrative*." *American Literature*, vol. 73, no. 2, 2001, pp. 245–75.

Dimock, Wai-chee. "The Economy of Pain: Capitalism, Humanitarianism, and the Realistic." *New Essays on the Rise of Silas Lapham*, edited by Donald Pease, Cambridge UP, 1991, pp. 67–90.

Dobson, Joanne. "Reclaiming Sentimental Literature." *American Literature*, vol. 69, no. 2, 1997, pp. 263–88.

Douglas, Ann. *The Feminization of American Culture*. Anchor, 1977.

Douglass, Frederick. *The Heroic Slave*. 1853. *The Oxford Frederick Douglass Reader*, edited by William L. Andrews, Oxford UP, 1996, pp. 131–63.

———. *Narrative of the Life of Frederick Douglass*. 1845. Edited by William L. Andrews and William S. McFeely, Norton, 1996.

Eastman, Mary Henderson. *Aunt Phillis's Cabin; Or, Southern Life as It Is*. Lippincott, Grambo & Co., 1852.

Edel, Leon. Introduction. *Henry James: Letters*. Edited by Edel, vol. 3, Belknap, 1980, pp. xliii–xx.

Engelsing, Rolf. *Der Bürger als Leser: Lesergeschichte in Deutschland, 1500–1800*. Metzler, 1974.

Eugenides, Jeffrey. *The Virgin Suicides*. 4th Estate, 2021.

Felsenstein, Frank, et al. *What Middletown Read: Print Culture in an American Small City*. U of Massachusetts P, 2015.

Felski, Rita. *The Limits of Critique*. U of Chicago P, 2015.

Festa, Lynn. *Sentimental Figures of Empire in Eighteenth-Century Britain and France*. Johns Hopkins UP, 2009.

Fields, Annie. *Life and Letters of Harriet Beecher Stowe*. Riverside Press, 1897.

Fields, Dynnelle, et al. "Disabling Assumptions: Inauthentic Deaf Characters in Traditional Literature." *English Journal*, vol. 105, no. 4, 2016, pp. 94–97.

Finkelstein, David, and Alistair McCleery. "Readers and Reading." *An Introduction to Book History*, 2nd ed., Routledge, 2013, pp. 101–18.

Finseth, Ian. "How Shall the Truth Be Told? Language and Race in the Marrow of Tradition." *American Literary Realism*, vol. 31, no. 3, 1999, p. 1–20.

Fish, Stanley. *Is There a Text in This Class? The Authority of Interpretive Communities*. Harvard UP, 1980.

Fisher, Philip. *Hard Facts: Setting and Form in the American Novel*. Oxford UP, 1985.

Fleissner, Jennifer L. "Earth-Eating, Addiction, Nostalgia: Charles Chesnutt's Diasporic Regionalism." *Studies in Romanticism*, vol. 49, no. 2, 2010, pp. 313–36.

Flück, Winfried. "The Power and Failure of Representation in Harriet Beecher Stowe's *Uncle Tom's Cabin*." *New Literary History*, vol. 23, no. 2, 1992, pp. 319–38.

Fludernik, Monika. *Towards a "Natural" Narratology*. Routledge, 2010.

Forster, E. M. *Aspects of the Novel*. Harcourt, Brace & World, 1927.

Fossett, Judith Jackson. Introduction. *The House Behind the Cedars* by Charles W. Chesnutt. Edited by Judith Jackson Fossett, Modern Library, 2003, pp. xi–xxiv.

Foucault, Michel. "What Is an Author?" *Language, Counter-Memory, Practice: Selected Essays and Interviews*, edited by Donald F. Bouchard and Sherry Simon, Cornell UP, 2012, pp. 113–38.

Frederick, John T. "Hawthorne's 'Scribbling Women.'" *New England Quarterly*, vol. 48, no. 2, 1975, pp. 231–40.

Fredrickson, George M. *The Black Image in the White Mind: The Debate on Afro-American Character and Destiny, 1817–1914*, Harper & Row, 1971.

Freeman, Elizabeth. "Connecticut Yankings: Mark Twain and the Masturbating Dude." *Unsettled States: Nineteenth-Century American Literary Studies*, edited by Dana Luciano and Ivy G. Wilson, New York UP, 2014, pp. 275–97.

"From the Negro Side." *Illustrated Buffalo Express*, vol. 19, 1900, p. 16. *Charles W. Chesnutt Archive*, https://chesnuttarchive.org/item/ccda.rev00295.

"From the *New York Times*, 15 Apr. 1899: 246." *The Conjure Stories* by Charles W. Chesnutt. Edited by Robert B. Stepto and Jennifer Rae Greeson, Norton, 2012, p. 231.

"From the *News and Observer* [Raleigh], 30 Apr. 1899: 3." *The Conjure Stories* by Charles W. Chesnutt. Edited by Robert B. Stepto and Jennifer Rae Greeson, Norton, 2012, pp. 233–34.

"From the *Southern Workman* 28 (May 1899): 194–95." *The Conjure Stories* by Charles W. Chesnutt. Edited by Robert B. Stepto and Jennifer Rae Greeson, Norton, 2012, pp. 231–33.

Garrison, William Lloyd. "Review of *Uncle Tom's Cabin; or Life among the Lowly*." *The Liberator*, vol. 22, no. 13, 1852, p. 50.

Garvey, Ellen Gruber. "Anonymity, Authorship, and Recirculation: A Civil War Episode." *Book History*, vol. 9, no. 1, 2006, pp. 159–78.

Gilbert, Sandra M., and Susan Gubar. *No Man's Land: The Place of the Woman*

Writer in the Twentieth Century, vol. 1, *The War of the Words*, Yale UP, 1988.

Glazener, Nancy. *Reading for Realism: The History of a U.S. Literary Institution, 1850–1910*. Duke UP, 1997.

Goodrich, Samuel G. *Recollections of a Lifetime, or, Men and Things I Have Seen in a Series of Familiar Letters to a Friend: Historical, Biographical, Anecdotical and Descriptive*. New York, 1856.

Grabes, Herbert. "Turning Words on the Page into 'Real' People." *Style*, vol. 38, no. 2, 2004, pp. 221–35.

Graff, Gerald. *Clueless in Academe: How Schooling Obscures the Life of the Mind*. Yale UP, 2003.

Greyser, Naomi. *On Sympathetic Grounds: Race, Gender, and Affective Geographies in Nineteenth-Century North America*. Oxford UP, 2020.

Guillory, John. *Professing Criticism: Essays on the Organization of Literary Study*. U of Chicago P, 2022.

Gustafson, Sandra M. *Eloquence Is Power: Oratory and Performance in Early America*. U of North Carolina P, 2000.

Habegger, Alfred. *Gender, Fantasy, and Realism in American Literature*. Columbia UP, 1982.

———. *Henry James and the "Woman Business."* Cambridge UP, 1989.

Hall, David D. "Readers and Reading in America: Historical and Critical Perspectives." *Proceedings of the American Antiquarian Society*, vol. 103, no. 2, 1993, pp. 337–57.

———. "The Uses of Literacy in New England, 1600–1850." *Cultures of Print: Essays in the History of the Book*, U of Massachusetts P, 1996, pp. 36–78.

Halpern, Faye. "Closeness through Unreliability: Sympathy, Empathy, and Ethics in Narrative Communication." *Narrative*, vol. 26, no. 2, 2018, pp. 125–45.

———. "In Defense of Reading Badly: The Politics of Identification in 'Benito Cereno,' *Uncle Tom's Cabin*, and Our Classrooms." *College English*, vol. 70, no. 6, 2008, pp. 551–77.

———. *Sentimental Readers: The Rise, Fall, and Revival of a Disparaged Rhetoric*. U of Iowa P, 2013.

Hamilton, Geordie. "Rethinking the Politics of American Realism through the Narrative Form and Moral Rhetoric of W. D. Howells' *The Rise of Silas Lapham*." *American Literary Realism*, vol. 42, no. 1, 2009, pp. 13–35.

Harris, Susan K. *19th-Century American Women's Novels: Interpretive Strategies*. Cambridge UP, 1990.

Harshav, Benjamin. *Explorations in Poetics*. Stanford UP, 2007.

Harvey, George. "Editor's Study." *Harper's Magazine*, vol. 121, 10 November 1910, pp. 961–64.

Hattenhauer, Darryl. "Racial and Textual Miscegenation in Chesnutt's *The House Behind the Cedars*." *Mississippi Quarterly*, vol. 47, no. 1, 1993, pp. 27–45.

Hawthorne, Nathaniel. "The Birth-Mark." 1843. *Hawthorne's Short Stories*. Edited by Newton Arvin, Vintage, 2011, pp. 177–93.

Healey, Christine. "The Antiquary and Literary Criticism in the Short Stories of Constance Fenimore Woolson." *Legacy*, vol. 29, no. 2, 2012, pp. 222–39.

Hendler, Glenn. "The Limits of Sympathy: Louisa May Alcott and the Sentimental Novel." *American Literary History*, vol. 3, no. 4, 1991, pp. 685–706.

Henson, Josiah. "Uncle Tom's Story of His Life." *An Autobiography of the Rev. Josiah Henson (Mrs. Harriet Beecher Stowe's "Uncle Tom"). From 1789 to 1876*. London, 1876. *Documenting the American South*, docsouth.unc.edu/neh/henson/henson.html.

Hewitt, Elizabeth. "Charles Chesnutt's Capitalist Conjurings." *ELH*, vol. 76, no. 4, 2009, pp. 931–62.

Hiebert, Elfrieda H., and D. Ray Reutzel. *Revisiting Silent Reading: New Directions for Teachers and Researchers*. International Reading Association, 2010.

Hochman, Barbara. "Devouring *Uncle Tom's Cabin*: Antebellum 'Common' Readers." *The History of Reading*, vol. 1, edited by Shafquat Towheed and W. R. Owens, Palgrave Macmillan, 2011, pp. 87–100.

———. "Reading Historically/Reading Selectively: *The Bostonians* in the *Century*, 1885–1886." *Henry James Review*, vol. 34, no. 3, 2013, pp. 270–78. *JSTOR*, http://muse.jhu.edu/journals/henry_james_review/v034/34.3.hochman.html.

———. *Uncle Tom's Cabin and the Reading Revolution: Race, Literacy, Childhood, and Fiction, 1851–1911*. U of Massachusetts P, 2011.

Hoeller, Hildegard. *Edith Wharton's Dialogue with Realism and Sentimental Fiction*. UP of Florida, 2000.

Homestead, Melissa. "Did a Woman Write the Great American Novel? Judging Women's Fiction in the Nineteenth Century and Today." *Tulsa Studies in Women's Literature*, vol. 29, no. 2, 2010, pp. 447–57.

Howells, William Dean. *Annie Kilburn*. 1888. *Novels, 1886–1888*. Library of America, 1989, pp. 641–865.

———. *Criticism and Fiction*. Harper and Brothers, 1891.

———. "Editor's Study." *Harper's New Monthly Magazine*, vol. 79, 1889, pp. 962–67.

———. "From Editor's Study." *The Norton Anthology of American Literature*, edited by Robert S. Levine, 9th ed., vol. C, Norton, 2017, pp. 957–60.

———. *A Hazard of New Fortunes*. 1889. Edited by David J. Nordloh et al., introduction by Arthur Schlesinger Jr., Modern Library, 2002.

———. *Literature and Life*. 1902. Project Gutenberg, 2006, https://www.gutenberg.org/files/3389/3389.txt.
———. "Novel-Reading and Novel-Writing." *Howells and James: A Double Billing*. Edited by William M. Gibson, New York Public Library, 1958, pp. 5–24.
———. "A Psychological Counter-Current in Recent Fiction." *North American Review*, vol. 173, no. 541, 1901, pp. 872–88.
———. "Recent Literature." *Atlantic Monthly*, vol. 35, no. 212, 1875, pp. 736-49.
———. "Recent Literature." *Atlantic Monthly*, vol. 43, no. 262, 1879, pp. 405–14.
———. *The Rise of Silas Lapham*. 1885. Edited by Don Lewis Cook, Norton, 1982.
"An Issue in the Race Problem." *Detroit Free Press*, vol. 66, 1900, p. 11. *Charles W. Chesnutt Archive*, https://chesnuttarchive.org/item/ccda.rev00139.
James, Henry. "The Art of Fiction." 1884. *Theory of Fiction: Henry James*. Edited by James E. Miller, U of Nebraska P, 1972, pp. 27–44.
———. *The Bostonians: A Novel*. 1886. Edited by Richard Lansdown, Penguin, 2000.
———. *Partial Portraits*. Macmillan, 1894. Project Gutenberg, https://www.gutenberg.org/files/58471/58471-h/58471-h.htm.
———. *Selected Letters*. Edited by Leon Edel, Belknap, 1987.
———. *A Small Boy and Others*. Scribner, 1913.
———. *Washington Square*. Harper & Bros., 1901.
Jameson, Fredric. *The Antinomies of Realism*. Verso, 2015.
Jarrett, Gene. "'This Expression Shall Not Be Changed': Irrelevant Episodes, Jim's Humanity Revisited, and Retracing Mark Twain's Evasion in *Adventures of Huckleberry Finn*." *American Literary Realism*, vol. 35, no. 1, 2002, pp. 1–28.
Johnson, Lee Ann. "The Psychology of Characterization: James's Portraits of Verena Tarrant and Olive Chancellor." *Studies in the Novel*, vol. 6, no. 3, 1974, pp. 295–303. *Periodicals Archive Online*, http://ezproxy.lib.ucalgary.ca/login?url=http://search.proquest.com/.
Kaplan, Amy. *The Social Construction of American Realism*. U of Chicago P, 1988.
Keen, Suzanne. *Empathy and the Novel*. Oxford UP, 2007.
Kete, Mary Louise. *Sentimental Collaborations: Mourning and Middle-Class Identity in Nineteenth-Century America*. Duke UP, 2000.
Knadler, Stephen. "Untragic Mulatto: Charles Chesnutt and the Discourse of Whiteness." *American Literary History*, vol. 8, no. 3, 1996, pp. 426–48.
Knapp, Steven. *Literary Interest: The Limits of Anti-Formalism*. Harvard UP, 1993.
Kuhn, Mary. "Chesnutt, Turpentine, and the Political Ecology of White Supremacy." *PMLA*, vol. 136, no. 1, 2021, pp. 39–54.
Lane, Rebecca, and Jeffrey Zamostny. "The Limits of Empathy: An Interview

with Marianne Noble." *disClosure: A Journal of Social Theory*, vol. 20, no. 1, 2011, pp. 160–64.

Lanser, Susan Sniader. "The 'I' of the Beholder: Equivocal Attachments and the Limits of Structuralist Narratology." *A Companion to Narrative Theory*, edited by James Phelan and Peter J. Rabinowitz, Oxford UP, 2008, pp. 206–19.

Larsen, Elizabeth. "The Progress of Literacy: Edward Tyrrel Channing and the Separation of the Student Writer from the World." *Rhetoric Review*, vol. 11, no. 1, 1992, pp. 159–71.

Lehane, Dennis. *Small Mercies*. E-book ed., HarperCollins, 2023.

Lesser, Wendy. *His Other Half: Men Looking at Women through Art*. Harvard UP, 1991.

Levine, Robert S. "*Uncle Tom's Cabin* in *Frederick Douglass' Paper*: An Analysis of Reception." *American Literature*, vol. 64, no. 1, 1992, pp. 71–93.

"The Literature of Slavery." *The New Englander*, vol. 10, November 1852, pp. 591–92.

Louwerse, Max, and Don Kuiken. "The Effects of Personal Involvement in Narrative Discourse." *Discourse Processes*, vol. 38, no. 2, 2004, pp. 169–72.

Lundeen, Kathleen. "Who Has the Right to Feel? The Ethics of Literary Empathy." *Style*, vol. 32, no. 2, 1998, pp. 261–71. *Academic OneFile*, http://go.galegroup.com.ezproxy.lib.ucalgary.ca/ps/i.do?p=AONE&sw=w&u=ucalgary&v=2.1&it=r&id=GALE%7CA54637195&sid=summon&asid=b75caeadbab1d6c58dc98cfc5d9f3c89.

Mabie, Hamilton Wright. "Two New Novelists." *The Outlook*, vol. 64, 1900, pp. 440–41. *Charles W. Chesnutt Archive*, https://chesnuttarchive.org/item/ccda.rev00222#more-metadata.

MacArthur, James. [Review of *The Conjure Woman*]. *The Outlook*, vol. 62, 1899, pp. 483–84. *Charles W. Chesnutt Archive*, https://chesnuttarchive.org/item/ccda.rev00026.

Manierre, William R. "The Rise of Silas Lapham: Retrospective Discussion as Dramatic Technique." *College English*, vol. 23, no. 5, 1962, pp. 357–61.

Martin, Matthew R. "The Two-Faced New South: The Plantation Tales of Thomas Nelson Page and Charles W. Chesnutt." *Southern Literary Journal*, vol. 30, no. 2, 1998, pp. 17–36.

McCaskill, Barbara. "The African American Novel after Reconstruction." *The Cambridge History of the American Novel*, edited by Leonard Cassuto, Cambridge UP, 2011, pp. 484–98.

McDowell, Deborah E. Introduction. *"Quicksand" and "Passing"* by Nella Larsen. Edited by McDowell, Rutgers UP, 1986, pp. ix–xxxv.

McElrath Jr., Joseph R. "Why Charles W. Chesnutt Is Not a Realist." *American Literary Realism*, vol. 32, no. 2, 2000, pp. 91–108.

McEntee, Grace. "'Have You Not Heard of Baptiste?': Educating the Reader in

Constance Fenimore Woolson's 'Jeannette.'" *American Literary Realism*, vol. 47, no. 2, 2015, pp. 151–68.

McGlothlin, Erin. "Empathetic Identification and the Mind of the Holocaust Perpetrator in Fiction: A Proposed Taxonomy of Response." *Narrative*, vol. 24, no. 3, 2016, pp. 251–76.

Millner, Michael. *Fever Reading: Affect and Reading Badly in the Early American Public Sphere*. U of New Hampshire P, 2012.

"The Mixture of Blood." *Denver Times*, November 11, 1900, p. 13. *Charles W. Chesnutt Archive*, https://chesnuttarchive.org/item/ccda.rev00171.

Minter, David. "Regionalism: A Diminished Thing." *Columbia Literary History of the United States*, edited by Emory Elliott et al., Columbia UP, 1988, pp. 761–84.

Moore, Julia A. *The Sentimental Song Book*. J. F. Ryder, 1877.

Morgan, Florence A. H. "Review of The Conjure Woman," *Bookman*, vol. 9, pp. 372–73. *Charles W. Chesnutt Archive*, https://chesnuttarchive.org/item/ccda.rev00023.

Morgan, William M. *Questionable Charity: Gender, Humanitarianism, and Complicity in U.S. Literary Realism*. UP of New England, 2004.

Morrison, Toni. "This Amazing, Troubling Book." *Adventures of Huckleberry Finn: An Authoritative Text, Contexts and Sources, Criticism*, edited by Thomas Cooley, 3rd ed., 1999, pp. 385–92.

"Mrs. Sigourney and Miss Gould." *North American Review*, vol. 41, no. 89, 1835, pp. 430–54.

Newkirk, Thomas. "The Case for Slow Reading." *Educational Leadership*, vol. 67, no. 6, 2010, pp. 6–11.

Nielsen, Henrik Skov, James Phelan, and Richard Walsh. "Ten Theses about Fictionality." *Narrative*, vol. 23, no. 1, 2015, pp. 61–73.

"Nineteen Negroes Shot to Death." *New York Times*, 11 Nov. 1898, p. 1.

Noble, Marianne. "The Courage to Speak and Hear the Truth: Sympathy and Genuine Human Contact in Harriet Beecher Stowe's *The Minister's Wooing*." *New England Quarterly*, vol. 81, no. 4, 2008, pp. 676–702.

———. *The Masochistic Pleasures of Sentimental Literature*. Princeton UP, 2000.

———. *Rethinking Sympathy and Human Contact in Nineteenth-Century American Literature: Hawthorne, Douglass, Stowe, Dickinson*. Cambridge UP, 2019.

———. "Sympathetic Listening in Frederick Douglass's 'The Heroic Slave' and *My Bondage and My Freedom*." *Studies in American Fiction*, vol. 34, no. 1, 2006, pp. 53–68.

Nowlin, Michael. "'The First Negro Novelist': Charles Chesnutt's Point of View and the Emergence of African American Literature." *Studies in American Fiction*, vol. 39, no. 2, 2012, pp. 147–74.

Nünning, Vera. "Unreliable Narration and the Historical Variability of Values and Norms: *The Vicar of Wakefield* as a Test Case of a Cultural-Historical Narratology." *Style*, vol. 38, no. 2, 2004, pp. 236–52.

Nussbaum, Martha Craven. *Love's Knowledge: Essays on Philosophy and Literature*. Oxford UP, 1990.

O'Hara, Daniel T. "Smiling through Pain: The Practice of Self in *the Rise of Silas Lapham*." *New Essays on the Rise of Silas Lapham*, edited by Donald Pease, Cambridge UP, 1991, pp. 91–106.

Ong, Walter. "The Writer's Audience Is Always a Fiction." *Cross-Talk in Comp Theory*, edited by Victor Villaneuva, 2nd ed., NCTE, 2003, pp. 55–76.

Pardey, Hannah. "Investigating Postcolonial Affective Online Communities: A Computational Analysis of Reader Reviews for Contemporary Nigerian Fiction." *ARIEL*, vol. 54, nos. 3–4, pp. 157–87.

Parfait, Claire. *Publishing History of "Uncle Tom's Cabin," 1852–2002*. Ashgate, 2008.

Pearson, P. David, and Susie M. Goodin. "Silent Reading Pedagogy: A Historical Perspective." *Revisiting Silent Reading: New Directions for Teachers and Researchers*, edited by Elfrieda H. Hiebert and D. Ray Reutzel, International Reading Association, 2010, pp. 3–23.

Pettis, Joyce. "The Literary Imagination and the Historic Event: Chesnutt's Use of History in *The Marrow of Tradition*." *South Atlantic Review*, vol. 55, no. 4, 1990, pp. 37–48.

Phelan, James. "Authors, Resources, Audiences: Toward a Rhetorical Poetics of Narrative." *Style*, vol. 52, nos. 1–2, 2018, pp. 1–34.

———. "Estranging Unreliability, Bonding Unreliability, and the Ethics of *Lolita*." *Narrative*, vol. 15, no. 2, 2007, pp. 222–38.

———. *Living to Tell about It: A Rhetoric and Ethics of Character Narration*. Cornell UP, 2005.

———. *Somebody Telling Somebody Else: A Rhetorical Poetics of Narrative*. The Ohio State UP, 2017.

Phelan, James, and Sarah Copland. "The Ideal Narratee and the Rhetorical Model of Audiences." *Poetics Today*, vol. 43, no. 1, 2022, pp. 1–26.

Rabinowitz, Peter J. *Before Reading: Narrative Conventions and the Politics of Interpretation*. Cornell UP, 1987.

———. "'Betraying the Sender': The Rhetoric and Ethics of Fragile Texts." *Narrative*, vol. 2, no. 3, 1994, pp. 201–13.

———. "Truth in Fiction: A Re-Examination of Audiences." *Critical Inquiry*, vol. 4, no. 1, 1977, pp. 121–41.

Radway, Janice. "Beyond Mary Bailey and Old Maid Librarians: Reimagining Readers and Rethinking Reading." *Journal of Education for Library and Information Science*, vol. 35, no. 4, 1994, pp. 275–96.

Rauterkus, Melissa Asher. "Racial Fictions and the Cultural Work of Genre in

Charles W. Chesnutt's *The House Behind the Cedars*." *American Literary Realism*, vol. 48, no. 2, 2016, pp. 128–46.

"Realism and Naturalism." *The Norton Anthology of American Literature*, edited by Robert S. Levine, vol. C, Norton, 2017, pp. 955–76.

"Recent Literature [including a review of *Uncle Tom's Cabin*]." *Atlantic Monthly*, vol. 43, 1879, pp. 405–08.

Review of *The Conjure Woman*. *Daily Inter Ocean*, 12 June 1899, p. 9. Charles W. Chesnutt Archive, https://chesnuttarchive.org/item/ccda.rev00044.

Review of *The Conjure Woman*. *Nebraska State Journal*, 1899, p. 4. Charles W. Chesnutt Archive, https://chesnuttarchive.org/item/ccda.rev00004.

Review of *The Conjure Woman*. *Philadelphia Press*, vol. 6, 1899, p. 6. Charles W. Chesnutt Archive, https://chesnuttarchive.org/item/ccda.rev00012.

Review of *The Marrow of Tradition*. *The Appeal*, vol. 17, 1901, p. 5. Charles W. Chesnutt Archive, https://chesnuttarchive.org/item/ccda.rev00292.

Review of *The Marrow of Tradition*. *Brooklyn Daily Eagle*, vol. 9, 1901. Charles W. Chesnutt Archive, https//chesnuttarchive.org/item/ccda.rev00288.

Review of *The Marrow of Tradition*. *Daily Time*, vol. 14, 1901, p. 5. Charles W. Chesnutt Archive, https://chesnuttarchive.org/item/ccda.rev00301.

Review of *The Marrow of Tradition*. *New York Press*, vol. 14, 1900, p. 7. Charles W. Chesnutt Archive, https://chesnuttarchive.org/item/ccda.rev00275.

Review of *The Marrow of Tradition*. *Times*, vol. 17, 1901, p. 5. Charles W. Chesnutt Archive, https://chesnuttarchive.org/item/ccda.rev00282.

Reynolds, David S. *Mightier Than the Sword: Uncle Tom's Cabin and the Battle for America*. Norton, 2011.

Rhoads, Bonita. "Henry James and the Plunder of Sentiment: Building the House of Modernism from the Spoils of Poynton." *Henry James Review*, vol. 33, no. 2, 2012, pp. 147–64.

Ricoeur, Paul. *Freud and Philosophy: An Essay on Interpretation*. Yale UP, 1986.

Rimmon-Kenan, Shlomith. *Narrative Fiction*. Routledge, 1983.

Rioux, Anne Boyd. "Anticipating James, Anticipating Grief: Constance Fenimore Woolson's 'Miss Grief.'" *Constance Fenimore Woolson's Nineteenth Century: Essays*, edited by Victoria Brehm, Wayne State UP, 2001, pp. 191–206.

———. *Constance Fenimore Woolson: Portrait of a Lady Novelist*. Norton, 2016.

———. "A New Era for the Appreciation of Constance Fenimore Woolson." *Woolson (pre)Fest*, 11 Mar. 2021. Keynote Address.

Ritzenberg, Aaron. "The Dream of History: Memory and the Unconscious in Charles Chesnutt's *The House Behind the Cedars*." *Passing in the Works of Charles W. Chesnutt*, edited by Susan Prothro Wright and Ernestine Pickens Glass, UP of Mississippi, 2010, pp. 51–65.

Robbins, Sarah. *Managing Literacy, Mothering America: Women's Narratives on Reading and Writing in the Nineteenth Century.* U of Pittsburgh P, 2004.

Romero, Lora. *Home Fronts: Domesticity and Its Critics in the Antebellum United States.* Duke UP, 1997.

Rowlandson, Mary. "A Narrative of the Captivity and Restoration of Mrs. Mary Rowlandson." 1682. *The Norton Anthology of American Literature*, edited by Robert S. Levine, vol. A, 9th ed., Norton, 2017, pp. 269–301.

Rowson, Susanna. *Charlotte Temple*, 1794. Oxford UP, 1986.

Ryan, Marie-Laure. "What Are Characters Made Of? Textual, Philosophical and 'World' Approaches to Character Ontology." *Neohelicon*, vol. 45, no. 2, 2018, pp. 415–29.

Ryan, Susan M. *The Grammar of Good Intentions: Race and the Antebellum Culture of Benevolence.* Cornell UP, 2003.

Sampson, John. "'A Catalogue of Wrong and Outrage': Undermining White Supremacist Discourse and Spatial Practice in Charles Chesnutt's *The Marrow of Tradition*." *American Literary Realism*, vol. 50, no. 3, 2018, pp. 189–213.

Sanchez-Eppler, Karen. *Touching Liberty: Abolition, Feminism, and the Politics of the Body.* U of California P, 1993.

Sand, George. "George Sand and Uncle Tom." *The National Era*, 1853. *Uncle Tom's Cabin & American Culture*, published by Stephen Railton and the University of Virginia, http://utc.iath.virginia.edu/notices/noaro1awt.html.

Scharnhorst, Gary. *In Defense of Literary Biography.* Ball State UP, 2005.

Schlesinger, Arthur, Jr. Introduction. *A Hazard of New Fortunes* by William Dean Howells. Edited by David J. Nordloh et al., Modern Library, 2002.

Scholes, Robert J. "The Transition to College Reading." *Pedagogy*, vol. 2, no. 2, 2002, pp. 165–72.

Sedgwick, Eve Kosofsky, and Adam Frank. *Touching Feeling: Affect, Pedagogy, Performativity.* Duke UP, 2003.

Sells, Laura R. "Maria W. Miller Stewart." *Women Public Speakers in the United States, 1800–1925: A Bio-Critical Sourcebook*, edited by Karlyn Kohrs Campbell, Greenwood, 1993, pp. 339–49.

Shaheen, Aaron. "Henry James's Southern Mode of Imagination: Men, Women, and the Image of the South in *The Bostonians*." *Henry James Review*, vol. 24, no. 2, 2003, pp. 180–92.

Sheridan, Thomas. *A Course of Lectures on Elocution: Together with Two Dissertations on Language.* W. Strahan, 1762.

Shi, David. *Facing Facts: Realism in American Thought and Culture, 1850–1920.* Oxford UP, 1995.

Shuman, Amy. *Other People's Stories: Entitlement Claims and the Critique of Empathy*. U of Illinois P, 2010.
Sicherman, Barbara. "Ideologies and Practices of Reading." *A History of the Book in America*, vol. 3, *The Industrial Book, 1840–1880*, edited by Scott E. Casper et al., U of North Carolina P, 2009, pp. 279–302.
Simmons, Ryan. *Chesnutt and Realism: A Study of the Novels*. U of Alabama P, 2006.
"Slavery in the Southern States." *Littell's Living Age*. 4 Dec. 1852, pp. 433–42.
Sloane, David E. E. "The N-Word in *Adventures of Huckleberry Finn* Reconsidered." *Mark Twain Annual*, vol. 12, no. 1, 2014, pp. 70–82.
Slote, Ben. "Listening to "The Goophered Grapevine" and Hearing Raisins Sing." *American Literary History*, vol. 6, no. 4, 1994, pp. 684–94.
Smith, Henry Nash. "The Scribbling Women and the Cosmic Success Story." *Critical Inquiry*, vol. 1, no. 1, 1974, pp. 47–70.
"Some Reminiscences of an Old Friend of Mrs. Stowe." *New York Times*, 9 Nov. 1888, p. 2.
Spillers, Hortense. *Black, White, and in Color: Essays on American Literature and Culture*. U of Chicago P, 2003.
Stokes, Claudia. "The Poetics of Unoriginality: The Case of Lucretia Davidson." *Legacy*, vol. 32, no. 1, 2015, pp. 31–52.
———. "The Religious Novel." *The American Novel, 1870–1940*, edited by Priscilla Wald and Michael A. Elliott, Oxford UP, 2014, pp. 168–83.
———. *Writers in Retrospect: The Rise of American Literary History, 1875–1910*, U of North Carolina P, 2006.
Stowe, Charles Edward. *Life of Harriet Beecher Stowe, Compiled from her Letters and Journals*. Riverside Press, 1890. *Project Gutenberg*, gutenberg.org/ebooks/6702.
Stowe, Harriet Beecher. *A Key to Uncle Tom's Cabin*. 1853. Applewood, 1970.
———. "Letter to Gamaliel Bailey." 1851. *Uncle Tom's Cabin & American Culture*, published by Stephen Railton and the University of Virginia, utc.iath.virginia.edu/uncletom/utlthbsht.html.
———. *The Minister's Wooing*. 1859. Edited by Sandra R. Duguid, Stowe-Day Foundation, 1978.
———. *Uncle Tom's Cabin*. 1852. Edited by Elizabeth Ammons, 2nd ed., Norton, 2010.
Suleiman, Susan Rubin. *Authoritarian Fictions: The Ideological Novel as a Literary Genre*. Columbia UP, 1983.
Sundquist, Eric. "Charles Chesnutt's Cakewalk." *To Wake the Nations: Race in the Making of American Literature*, Belknap, 1993, pp. 272–454.
Terrell, Mary Church. *Harriet Beecher Stowe: An Appreciation*. Murray Bros, 1911. *Uncle Tom's Cabin & American Culture*, published by Stephen Railton

and the University of Virginia, http://utc.iath.virginia.edu/africam/afesmctt.html.

Tharaud, Jerome. "The Evangelical Press, Harriet Beecher Stowe, and the Human Medium." *Arizona Quarterly*, vol. 69, no. 2, 2013, pp. 25–54.

Thayer, William Roscoe. "The New Story-Tellers and the Doom of Realism." *Forum*, vol. 18, 1894, pp. 470–80.

Thomas, Brook. "*Adventures of Huckleberry Finn* and Reconstruction." *American Literary Realism*, vol. 50, no. 1, 2017, pp. 1–24.

———. "The Construction of Privacy in and around *The Bostonians*." *American Literature*, vol. 64, no. 4, 1992, pp. 719–47.

Thompson, Katrina Dyonne. "'Taking Care a White Babies, That's What I Do': *The Help* and Americans' Obsession with the Mammy." *From "Uncle Tom's Cabin" to "The Help": Critical Perspectives on White-Authored Narratives of Black Life*, edited by Claire Oberon Garcia, Vershawn Ashanti Young, and Charise Pimentel, Palgrave Macmillan, 2014, pp. 57–72.

Thrailkill, Jane. *Affecting Fictions: Mind, Body, and Emotion in American Literary Realism*. Harvard UP, 2007.

Tinkle, Teresa, et al. "Teaching Close Reading Skills in a Large Lecture Course." *Pedagogy*, vol. 13, no. 3, 2013, pp. 505–36.

Tóibín, Colm. Foreword. *"Miss Grief" and Other Stories* by Constance Fenimore Woolson. Edited by Anne Boyd Rioux, Norton, 2016, pp. ix–xvi.

Tompkins, Jane. "Sentimental Power: *Uncle Tom's Cabin* and the Politics of Literary History." *Sensational Designs: The Cultural Work of American Fiction, 1790–1860*, Oxford UP, 1985, pp. 122–46.

Torsney, Cheryl B. *Constance Fenimore Woolson: The Grief of Artistry*. U of Georgia P, 1989.

———. *Critical Essays on Constance Fenimore Woolson*, edited by Torsney, Macmillan, 1992.

———. Introduction. *Critical Essays on Constance Fenimore Woolson*, edited by Torsney, Macmillan, 1992, pp. 1–16.

———. "Introduction to 'Miss Grief.'" *Legacy*, vol. 4, no. 1, 1987, pp. 11–13.

Twain, Mark. *Adventures of Huckleberry Finn*. 1885. Edited by Gerald Graff and James Phelan, 2nd ed., Bedford Books, 2004.

———. *Adventures of Huckleberry Finn*. 1885. Edited by R. Kent Rasmussen, Penguin, 2014.

———. *A Connecticut Yankee in King Arthur's Court*. 1889. Edited by Bernard L. Stein, U of California P, 2011.

———. "Fenimore Cooper's Literary Offenses." 1895. *Collected Tales, Sketches, Speeches & Essays, 1891–1910*. Edited by Louis J. Budd, Library of America, 1992, pp. 180–92.

Veeder, William R. *Henry James—The Lessons of the Master: Popular Fiction and Personal Style in the Nineteenth Century*. U of Chicago P, 1975.

Wallace, James D. "Hawthorne and the Scribbling Women Reconsidered." *American Literature*, vol. 62, no. 2, 1990, pp. 201–22. *JSTOR*, doi:10.2307/2926913.

Wandler, Steven. "Hogs, Not Maidens: The Ambivalent Imperialism of *A Connecticut Yankee in King Arthur's Court*." *Arizona Quarterly: A Journal of American Literature, Culture, and Theory*, vol. 66, no. 4, 2010, pp. 33–52.

Wardley, Lynn. "Woman's Voice, Democracy's Body, and *The Bostonians*." *ELH*, vol. 56, no. 3, 1989, pp. 639–65.

Warhol, Robyn. "As You Stand, So You Feel and Are: The Crying Body and the Nineteenth-Century Text." *Tattoo, Torture, Mutilation, and the Denaturalization of the Body in Culture*, edited by Frances E. Mascia-Lees and Patricia Sharpe, State U of New York P, 1992, pp. 100–25.

———. "Poetics and Persuasion: *Uncle Tom's Cabin* as a Realist Novel." *Essays in Literature*, vol. 13, no. 2, 1986, pp. 283–98.

———. "Reader, Can You Imagine? No, You Cannot: The Narratee as Other in Harriet Jacobs's Text." *Narrative*, vol. 3, no. 1, 1995, pp. 57–72.

Warner, Charles Dudley. "Editor's Study." *Harper's Monthly Magazine*, vol. 88, no. 528, 1894, pp. 966–67.

Warner, Michael. "Uncritical Reading." *Polemic: Critical or Uncritical*, edited by Jane Gallop, Routledge, 2004, pp. 13–38.

Weimer, Joan Myers. Introduction. *Women Artists, Women Exiles: "Miss Grief" and Other Stories* by Constance Fenimore Woolson. Edited by Weimer, Rutgers UP, 1988, pp. ix–xlvii.

Weinstein, Cindy. *Family, Kinship, and Sympathy*. Cambridge UP, 2004.

Werner, Craig. "The Framing of Charles W. Chesnutt: Practical Deconstruction in the Afro-American Tradition." *Studies in English*, vol. 9, 1990, pp. 1–25.

Wharton, Edith. *The Writing of Fiction*. Charles Scribner's Sons, 1925.

Whicher, George F. "Literature and Conflict." *Literary History of the United States*, edited by Robert Ernest Spiller et al., vol. 1, Macmillan, 1948, pp. 563–86.

White, Thomas. *A Little Book for Little Children*. Boston, 1702.

Wideman, John. "Charles W. Chesnutt: *The Marrow of Tradition*." *The American Scholar*, vol. 42, no. 1, 1972, pp. 128–34.

Williams, Raymond. *Marxism and Literature*. Oxford UP, 1977.

Wilson, Matthew. *Whiteness in the Novels of Charles W. Chesnutt*. UP of Mississippi, 2009.

———. "Who Has the Right to Say? Charles W. Chesnutt, Whiteness, and the Public Sphere." *College Literature*, vol. 26, no. 2, 1999, pp. 18–35.

Wimsatt, William K., and Monroe C. Beardsley. "The Affective Fallacy." 1949. *The*

Norton Anthology of Theory and Criticism, edited by Vincent B. Leitch, Norton, 2010, pp. 1246–61.

———. "The Intentional Fallacy." 1946. *The Norton Anthology of Theory and Criticism*, edited by Vincent B. Leitch, Norton, 2010, pp. 1374–87.

Windell, Maria A. *Transamerican Sentimentalism and Nineteenth-Century US Literary History*. Oxford UP, 2020.

Wolfe, Joanne, and Laura Wilder. *Digging into Literature: Strategies for Reading, Analysis, and Writing*, Bedford/St. Martin's, 2016.

Wolff, Simone. "An Interview with Anne Boyd Rioux." *Bookslut*, May 2016, doi:http://www.bookslut.com/features/2016_05_021444.php.

Wooley, Christine A. "African American Realism." *The Oxford Handbook of American Literary Realism*, edited by Keith Newlin, Oxford UP, 2019, pp. 185–200.

Woolson, Constance Fenimore. *Collected Stories*. Edited by Anne Boyd Rioux, Library of America, 2020.

———. "Felipa." *Rodman the Keeper: Southern Sketches*. Harper & Brothers, 1886, pp. 197–220.

———. "Jeannette." *Selected Stories and Travel Narratives*. Edited by Victoria Brehm and Sharon L. Dean, U of Tennessee P, 2004, pp. 32–55.

———. "'Miss Grief.'" *Miss Grief and Other Stories*. Edited by Anne Boyd Rioux, Norton, 2016, pp. 157–86.

———. *Miss Grief and Other Stories*. Edited by Anne Boyd Rioux, Norton, 2016.

———. *Selected Stories and Travel Narratives*. Edited by Victoria Brehm and Sharon L. Dean, U of Tennessee P, 2004.

———. "Solomon." *Miss Grief and Other Stories*. Edited by Anne Boyd Rioux, Norton, 2016, pp. 43–70.

———. "St. Clair Flats." *Miss Grief and Other Stories*. Edited by Anne Boyd Rioux, Norton, 2016, pp. 3–40.

Xine, Yao. *Disaffected: The Cultural Politics of Unfeeling in Nineteenth-Century America*. Duke UP, 2021.

Zboray, Ronald J. *A Fictive People: Antebellum Economic Development and the American Reading Public*. Oxford UP, 1993.

Zwarg, Christina. "Fathering and Blackface in *Uncle Tom's Cabin*." *NOVEL: A Forum on Fiction*, vol. 22, no. 3, 1989, pp. 274–87.

Index

Abeln, Paul, 88
actual reader, 37, 44, 71, 180, 193
affective fallacy, 10, 12, 17, 191, 217n2
affordances, narrative, 19, 60, 84, 93, 116, 159
affordances of sentimentality, 5, 53, 192
African American literary tradition, 5, 27, 156–57, 215n20
American literary realism, initial discussion of role of sympathy and sentimentality in, 3–4
Anderson, Benedict, 33
Andrews, William L., 213n3
apostrophes, 38, 48–49, 142, 165, 204n34
Artese, Brian, 97–98
    "Overhearing Testimony: James in the Shadow of Sentimentalism," 97
Atlantic Monthly, 59, 120–21, 123, 139, 144, 146–47, 167, 198n15
attachments, sympathetic, 142
audience
    actual, 76
    authorial, 167, 203n24, 212n23
    discerning, 120
    double, 95
    extradiegetic, 100
    gullible, 119, 127, 143–45
    ideal narrative, 203n27
    intended, 44
    interdiegetic, 102
    masterful, 120, 127
    model of, 31, 44–46, 162, 188, 199n21
    narrative, 44
authoritarian fiction, 164
authors
    American literary realist, 25, 123, 142
    didactic, 149

    marginalized, 27, 134–35
    strategizing, 137
    women, 116–17, 136

Baldwin, James, 26
Balzac, 57, 205n14
Banks, Marva, 201n3, 203n25
Barnes, Elizabeth, 95, 202n13
Barrish, Phillip, 197n5, 206n27
Barthes, Roland, 213n28
Batson, C. Daniel, 5–6, 8, 83–84
Bayley, John, 97, 111–12, 209n9, 209n10
Baym, Nina, 98, 197n1, 213n27
    Woman's Fiction, 199n20, 211n7
Beam, Dorri, 110
Beardsley, Monroe C., 10, 213n28
Beckman, John, 206n21
Beecher, Eunice, 39
Beecher, Henry Ward, 39, 42, 132, 200n28
benevolence, culture of, 34, 54, 62, 97, 205n17. *See also* charity
Bentley, Nancy, 94, 111, 198n13
    Frantic Panoramas, 206n26
Berlant, Lauren, 8, 199n18
    The Female Complaint, 11, 198n9
Bernstein, Susan, 198n9
Booth, Wayne, 12, 15, 190, 217n1
Borus, Daniel H., 10, 63, 138, 155, 198n16
Boudreau, Kristin, 2–3, 54, 205n16, 207n33
Brehm, Victoria, 26, 117–18
Bremer, Sidney H., 72, 206n25
Brodhead, Richard H., 121, 125–26, 180, 188
Brown, Candy Gunther, 36
Brown, Gillian, 201n1
Brown, Herbert Ross, 59, 209n17
Bufkin, Sydney, 180–81, 184, 216n34

Camfield, Gregg, 19, 54, 90, 198n7
    Sentimental Twain, 2
Campbell, Donna, 120
Carr, Stephen L., 201n4
Carter, Everett, 71
Castiglia, Christopher, 31
Century Illustrated Magazine, 92
Chakkalalal, Tess, 156
Chapman, Mary, 205n13
character-narrator, 121, 129
characters
    amalgamated, 164
    focalized, 14–15, 102, 106, 143, 151–52, 160, 164, 206n22, 209n18, 211n9, 213n4
    See also focalization
    lifelike, 20
    round, 19, 57
    unreliable, 15, 107, 109, 183, 211n9
    vivid, 18–25, 89
character types and typicality, 13, 20, 73, 200n29
charity, 61–62, 83, 184, 205n16. *See also* benevolence, culture of
cherished cultural narratives, 21, 23, 38, 89, 111, 200n29
cherished cultural stories, 22–23, 67
Chesnutt, Charles
    "Baxter's *Procrustes*", 213n5
    The Colonel's Dream, 213n5, 216n33
    conflicting portraits of, 141, 148, 213n6
    conjure tales, 14, 27, 139–43, 146–48, 156–57, 169, 187–88, 213n3, 215n21
    The Conjure Woman, 139, 142, 144, 147, 213n5, 214n8
    and critical distance, 179
    critique of modern literary critical practice, 187
    "The Goophered Grapevine," 144–48, 213n3, 214n9
    The House Behind the Cedars, 142, 148–56, 161, 163–64, 168–69, 213n4, 213n5
    journals of, 141, 189
    The Marrow of Tradition, 14–15, 27, 139–40, 156–86, 188, 190–91, 213n1, 213n4, 213n5, 215n25, 215n26, 216n27, 216n30, 216n31, 216n35
    narrative methods of, 140
    and narrative unreliability, 27, 140–41, 152–53, 155–56, 162

    and rhetorical passing, 141, 146–48, 190
    and sentimental self-identification, 27, 138, 141, 179, 185–86
    and sympathy, 26–27, 140, 142, 156, 160–61, 164, 167, 169, 173, 177–80, 186, 191
    views on race, 142–43, 154, 157, 159, 171, 176, 183, 213n3, 214n7, 215n19, 215n25, 215n26
chiasmus, 34
Claybaugh, Amanda, 84–86, 91, 205n10, 205n17, 207n30, 207n36
Clemens, Samuel L, 2, 198n7
Clemens, Samuel L., relationship to moral philosophy, 2
Clemens, Samuel L. *See also* Twain, Mark
Cohn, Dorrit, 214n13
    The Distinction of Fiction, 199n24
Comment, Kristin M., 212n17
Cooper, James Fenimore, 19, 57, 205n11
Coplan, Amy, 6
Copland, Sarah, 199n19
Coulson, Victoria, 111, 116, 118, 209n16
coverplot, 135–37
Cox, James, 91
Crane, Stephen, *Maggie*, 13, 51–53, 69, 199n20
critical distance
    as feature of professional reading, 1, 4, 46, 50, 189, 191, 203n28
    as feature of realist works, 53, 60, 74, 83, 119, 172, 174, 176, 179, 186, 191
    and sympathetic reading, 9, 16, 95, 131, 191–92
    and unreliability, 15
Culler, Jonathan, 48–49, 199n23, 209n18

Darnton, Robert, 202n16
Dauber, Kenneth, 202n14
Daugherty, Sarah B., 61–62
Dawson, Melanie, 20, 22, 70, 73, 123
Dean, Sharon L., 117
DeForest, John, 110
Dickinson, Anna, 99
Dixon, Thomas, 157
Dobson, Joanne, 97, 110–11
    "Reclaiming Sentimental Literature," 208n7
Douglas, Ann, 59, 96, 101, 105, 113, 209n17
    The Feminization of American Culture, 101

Douglass, Frederick, 34, 49, 202n21, 204n35

Eastman, Mary Henderson, *Aunt Phillis's Cabin*, 159, 189
Edel, Leon, 116, 210n5
Engelsing, Rolf, 40
Eugenides, Jeffrey, 152

feeling politics, 8
Felski, Rita, 9–10, 18, 119
 The Limits of Critique, 189, 199n26
feminist rescue of nineteenth-century American women writers, 59, 97, 110, 116–17, 135–38, 211n7
Fern, Fanny, 204n6
Festa, Lynn, 198n9
Fields, Annie, 212n21
Finseth, Ian, 215n20
Fleissner, Jennifer, 213n3
Flück, Winfried, 22, 170, 200n31
Fludernik, Monika, 199n24
focalization, 14, 51, 102, 151–53, 172, 209n18, 211n9. *See also* characters, focalized
Forster, E.M., 19–20, 78
Fossett, Judith Jackson, 148
Foucault, Michel, 31, 213n28
Frederick, John T., 204n6
Fredrickson, George M., 201n5
Freeman, Elizabeth, 84
Fugitive Slave Bill, 34

Garrison, William Lloyd, 39
Garvey, Ellen Gruber, 63, 206n19
Gilbert, Sandra, 103–5, 110
Glazener, Nancy, 14, 198n15, 199n25, 210n20, 215n24
Goodrich, Samuel, 40
Grabes, Herbert, 20–21, 23
Graff, Gerald, 194
Greeson, Jennifer Rae, 146
Greyser, Naomi, 212n24
Gubar, Susan, 103–5, 110
Guillory, John, 9, 192
 Professing Criticism, 199n17
Gustafson, Sandra, 212n18

Habegger, Alfred, 92–93, 98, 197n3, 208n1
Hall, David D., 40, 202n17

Halpern, Faye, *Sentimental Readers*, 1, 13, 199n20, 204n34, 206n23
Hamilton, Geordie, 167
Hardwick, Elizabeth, 104
Harper's Monthly Magazine, 120, 139, 167, 210n4, 210n6
Harris, Susan K., 135–36
Harvey, George, 116, 210n6
Hatch, Cora L.V., 92
Hattenhauer, Darryl, 213n4
Hawthorne, Nathaniel, 18, 49, 55, 93, 109, 204n34, 204n6
 "The Birth-Mark," 132, 212n20
Haymarket Affair, 78–79
Healey, Christine, 135
Hendler, Glenn, 37, 205n13, 210n19
Henson, Josiah, 47, 203n32
Hewitt, Elizabeth, 213n6
Hochman, Barbara, 39, 106, 201n2, 202n15, 205n13, 208n3, 208n4, 215n22
Hoeller, Hildegard, 2, 10, 197n6, 203n29, 204n7, 205n9, 205n14
Homestead, Melissa, 110
Howells, William Dean
 Annie Kilburn, 22, 26, 54, 60–74, 80–81, 83, 205n16
 on Charles Chesnutt, 139, 181
 on Constance Fenimore Woolson, 122–23
 Criticism and Fiction, 199n27, 212n22
 "Editor's Study," 2, 53, 66, 113, 116
 on Harriet Beecher Stowe, 4, 25, 59
 A Hazard of New Fortunes, 15, 19–20, 60–61, 72–84, 206n26, 210n3
 on how to represent emotion, 20, 22
 interest in home decor, 210n3
 "Novel-Writing and Novel-Reading," 57
 on realism, 10, 18, 53, 57, 62, 68, 72, 77, 113, 123, 206n27
 The Rise of Silas Lapham, 23, 26, 47, 55–56, 60, 88–89, 167, 205n9, 207n39, 210n3
 on sentimentality, 57, 88, 93–94, 114, 157–58, 205n18

Jacobs, Harriet, 185
James, Henry, 92–113, 132, 156, 197n3, 198n13, 208n41, 208n1, 208n2, 209n16
 and ambiguity, 96–97
 and the American woman question, 62

James, Henry (*continued*)
  The Bostonians, 13–14, 26, 69, 76, 93–114, 208n41, 209n18, 210n19
  Partial Portraits, 116
  response to sentimentality, 26, 60, 92–93, 97–99, 114, 208n1, 208n2, 210n19
  Washington Square, 98–99
  and William Dean Howells, 76
Jameson, Fredric, 12, 206n21
Jarrett, Gene, 90

Kaplan, Amy, 197n2
Keen, Suzanne, 5, 52, 182, 206n24
Kete, Mary Louise, 197n1
Knadler, Stephen, 156–57, 159–60, 213n1, 214n7, 215n19, 215n26
Kuhn, Mary, 213n3

The Lamplighter, 99, 112
Lanser, Sue, "The 'I' of the Beholder," 211n8
Larsen, Nella, 119, 190
  Passing, 119–20, 211n12
Lehane, Dennis, *Small Mercies*, 200n32
Lesser, Wendy, 103
Levine, Robert S., 201n3, 203n25
Lundeen, Katherine, 198n9

Mabie, Hamilton Wright, 214n10
Martin, Matthew, 157, 161, 213n3, 215n21
May, Georgiana, 39, 41, 132, 200n28
McCaskill, Barbara, 157
McElrath Jr., Joseph R., 159, 215n24
McEntee, Grace, 117, 135
McGlothlin, Erin, 7, 198n12
Millner, Michael, 10
Moore, Julia A., 54
Morgan, William, 76
  Questionable Charity, 2
Morrison, Toni, 90
"Mortally Wounded," 63, 206n19

narratological analysis, 12
narratological approach to realism, 12
Newkirk, Thomas, 43–44, 202n22, 203n22
Nielsen, Henrik Skov, 203n33
Noble, Marianne, 2, 36, 202n12
  Rethinking Sympathy and Human Connection in Nineteenth-Century Literature, 2, 5
Nowlin, Michael, 213n6
Nussbaum, Martha, *Love's Knowledge*, 207n32

O'Brien, Edward J., 116
O'Hara, Daniel T., 88–89
Ong, Walter, 204n36
orality, 25, 201n8, 212n18

Page, Thomas Nelson, 157, 181, 213n3, 215n21
Parfait, Claire, 59
Peabody, Elizabeth, 109
Pettis, Joyce, 173
Phelan, James, 3, 12, 14–15, 45, 130, 198n14, 199n22, 203n26, 203n33, 207n35, 211n10
  ARA (author-resources-audience) model, 12, 71
  "Estranging Unreliability, Bonding Unreliability, and the Ethics of *Lolita*," 217n37
professional readers and reading, 11, 44, 111, 195
  characteristics of, 9
Purity Principle of realism, 143, 148, 159, 172–73, 181, 192, 215n26

Rabinowitz, Peter J., 12, 161
  "Betraying the Sender: The Rhetoric and Ethics of Fragile Texts," 119
  model of audience, 24, 44–45, 94, 199n21, 203n24, 203n27
  rhetorical passing, 26, 119–20, 143–47
Radway, Janice, 45–46, 193
  "Beyond Mary Bailey and Old Maid Librarians," 46
Rasmussen, Kent, 204n4
Rauterkus, Melissa Asher, 152
realist narrative techniques, 12, 26, 94, 112, 155, 171–72, 174
regionalism, 121, 125–28, 131, 136, 138, 144, 205n12, 213n3
Reynolds, David, 95
rhetorical narrative analysis, 12–14, 67, 198n14
Rhoads, Bonita, 98, 208n1

Rioux, Anne Boyd, 117, 119, 129, 132, 135, 210n1, 210n4, 211n7, 211n10
  "Anticipating James, Anticipating Grief," 211n10
Ritzenberg, Aaron, 152
Robbins, Sarah, 29
Romero, Lora, 97
Ryan, Marie-Laure, "What Are Characters Made Of?," 212n25
Ryan, Susan M., 8, 97

Sanchez-Eppler, Karen, 209n11
Sand, George, 21
Scholes, Robert, 198n11
Sedgwick, Eve, 9
sentimental
  antebellum authors, 204n6
  antebellum tradition, 2
  antebellum writers, 1, 7, 92, 97, 116, 130, 197n3, 211n6
  antebellum writing, 48, 54, 60–61, 93
artifice, 17, 62, 128, 199n21
attachment, 16, 22, 118, 135
sentimentality
  association of women with, 60, 205n13
  attacks on, 53–54, 56–59, 62–64, 67, 70–71, 75, 84, 88, 94, 205n13, 206n18
  See also Howells, William Dean on sentimentality
sentimental narrative techniques, 3–4, 78, 112, 158, 192
sentimental sympathy
  characteristics of, 6, 22, 37–38, 95, 177–79
  definition of, 4–6, 12
  ethical nature of, 3, 6–9, 57, 189
  as narrative resource, 3, 18, 60, 71, 142, 192
  as reading practice, 9, 11, 189, 191–92
Sheridan, Thomas, 174
Shi, David, *Facing Facts*, 197n2
Shuman, Amy, 28, 198n9
Sigourney, Lydia, 59, 101, 105
Simmons, Ryan, 14–15, 153, 158–59, 169, 171–72, 215n24, 216n31
Smith, Henry Nash, 98
Spillers, Hortense, 32, 159
Stepto, Robert B., 146
Stokes, Claudia, 204n2, 207n34, 209n12

Stowe, Harriet Beecher, 39, 58–59, 65, 153, 173, 177
  "Concluding Remarks" in *Uncle Tom's Cabin*, 37, 47–48, 201n10
  A Key to Uncle Tom's Cabin, 47, 154, 199n21
  The Minister's Wooing, 65, 202n12
  as popular woman writer, 117, 138
  and regionalism, 58, 205n12
  Uncle Tom's Cabin, 4–6, 19, 21–22, 25, 27–50, 58–59, 95–96, 99–100, 110–13, 137–38, 149–50, 153–55, 157–64, 172–76, 181–84, 187–89, 202n14, 208n7, 211n8, 212n21
  anti-literacy in, 30, 40, 42, 46, 48–49
Suleiman, Susan, 34, 42, 149, 154, 156, 164, 201n11
Sundquist, Eric, 216n27
Symonds, John Addington, 62
sympathy, 7–9, 16, 57
  aspirational nature of, 180, 182–84
  distinction between sympathy and empathy, 5, 198n8
  See also sentimental sympathy

Terrell, Mary Church, 157–58
Tharaud, Jerome, 202n18
Thayer, William Roscoe, 10, 19, 198n16
thematic analysis, 3, 16, 61, 67, 205n16
Thomas, Brook, 89, 207n39
Thompson, Katrina Dyonne, 162, 216n28
Thrailkill, Jane, 10, 208n6, 217n2
  Affecting Fictions, 10, 208n6, 217n2
Tinkle, Teresa, 11
Tóibín, Colm, 117
Tolstoy, Leo, influence on Howells, 61–62, 64
Tompkins, Jane, 19, 30, 96, 162, 200n31, 213n27
  Sensational Designs, 208n3
Torsney, Cheryl B., 117, 129
Twain, Mark
  Adventures of Huckleberry Finn, 2, 11, 13–14, 23, 26, 54–56, 86, 88–91, 204n3, 204n4, 205n10, 205n13, 207n39, 210n3
  A Connecticut Yankee in King Arthur's Court, 14, 26, 84–88, 205n10

"Fenimore Cooper's Literary Offenses," 10–11, 18–19, 25–26, 53–57, 59–60, 70–71, 84, 87–88, 90–91, 93, 204n8, 205n11, 205n13, 206n21, 210n3
   on home decor, 210n3
   on sentimentality, 54, 56, 114, 158
   use of sentimentality, 60, 88
   See also Clemens, Samuel L.

uncritical reading, 9, 189, 193–94, 217n4
unreliability
   characteristics, 15–16, 130, 140, 199n24, 212n16
   in Charles Chesnutt's works, 27, 140–41, 145, 153, 156, 169, 183
   in Constance Fenimore Woolson's works, 118, 120, 124, 128–30, 213n26
   definition, 15
   in Mark Twains's works, 55, 91
   in narrative theory, 211n10
   in rhetorical passing, 120–21
unreliability in American literary realism, 14–15, 27
unreliable focalization
   characteristics, 69–71, 74, 80, 83, 102, 104, 107, 140, 151–53, 155–56, 162–63, 165, 179, 206n22, 211n9
   definition, 69, 206n22, 211n9
   in Henry James's works, 128
   in William Dean Howells's works, 69, 74

Veeder, William, 98

Wandler, Steven, 207n38
Wardley, Lynn, 209n15
Warhol, Robyn, 21, 38, 185, 193, 200n29, 201n10, 202n13
Warner, Charles Dudley, 210n4
Warner, Michael, 9, 194, 217n4
Weimer, Joan Myers, 212n15
Weinstein, Cindy, 47, 97, 203n31, 209n8
Werner, Craig, 141, 213n5, 214n7
Wharton, Edith, 2, 10, 60, 93, 200n27, 205n14, 211n11
Whicher, George, 138
White, Thomas, 40
Wideman, John, 159, 165, 169, 173
Williams, Raymond, 40, 200n32
Wilmington massacre, 66, 139–40, 143, 160, 173, 181
Wilson, Matthew, 140, 157, 160, 213n1, 213n7
Wimsatt, William K., 10, 20, 213n28
Windell, Maria, 215n18
Wolfe, Joanna, 194
Wooley, Christine, 216n33
Woolson, Constance Fenimore
   failed artists, 127–28
   and Henry James, 116
   "Jeannette," 135, 213n26
   "Miss Grief," 14, 26, 93, 110, 117, 120, 128–38, 210n1, 211n10, 212n17, 212n20
   rescue of from critical obscurity, 115–17
   "Solomon," 14, 26, 120–29, 133–34, 138

Yao, Xine, *Disaffected*, 8, 23

Zwarg, Christina, 201n6